CONCORDIA UNIVERSITY
DA495.M14
THE REIGN OF QUEEN ANNE

3 4211 000022054

THE REIGN OF
QUEEN ANNE

BY

JUSTIN McCARTHY

AUTHOR OF "A HISTORY OF OUR OWN TIMES"
"A HISTORY OF THE FOUR GEORGES AND WILLIAM IV." ETC.

IN TWO VOLUMES

VOL. I.

HARPER & BROTHERS PUBLISHERS
NEW YORK AND LONDON
1903

Copyright, 1902, by HARPER & BROTHERS.

All rights reserved.

Published October, 1902.

TO MY DAUGHTER

CHARLOTTE ELY McCARTHY

I DEDICATE THIS BOOK

CONTENTS

CHAPTER		PAGE
I.	THE WOMAN BORN TO BE QUEEN	1
II.	WHAT THE QUEEN CAME TO—AT HOME	13
III.	WHAT THE QUEEN CAME TO—ABROAD	32
IV.	THOSE AROUND QUEEN ANNE	49
V.	DISSENT AND DEFOE	66
VI.	ON THE ROUGH EDGE OF BATTLE	81
VII.	"THE CAMPAIGN"—BLENHEIM	98
VIII.	PETERBOROUGH IN SPAIN	122
IX.	EVENTS AND PARTIES AT HOME	139
X.	THE UNION WITH SCOTLAND	160
XI.	"THE TRIVIAL ROUND—THE COMMON TASK"	179
XII.	THE LONDON OF QUEEN ANNE	200
XIII.	JONATHAN SWIFT	222
XIV.	RAMILLIES AND ALMANZA	245
XV.	THE FIRST PARLIAMENT OF THE UNION	262
XVI.	SACHEVERELL	282
XVII.	"HARLEY, THE NATION'S GREAT SUPPORT"	306
XVIII.	THE TRIUMPH OF THE TORIES	324
XIX.	WHAT THE WAR WAS COMING TO	342
XX.	JONATHAN SWIFT'S VIEWS	366

THE REIGN OF QUEEN ANNE

THE REIGN OF QUEEN ANNE

CHAPTER I

THE WOMAN BORN TO BE QUEEN

ONE of the poets of the later Victorian literature, William Morris, has told in his melodious verse the story of the "Man born to be King," the idea of which is taken from that rich treasure-house of fantasy, the *Gesta Romanorum.* The story, however, is very different from that which begins under the heading of this first chapter—the story of the Woman born to be Queen. William Morris's hero becomes king in default of every hereditary claim to such a position and in despite of all disadvantages, difficulties, and seeming impossibilities, just because nature had endowed him with the special gifts which are sure to win for their owner a complete success. Queen Anne, on the contrary, was born to be a queen, and under no other conditions could have had the slightest chance of becoming the ruler of a great monarchy. Anne was the last of the Stuart sovereigns. She was the second daughter of James the Second by his first wife, Anne Hyde, who was the daughter of Edward Hyde, afterwards Earl of Clarendon, the famous lawyer, politician, and historian. The marriage between James and Anne Hyde was one of the sensations—and indeed, in a certain sense, one of the conventional scandals—of the time, for public opinion was much shocked when it became known that a marriage, secretly contracted, had been carried out between the daughter of a man who, no matter what his capacity, was born a commoner, and James, the Duke of York as he then was, heir-presumptive to the throne of England. Edward Hyde was known to have felt, or at all events to have feigned, great indignation when he found that his daughter had allowed the Duke of York to contract an alliance with one who was not a princess.

Anne was born at Twickenham on February 6, 1664, and she came into the world at a time as full of threatening change and movement at home and abroad, politically, morally, and intellectually, as the history of England can picture. The child thus born was destined to a place in history which may well be described as unique. The mere mention of her name brings with it to the mind of every one who has had any education, or even any opportunity of desultory reading, the idea of an age illustrious in war, in politics, in literature, and in art. It brings with it, too, the thought of an age which became a turning-point not only in the history of England but in the history of Europe. The old world of political life seems to have closed for England and the world of modern politics to have begun with the reign of Queen Anne. "Parliamentary government," says Lord Macaulay, "is government by talking," and the true reign of debate as the over-mastering power in parliamentary and political life established itself with the reign of Queen Anne. England never, perhaps, had so great a soldier as Marlborough. Except for the name of Wellington, there is no name to be compared with his in the modern history of England. English political history down to the latest days recalls the name of no parliamentary debater greater, on the whole, than Bolingbroke. The reign of Anne saw the most momentous struggle in which England was ever engaged on the continent of Europe until we come to the days of the French Revolution and the First Napoleon.

The age of Queen Anne stands out a distinct epoch in the history of the world. It takes rank with the age of Pericles in Greece, with the Augustan era in Rome, with the Elizabethan era in England. The mere mention of any one of these eras brings with it the thought of a peculiar success as great in the achievements of peace as in the achievements of war, as great in arts as in arms. But in such instances as those, when we associate an era with one name we bear with us the natural and well-sustained impression that the owner of the name had at least something to do with the greatness of the era. When we speak of the age of Queen Anne we cannot possibly associate the greatness of the era with any genius of inspiration coming from the woman whose name it bears. Anne was born to a great era, just as she was born to a crown, and had no more to do personally with the making of its greatness than if she had been born in a garret to a life of commonplace obscurity. Even the worst faults of Elizabeth may be seen to have had some share in creating much of the picturesque greatness at least which belongs to the Elizabethan age. But even the best virtues of Anne had little or nothing to do with the inspiration or the promotion of the greatness which marks her reign.

The writer has thought it not amiss to begin his survey of Queen Anne's life and reign by observations which might naturally have seemed to belong rather to a closing review of the whole, because he is anxious to direct the reader's attention from the very outset to the curious contrast which the history of the regin presents between the extraordinary character of the age and the utterly commonplace character of the woman whose name it bears. In more than one fairy legend we read of a princess over whom a magical spell has been cast, and who sleeps all her life away in an aërial tower while wars are carried on in her name and conquests are added to her domain, and wonders of art and letters are accomplished in her capital, and all the world knows of these thrilling and marvellous doings except the poor princess herself who reigns but does not know it. The story of Queen Anne might, in a certain sense, seem to belong almost as completely to the world of enchantment. The sleeping princess in the magical tower had about as much to do with the great triumphs which were accomplished in every field during her reign, and in her name, as Queen Anne in the whole course of her mature life had to do directly and personally with the achievements of England abroad and at home.

History has done stern justice to the rule and to the policy of James the Second, but it has not done justice to his motives or to his personal character. As to his rule and his policy there can hardly be a second opinion among responsible historians and impartial critics anywhere. But there seems a great deal to be said for the personal character and the public motives of the man, which most historians and critics, and popular opinion generally in our own days and earlier, have left altogether unsaid. The history of Europe hardly contains the name of any ruler who is so completely out of public favor. Richard the Third has found his champions, but no such stroke of good luck has fallen to the fortune of James the Second. Charles the First has even still a select circle of devotees in England, and his has always been a picturesque figure which romance and the drama have loved to illustrate. Macaulay said with great truth that Vandyke's brush created for generations a hero whom the judgments of history could never dethrone. Some of the most uncompromising opponents of the divine-right theory are quite ready to recognize good qualities in Charles the Second, to see that he was a man of wit and culture, with better education than that of most princes at his time and after, and with at least some generous instincts and enlightened purposes. But hardly any one has a word to say in favor of James the Second. In Ireland, where so many brave men laid down their lives in defence of his cause, it has become an accepted legend that James was a positive coward, and that the battle of the Boyne might have ended quite differently if James had had to sustain him one spark of the courage possessed by William the Dutchman. Yet it is certain that James in his earlier days was highly praised for his courage by the great Turenne, under whom he served, and who may surely be regarded as competent to form an opinion on the merits of a soldier.

There is a common impression in England that James was a man of no principles, although it is certain that at more than one crisis of his life the Stuart cause might have had a fair chance of success if James could have been prevailed upon to change his religion, or even to announce that he had changed it. The fact probably is that James meets with universal condemnation because the principle which he advocated is either universally condemned or wholly out of fashion among Englishmen. In order to do anything like justice to the unfortunate James, we must judge his personal character and his personal doings by the light of his own principles and not by the light of ours. It is not too much to say for him that he was a sincere martyr to the cause of divine right. It is so hard for a reasonable Englishman of our day to get into his mind the possibility of any sane person sincerely believing in the right of a king to govern a people exactly according to his own liking, that he can only explain James's conduct by assuming that James was an utterly insincere and self-seeking personage. But all that we read of James, even in the writings of those who most strongly condemn his policy, will give warrant for the conviction that he was an unqualified believer in the principle of divine right, as Richard Cobden was in the doctrine of free-trade, or Father Mathew in the doctrine of total abstinence from intoxicating liquors. James was a fanatic in his way, and a fanatic whom evil fortune for himself and others had put in a position to do immense harm by the enforcement of his doctrine, but we may at least concede to him the merit of having been sincere in his fanaticism.

There is absolutely nothing to be said in defence of James's system of rule unless it be said by those, if any there be at present among civilized men, who not only believe in the principle of divine right, but also believe that a king thus called to the throne can never do wrong. It would hardly be possible to find in history the accredited records of any sovereign who governed, when he had the chance, with a more absolute disregard for all the principles and practices of constitutional liberty, even as these were recognized in the England of his time. Then, again, in his private life he was quite as immoral as Charles the Second, and indeed many chapters of his personal history would seem as if they might have been suitably chronicled by Saint-Simon. Even his marriage—his first marriage, that is to say—was contracted under conditions which made it a sort of public scandal. James had large families of children, legitimate and illegitimate, but among the children borne to him by both his wives very few attained to anything like maturity. After the death of his eldest daughter, Mary, who reigned with William the Third, Anne became heir to the English crown. Of her father's character and temperament Anne seems to have inherited little more than a strong inclination towards the doctrine of divine right, especially when that right was illustrated in the claims of the house of Stuart. None of her father's worst qualities seem to have descended to her. If she had as little sense of humor as he had, and if she showed that she could sometimes be as silently obstinate as he habitually was, she had none of his moral corruptness, and, happily for the people over whom she came to rule, she had none of his self-conceit. It is necessary to enter a protest against the unqualified and unconditional censure which history in general has pronounced upon James the Second, but the protest only refers to certain articles of the censure. James has often been set down as a coward, which he certainly was not, and he has been almost universally accused of insincerity and of mere self-seeking, when he was positively acting in his wrong-headed, narrow-minded way under the influence of what he firmly believed to be his divine right to rule his people.

Anne had not been fortunate in the husband whom fate and family convenience had imposed upon her. She was married in her twentieth year to Prince George of Denmark, brother of the reigning sovereign of that country, and Prince George was perhaps as characteristic a specimen of the good-for-nothing as any age or condition could have produced. He was not exactly a bad man, but nobody seemed to find anything to say in his praise. He had no opportunity of doing much harm during his lifetime, and he kept himself for the most part conveniently in the background. Historical controversy has not troubled itself about him. It is said that he was the occasion of the one only joke ever made by his father-in-law, James the Second. The story goes that when James, in his hours of political danger, was receiving successive announcements that this, that, or the other public man had gone over to the side of the invader William, Prince George always greeted the news with the words, "Est-il possible?" The hour came at last when George himself went over to the side of the invader, and then King James asked, with a smile, "Has 'Est-il possible?' gone too?"

Anne was brought up in the Protestant faith, and always adhered to it. When the great crisis came she abandoned the cause of her father, which had indeed become already quite hopeless, and in 1689 the crown of Great Britain was settled upon her in succession to William the Third, by the Bill of Rights, as the act making the decree was called.

Anne had a large family of children, but all except one died at birth or in mere infancy, and even the one surviving child, the little Duke of Gloucester, looked upon the earth but for a few years. Therefore when William's wife, Mary, eldest sister of Anne, died and left her husband a childless widower, it became necessary to cast about for some new arrangement which might secure the succession in such a manner as to exclude the exiled Stuart claimants. Not often in history has this sort of quest been rendered necessary, and in thinking it over one is sometimes reminded oddly of the story based on some historical evidence that the rightful successor to a Byzantine throne was absolutely advertised for by public proclamation. In the instance of the English monarch the quest was rendered all the more embarrassing because there were so many relatives and connections of English royal families scattered all over the continent of Europe. The object was to hit upon some order of succession which should seem to have a legitimate and reasonable claim to justify it, and, at the same time, should shut out as strictly as possible any connection with the banished Stuarts.

This end was at last accomplished by selecting the Electress Sophia of Hanover, who had on her mother's side some family connection with Charles the First, and who was the head of a German house which was not likely to have much sympathy with Charles the First's exiled and proscribed descendants. The Electress Sophia had a son, George, and therefore if she should accept the arrangement there seemed good reason to count on continuity of succession. The Electress Sophia was not particularly anxious to assume the responsibilities imposed upon her, but she was a shrewd, clever woman, and although at first she saw no reason why she should accept the offer, yet by the force of thinking the matter out, she made up her mind that there was no reason why she should not accept it, and that it might on the whole bring many advantages to her family. The matter was therefore satisfactorily arranged by the Act of Settlement which was passed on March 12, 1701. Anne had not long to wait for her succession to the throne. William the Third was in very feeble health. His physical frame was thoroughly worn out by a life of what the Scotch balladist calls "sturt and strife." No one, however, expected his immediate death, and indeed for some little time it had been thought that his health was improving. One evening in the end of February, 1702, he rode out, as he had lately been in the habit of doing, to Hampton Court. On the way the King's horse stumbled over a molehill, and William was thrown to the ground and broke his collar-bone. He never recovered from the effects of this accident, and he died at Kensington Palace on March 8, 1702, in the fifty-second year of his age—an early death, if estimated according to the ordinary rate of human life, but not too early for the accomplishment of a great revolution in the history of England.

Anne was then the Queen of England. She had but lately entered her thirty-eighth year. Bishop Burnet tells us that " upon the King's death, the Privy Council came in a body to wait on the new Queen; she received them with a well-considered speech." In this well-considered speech " she expressed great respect to the memory of the late King, in whose steps she intended to go, for preserving both Church and State, in opposition to the growing power of France, and for maintaining the succession in the Protestant line: she pronounced this, as she did all her other speeches, with great weight and authority, and with a softness of voice, and sweetness in the pronunciation, that added much life to all she spoke." The two Houses of Parliament met that same day and agreed to send addresses to her, " full of respect and duty," as Burnet describes them. The Queen " answered both very favorably, and she received all that came to her in so gracious a manner that they went from her highly satisfied with her goodness, and her obliging deportment; for she harkened with attention to everything that was said to her." It does not even need the high authority of Bishop Burnet to make us well assured that the capacity to be, or seem to be, a good listener is an invaluable quality in a new sovereign. " Two days after," Burnet tells us, " she went to the Parliament, which, to the great happiness of the nation, and to the advantage of her government, was now continued to sit, notwithstanding the King's demise, by the act that was made five years before, upon the discovery of the assassination plot. In her speech she repeated, but more copiously, what she had said to the council upon her first accession to the throne. There were two passages in this speech that were thought not so well considered; she assured them her heart was 'entirely English'; this was looked on as a reflection on the late King: she also added, that they might 'depend on her word.' Both these expressions had been in her father's first speech, how little soever they were afterwards minded by him." Bishop Burnet lays some stress on the fact that these two passages produced an unsatisfactory impression, and his remark would be worthy of citation if only that it illustrates a difficulty which beset Queen Anne from the very outset of her career. If anything she happened to say should remind the public of her father, the majority of people might be filled with the dread that she was likely to prove just such another sovereign as he had been, and if her style of reply seemed obviously and purposely unlike his mode of speech, a certain number of other people would be sure to set her down as an ungrateful daughter who was only too anxious to stand aloof from any manner of association with her father, who had died dethroned and exiled.

If one were to compare the ruling capacity of Queen Anne with that of the sovereign whom she followed on the throne of England, it might seem as if an anticlimax had come to pass not less strange and striking than that which was seen when the rule of Oliver Cromwell was followed by the rule of Richard Cromwell. The mere mention of the names, however, is enough to illustrate the difference between the one succession and the other. The name of Richard Cromwell means an ignoble blank in English history following immediately after the masterful and momentous domination of the great Protector. The reign of Queen Anne must be forever memorable in the history of the English constitution, of English letters, and of English arms, even although it came immediately after the reign of William the Third.

CHAPTER II

WHAT THE QUEEN CAME TO—AT HOME

Now that Queen Anne has been solemnly enthroned as sovereign of Great Britain, and is receiving addresses of loyal congratulation from various cities and towns and corporate bodies of all kinds, it is well to take a rapid survey of the political and social conditions presented for her study, if she had the capacity or the inclination to study them, by the England of that day. Anne, the last of the Stuart sovereigns, may fairly be described as the first of the constitutional sovereigns in these countries. William the Third had indeed laid the foundations of the constitutional system, by which we mean the political system that depends avowedly on some sort of representative principle and is not merely the expression and realization of the sovereign's will and pleasure. But William had not much time or opportunity to settle down into the sheltered condition of a constitutional ruler. He had had to fight in order to gain his throne, he had to fight in order to maintain it, he had to fight in order to secure for England that place among the states of Europe which he believed her entitled to assert, and it was still not by any means out of the question that he might have had to resist a counter-revolution at home. He was a great statesman as well as a great soldier, he could read the signs of the times, and he saw clearly enough that the day of absolute monarchy was gone by for England. He saw, however, much more than that: he saw how the new constitution was to be constructed and how it was to act in the future. He was like the inventor and the constructor of some new model of sailing-ship who has got the vessel ready for sea and has even taken the command, but is for a time prevented by stress of weather from giving his experiment a fair trial and is cut off by death before the ship can make her first trial.

Parliament in the days of Queen Anne was more like the Parliament which we know in our own times than any of its predecessors had ever been. The conditions under which William the Third had settled into the sovereign position gave to the parliamentary chambers a power of control over the will of the sovereign which had not existed during any previous reign. The King could no longer maintain his army except through supplies which were voted by Parliament, and therefore the King was no longer able to put off the summoning of a Parliament as long as it was his royal pleasure to act for himself, without taking the trouble to consult the parliamentary representatives. The relations between the sovereign and his ministers had now, for the first time, taken the form in which they are familiar to the political life of our own generation. Up to the time of William the Third the institution which we now know as the cabinet had not come into existence. At the present day it would be hard, indeed, to find any legislative authority establishing the existence and defining the functions which are as certain, as practical, and as essential to the working of our political constitution as any other part of our whole parliamentary system.

In the days before William the Third the King consulted with such of his ministers as he thought fit, **and** left some of them out of the consultation altogether according as his humor directed him. The King intrusted any one of his ministers with such duties as he thought that minister most likely to discharge in a manner satisfactory to the royal purposes. A favorite minister was often intrusted with negotiations or other business of the utmost importance concerning which his companions in office, for they could hardly be called his colleagues, were favored with no information whatever. There was no collective responsibility involving all the ministers, even those who formed what may be called the inner circle of the King's advisers. There was, in point of fact, no recognized and official prime-minister as we now understand the meaning of the title. The prime-minister and the cabinet became established and recognized realities about that time in English history when Queen Anne was called to the throne. The policy of the state in home or foreign affairs could no longer be settled by the sovereign's own will and pleasure or by the decision of the sovereign acting in consultation with this or that member of the ministry. There was a prime-minister and there was a cabinet of ministers, every one of whom was entitled to be consulted on each great question coming up for decision, and every one of whom was understood to have his share in the responsibility which each decision brought with it. There was, therefore, a body of men having seats in one or the other House of Parliament who were responsible for the defence and the maintenance of their policy in either assembly, who could be questioned as to their policy and attacked because of it, or censured because of it, if they failed to command support enough to sustain them, or failed to convince their habitual opponents that in this particular instance their policy was just. Parliamentary debate was, therefore, growing more and more to be one of the vital forces in the working of the constitutional system.

Then, again, that which we are accustomed in more modern times to speak of as the power of the press had been endowed with something like a reasonable freedom of utterance during the reign of William the Third. It was no longer part of the recognized system of government to come down with sharp and sometimes savage punishments on any audacious offender who presumed to put into print some opinions of his own which seemed offensive or even untimely to men in power. Of course there were severe laws in existence against newspaper criticism of personages in high office for many generations after Queen Anne had passed away and down to a time not far remote from our own. But the legislation by virtue of which William the Third had been able to secure his place on the throne of England had distinctly conferred a degree of tolerance to printed comment and criticism which did not exist under the Stuart dynasty or in the days of the Commonwealth. During Queen Anne's reign, the political air may be said to have been thick with whole flights of pamphleteering criticism coming from all quarters and descending on every field of politics, letters, art, and social life. Most of these, although certainly not all, were allowed to go unpunished.

Much of the work of criticism which is done by the daily or weekly newspaper now was done by the pamphlet in the time of Queen Anne. The most casual and cursory reader can observe the difference in all that concerned political and parliamentary debate between the reign of Queen Anne and that of James the Second. Queen Anne's reign seems, in this part of its history at least, like the opening of some new chapter in civilization. The centre of public interest is no longer in the palace of the sovereign, but is within the precincts of Parliament. The statesman who desires to maintain his place must now carry along with him the public opinion of the country, and can no longer silence, by the mere threat of his prohibition, the voices of any critics who might feel audacious enough to disparage his policy or to question his motives. The place from which he can best command the attention of the public is his place in the House of Commons or the House of Lords, and if he has in him the genuine capacity for debate, he is only too glad to throw his whole energy and his whole soul into the splendid parliamentary battle. The power of eloquence is in fact resuming that place in the government of states which it had held in the days of Pericles and in the days of Julius Cæsar, and had lost during the long ages when kings and soldiers managed the government of states among them. It is not too much to say that we can picture several of the leading figures of Queen Anne's Parliament in many of the great parliamentary debates of Queen Victoria's reign, just as we can imagine Sir Roger de Coverley taking a turn in the Temple Gardens with Colonel Newcome.

The awakening power of the English Parliament was accompanied by a corresponding activity on the part of the English press. The press, however, as has been said already, made its activity felt more through the influence of the pamphlet than of the newspaper. We shall have occasion to notice how one of the greatest Englishmen of his time — in his own field of literature one of the greatest Englishmen of any time — Daniel Defoe, made himself a genuine popular power in the political and religious controversy of the day. We hear a good deal about Daniel Defoe in the commentary of Bishop Burnet on some of the great questions, the "burning questions," as they would have been called at a later day, which were occupying the attention of Parliament and came under the special notice of the historian of the Reformation with whom these pages have more to do as the author of *The History of My Own Times*. The name of Bishop Burnet is almost as completely identified with the life and politics of Queen Anne's reign as that of Daniel Defoe himself, or any other of the eminent writers whose literature helps to make up the glory of that reign in one way, as did the genius of Marlborough in another. Bishop Burnet was not a great man in the nobler sense, and perhaps we are not entitled to give him any higher position as a chronicler of the reigns of William the Third and Anne than that which Boswell holds in regard to Samuel Johnson. But just as we have to construct our Samuel Johnson with the help of the illumination shed by Boswell, so we are compelled in a great measure to form our ideas as to the men and the movements of the reign of William and of Anne under Bishop Burnet's guidance.

Bishop Burnet's history has become a sort of classical authority, in a certain sense, with all readers who study the events and the persons belonging to the reigns of King William the Third and Queen Anne. The good Bishop called his book a *History of My Own Times,* but the more modern editions of the book and the references to it by more modern writers almost invariably entitle it for some unexplained reason Burnet's *History of His Own Times*. The book is undoubtedly a work of great historical value. Burnet's views are not always quite impartial, and even his statements of mere fact are occasionally inaccurate. The estimates he forms and the conclusions he draws are not always in keeping with the judgment which events unknown to Burnet,

WHAT THE QUEEN CAME TO—AT HOME

events which could not have been known in his time, have compelled later historians and readers to adopt. But the value of the book to any careful student of history is not much depreciated by Burnet's occasional mistakes as to fact or misconception as to character. The history has the inestimable advantage of being a history of the man's own times, and even when we can clearly see that he was mistaken in this or that statement or opinion, it is nevertheless a matter of the greatest importance to the reader to know that such were the impressions formed and the opinions accepted by an observer who was living and moving among the scenes and the persons described in the work. When Bishop Burnet tells us casually that he conversed with King William on this or that event the day after it happened, or that he received directly from Queen Anne such opinions as she thought fit to give him on some question of importance at the time, we cannot help feeling that anything coming from such a man must have a distinct value quite apart from the narrator's own capacity to form an impartial historical judgment.

No figure is more often made the mark of satire than the self-sufficient person who settles every question relating to the condition or the ways of any foreign country by the declaration that he has been there and ought to know. In private life, to this day, we are apt to be put out by the dogmatic self-satisfaction of this authoritative personage, and we are for that reason often inclined to attach little importance to his testimony, even where we have no positive evidence to discredit his statements. Perhaps one feels sometimes inclined to entertain a like sentiment towards the good Bishop Burnet when he invites us to believe that he understands the characters and the motives of all the illustrious men and women whom he was in the habit of meeting. It is certain that in his own days he was the object of much sarcasm from the satirists and wits of the time, and that men like Pope and Swift were not slow to make it clear that they saw a very comic side to his character. Still it is no less certain that Burnet continues to be regarded as an authority on the history of his own times, and that the clever things which Pope and Swift said about him are forgotten by the great majority of readers. Any one who reads the book will easily see for himself the principal weaknesses of Bishop Burnet's nature and temperament, just as anybody can see for himself the principal weaknesses in the character of Mr. Pepys. But we can hardly understand to the full the history of the court of Charles the Second without taking into account the testimony of Mr. Pepys, and in the same way, and to a still greater extent, we should fail to understand the real history of the reigns of William the Third and Anne if we failed to give due weight to the testimony of Bishop Burnet.

The History of My Own Times has a fascination for the reader which does not depend on vivacity of narrative or beauty of style. There is no reason to question the sincerity and the good faith of the man who lived in such times and moved among such personages. We can always take it that he is giving us what he believes to be genuine evidence. His own personal, political, and religious partialities are made so clear to us that we can easily allow for any bias in his judgment, and we are not likely to follow him into wrong conclusions because he has allowed his own judgment to grow color-blind here and there, or to be led astray from the main track because he has occasionally made an unsuccessful attempt at a short-cut in his eagerness to show that he knew the right way better than any one else could know it.

The realm over which Queen Anne came to **reign**

WHAT THE QUEEN CAME TO—AT HOME

could not be described in any sense as the United Kingdom of Great Britain and Ireland. Scotland had her own Parliament and her own laws, and even claimed a distinct and separate order of succession in her sovereigns. There was almost as much rivalry of trading and commercial interest between England and Scotland as between England and the United Provinces of the Netherlands. We shall presently see that these very jealousies and rivalries of trade and shipping had more to do than even political influences with the condition of things which was soon to force on public attention the momentous question whether England and Scotland were really to unite into one political system or were actually to separate into rival states. Ireland was still merely a conquered country, held by force under the dominion of the English sovereign. Ireland was still suffering severely from the effects of the iron rule and the remorseless conquests of Oliver Cromwell. In the interesting and really instructive life of the great Protector, by the distinguished American soldier and politician, Theodore Roosevelt, now President of the United States, the author, whose admiration of Cromwell is never allowed to interfere with his impartial judgment, tells us that the only excuse for Cromwell's dealings with Ireland is to be found in the fact that other English rulers before and after Cromwell had dealt as severely with what is commonly called the sister island. The fact is that at the time of Queen Anne's accession the greater part of the Irish population were in sympathy with the claims of the Stuarts merely because they still remembered with bitterness and passion the manner in which Cromwell had dealt with their country, and were willing to welcome as a friend the descendant of the sovereign who had been dethroned and done to death by the over-mastering Protector.

THE REIGN OF QUEEN ANNE

The people, as we understand the expression in our modern days, could hardly be said to have any influence on political movements at the time when the reign of Queen Anne opened. The voice of what might, perhaps, be called the people, occasionally made itself heard, in approval or in disapproval, through the lungs of noisy mobs in some of the larger cities or towns. But there was no clear idea of any such thing as popular representation, or even of any popular organization which might represent in political and social controversy the views and the interests of the working classes. The bitterness of dispute among the various religious denominations was keen and sometimes even ferocious. Many an English Protestant seemed to be in serious doubt as to the grave question whether he ought to dread and hate the Roman Catholics more than the Dissenters, or the Dissenters more than the Roman Catholics.

Readers of this generation, looking composedly back over the history of Queen Anne's reign, are naturally inclined to set it down as a matter of fact that the principle of constitutional government has been generated by the process of political evolution, and that there can be no return on the part of England to the earlier stage of historical development. But even the shrewdest observers who were contemporaries of Bishop Burnet and Daniel Defoe could not be expected to regard the existing state of things as a finally accomplished stage of political growth from which there could be no retrogression, and to which there could be no interruption. The struggle for the Stuart family was, in fact, a struggle for the principle of the divine right of kings. A devotion personal, sentimental, and religious for the Stuarts had much to do with the persevering adhesion of so many in England, Scotland, and Ireland

WHAT THE QUEEN CAME TO—AT HOME

to the cause of the family which went into exile with James the Second. But there was more involved, although to a great extent unconsciously, than any question of personal or even of religious achievement. The time had come when the principle of divine right had to give place to the principle of hereditary succession, originating avowedly in the national choice, and not in any supposed investiture of the sovereign and his successors by divine ordination. So far as the formal choice of the country itself was concerned, there was perhaps not much more to be said for the principle of hereditary succession than for that of succession by divine right. It would be impossible to contend that the great majority of Englishmen, Irishmen, Scotchmen, and Welshmen had been in any way invited to consultation and decision on the question whether the crown of these realms was to be given thenceforward to those who represented the house of Orange-Nassau, and not to those who represented the house of Stuart. But the idea of inviting the majority of the people to any consultation as to the form of government had not then come up in the state affairs of modern Europe, and the choice of the nation was always assumed to be determined by the relative influence of leading statesmen and leading families on the one side of the question or on the other.

The weakness of the Stuart cause consisted in the fact that England had by this time outlived the principle of divine right. That principle had become an anachronism, and was no more to be maintained against the newer principle of hereditary succession than, at a much later day, the old-world fashion of travelling by horse-drawn coaches could be maintained against the newer practice of travelling on lines of railway.

THE REIGN OF QUEEN ANNE

There was much blood yet to be shed in defence of the divine-right principle. It had for many succeeding generations large masses of followers devoted to its cause, and indeed there are, even in our own age and in these countries, intelligent men and women who still believe in the divine right of the Stuarts to go on governing the realm after their own fashion. But so far as practical politics in these countries were concerned, the divine-right system was outworn and was already becoming a mere tradition of the past. A power stronger than that of any mere set of Whig statesmen was against the old-fashioned system. The process of political evolution was the enemy against which no courage or self-sacrifice on the part of those who still upheld the Stuart dynasty could possibly prevail. In order to understand fully the whole story of Queen Anne's reign, we must bear in mind that to those who were living at the time it was still quite an unsettled question whether the fortunes of the house of Stuart might not yet rise to a restoration of the dynasty, for all that had come and gone. We can often read, even in the writings of grave historians, who came long after Queen Anne had passed away, dissertations on what might have happened if only this or that event had not happened—if James the Second could have been prevailed upon to renounce his religious principles and become a Protestant; if Queen Anne had made up her mind resolutely a little earlier; if she had trusted herself altogether to this and not to that set of statesmen.

We can easily see at this distance of time that it was after all mainly a question of political evolution, and that the English world had outgrown the principle of divine right. But when we have to study the character of Queen Anne herself and the comparative

WHAT THE QUEEN CAME TO—AT HOME

capacity and trustworthiness of the statesmen who struggled for ascendency in her time, we must always remember that even to the shrewdest and most far-seeing on either side of the political field, it still seemed quite within the range of ordinary possibilities that some sudden turn of affairs, the influence of some daring energy, or even the mere chapter of accidents, might bring the Stuarts to the front again, and set up a divine-right sovereign once more upon the throne of England.

There was, it is almost needless to say, no sentimental passion attaching anywhere in England to the memory of William the Third or to the order of succession which his reign had established. William the Dutchman, as he was commonly called for generations after by those who belonged to the opposite party, had never been particularly popular in the country over which he came to rule. He was a foreigner, to begin with, and his ways were not the ways of Englishmen. He had not even a son to succeed him, and the hereditary principle could not therefore work by its own direct movement. A new arrangement, a new compromise of some kind, had to be sought out and adopted in order to keep the new principle in continuous action. If William the Third had been the father of some prince who gave promise of being another Henry the Fifth, or even another William the Third, then everything might have gone steadily and naturally on, and there would have seemed little chance for the exiled representatives of the Stuart cause. But it was a serious crisis for England when it became apparent that nothing had been definitely settled by the kingship of William the Third, and that it required no less than a new Act of Settlement to keep the hereditary government going on. Then it soon became apparent also that the only practical way of attempting any reasonable form of adjustment was by accepting for the time a sovereign who belonged to the house of Stuart, and taking the opportunity of her childless condition to arrange for a succession which should declare the Stuart family cut off forever.

Seldom has there been in the history of any modern state a crisis more serious and, if we may use an expression which seems to carry something of triviality with it, a crisis more peculiarly inconvenient. England had been impressed, so far as statesmanship could effect the impression, with the belief that the coming of William of Nassau would bring with it a rule of steady and abiding government, and would get rid of the Stuart claims, the Stuart succession, and all the essential conditions of the disturbance forever. Now it had to be admitted by King William's own chosen followers that it would be necessary to accept the succession of a Stuart princess, and to devise some arrangement by means of which other princes, but not the Stuarts, must be brought from abroad to occupy in their turn the throne of England.

Therefore, even when the Act of Settlement had been passed, the Hanoverian line had been invested in anticipation with the succession to the English throne, and the work, so far as the agreement among recognized statesmen and the decree of Parliament could secure it, had been accomplished, the mind of Anne herself and of many around her must have had frequent anxious hours. At any moment the Stuart claimant might come over from France, land on the Scottish coast, and obtain the help of the Scottish clans to make good his claim by force of arms.

The England Queen Anne had come to rule was a country which, even if we include Wales, must have had a population of somewhat under seven millions. With the exception of London, and perhaps Bristol, there were really no large cities according to the proportions of modern estimates. It has to be noticed as a curious characteristic of the time that in the opening of Queen Anne's reign the populous and busy communities were found in the south and in the east of the kingdom. In our times it is very much the other way. With the exception of London alone, the great manufacturing cities, the strongholds of the country's business and population, are found in the northern counties, in Manchester and Liverpool, and the great and growing towns which cluster around them, or in such places as Birmingham and other parts of the Midlands. Bristol was the great seaport of Queen Anne's time, and now its shipping hardly comes into consideration when we speak of the docks and the merchant fleets of Liverpool. It is not so much that Bristol has gone down as that Liverpool has gone up.

At the time of Queen Anne's accession the most important towns after London itself were Bristol, York, Nottingham, Exeter, Shrewsbury, Winchester, and Canterbury. Bath has indeed to be mentioned, but only because of its claims to recognition as a watering-place and because of its history going back to the time of the Roman Conquest, and by no means for any importance which it could profess to have as a centre of manufactures or of commerce. Bath had always been regarded as a specially endowed health resort so far back as the history of its existence can be traced, but it was only in the first year of Queen Anne's reign that it acquired its fashionable reputation and became recognized as the place which everybody ought to visit who desired to claim a position in what would now be called smart society. The once celebrated Beau Nash may be said to have created the fame of Bath for this particular purpose, and it made its influence felt in this way through the literature of Queen Anne and in that of Jane Austen and Charles Dickens. London itself was then a city of what may fairly be called enormous size when we consider the proportion of its inhabitants to the whole population of England. The great metropolis at the opening of Queen Anne's reign contained a population approaching in number to very nearly three-quarters of a million, or rather more than a tenth of the population which the best calculations give to England and Wales. In the years which have passed since that time London has not merely maintained her relative supremacy, but has positively increased it, for the proportion of her population is even higher now, when compared with that of the whole country from the Scottish border to the English Channel, than it was in the days when Anne came to the throne.

London and Westminster were then two separate communities, divided from each other by distance as well as by name. The city of Westminster contained the famous historic Abbey and the Houses of Parliament, while the centre of London life was the Exchange. The stranger who in the present year happens to be in the lobby at the close of a night's sitting in the House of Commons will hear the words called out in stentorian tones, "Who goes home?" through all parts of the building, thus recalling to his mind the distant days when such an invitation was necessary in order that members might make up parties to journey home together through the dangerous roads which still lay between Westminster and London. The tendency of fashion in the capital was then, as it has ever since been and as it shows itself in most cities, to grow westward,

WHAT THE QUEEN CAME TO—AT HOME

but the fashionable London of those days would be regarded as a midland region at best by the dwellers in our West End of the present century. London and Westminster were miserably lighted by few and wretched oil-lamps, and there was no police force to take efficient charge of belated travellers. The only organized protection which the wayfarers knew was that afforded by the incompetent and miserable civic watch which the local authorities provided in order to keep up something like an appearance of security for those who had to make use of the public thoroughfares at night. In Gay's "Trivia," in the *Spectator,* in some of Swift's letters, and in various records of the time we find ample and telling evidence of the nightly dangers which beset the path of the luckless ones who had to seek their homes unguarded by a retinue of servants after darkness had fallen upon the streets of London and Westminster. To add to the troubles of those days, it should be said that London had not yet recovered from the effects of the great fire in 1666, and some of the new streets which it had been found necessary to begin at once, after the wrecks of the conflagration had been cleared away, had not yet been brought to what even in those days would have been regarded as a state of completion.

The England of Queen Anne's early reign held more than a million and a quarter of pauper inhabitants, pauperism thus, in fact, absorbing about one-fifth of the whole population. For a long time in the history of England the poverty of the country, when the laborer had ceased to be a mere serf, was left to the ministration of private charity, so far as it obtained any ministration at all. The monasteries and other religious houses did the work of charity, and after the suppression of the monasteries the clergy and the landlords of the parishes either did the work or left it undone. In the reign of Henry the Eighth the Statute of Vagrants, as it was called, made some attempt to deal with the vast mass of idle pauperism, which indiscriminate alms-giving was encouraging and even calling into existence, by enacting that sturdy beggars who were able to work and would not work might be whipped for their idleness. Then there came the statute of Elizabeth, which dealt even more severely with the sturdy vagrant by enacting that he should not merely be liable to whipping, but that he might be taken as a sort of serf and set to work compulsorily by anybody who wanted to make use of his services. But in the mean time laws were passed which set up something like a system for the employment of the poor who were willing to work and could not find work for themselves. The poor law of Henry the Eighth recognized the fact that it was the duty of the state to make some provision for the deserving poor in order that suitable employment should be found for them, or that relief should be given to them if they were physically unable to work, disabled by old age or by weakness, and that they should be kept alive either out-of-doors or in some sort of parochial institution. The statute of Elizabeth further extended and organized this system of relief, and made it the duty of church-wardens and overseers to "provide work, build poor-houses, and apprentice paupers." Not much change was made in this system until the great impulse to economical and social reform which set in with political reorganization in the reign of William the Fourth.

The new reign had some bright omens to welcome its opening. A wonderful era of literature had begun along with it. The new era was not, indeed, one of great originality in poetry of a high order, but it will always be remembered for its masterpieces in every department of prose. We shall have to tell in later chapters of the men of literature who contributed so much to make Queen Anne's reign immortal, and we now only stop to note the fact that the new reign and the new era of literature may be said to have begun together.

CHAPTER III

WHAT THE QUEEN CAME TO—ABROAD

QUEEN ANNE came in for an inheritance of continental war. The sovereignty created by William the Third had been born in bitterness and nurtured in convulsion. The political principles of his time had not allowed William to settle steadily down to the work of keeping his own kingdom safe and strong against any efforts which might be made by the dethroned Stuarts. Even so great a soldier and statesman as he might have found it hard business enough to make efficient preparation against all such attempts and possibilities, and at the same time to foster and watch over the internal prosperity of his new kingdom. It was his fate to have to take part in a great continental war which may be said to have involved the whole of the European states at one time or another in the long struggle. That war, of which we shall have to speak more fully a little later, was not one which, according to the ideas of the present day, had any direct bearing on the interests of England. Some impulse was undoubtedly given to the war spirit in England by the utterly unwise provocation which came from the King of France when he recognized the son of the exiled James the Second as the legitimate sovereign of England. But even if no such provocation had been given, it may be regarded as almost certain that, under the conditions of the times, England would have been drawn into the great struggle which was then convulsing the continent for the maintenance of what was called the balance of power. That was the struggle which Queen Anne inherited, and she assumed it to be a necessary part of her duty and her business to carry it on. It had divided itself into two great military and political chapters, one of which came to an end before William's death, but the second chapter may be described as a necessary development of the first.

The one great endeavor of the statesmanship of Europe seemed then to be the endeavor to maintain the balance of power on the European continent. We hear but little of the balance of power in our own days, and many years have passed since it was a subject of any serious account in the parliamentary debates of Westminster Palace. It is perhaps not unreasonable to say that it ceased to occupy the attention of the Houses of Parliament since the doctrine of nationalities came to be accounted a living principle in political affairs. There was a time, however, when statesmanship distracted its brains with schemes for the maintenance, or the redress, of the balance of power. It would not be easy to reduce the principle to any theory capable of definite expression, and perhaps even the rival statesmen who disputed in Parliament about the balance of power would have found it as difficult to agree on the precise meaning of the words as they found it difficult to agree on the practical application of the doctrine. Yet it may safely be said that during a long period of European history the balance of power had quite as much to do with the promotion of war as the passion for conquest or the rival claims of dynasties.

The central idea, however, of the policy which went in for adjusting the balance of power was the idea that certain European states had acquired, rightly or wrong-ly, by fair means or by foul, a title to divide the continent of Europe among them, and that an innovation made by any of them, or by any new power arising outside them or within them, was an unlawful attempt to disturb the recognized order of things, and ought to be immediately put down by force. It was, perhaps, the doctrine of divine right breaking out upon the world in a new form and under a new name. The embodied statesmanship of the ages which succeeded the recognized reign of mere conquest for the avowed purpose of conquest would seem to have set itself to find some basis of compromise and arrangement, and to have found it in the principle of the balance of power. This newer statesmanship said to itself: "Behold!—here we have Europe divided practically among three or four great predominant states, and this arrangement must undoubtedly be the direct dispensation of Providence. Let it, therefore, be regarded as an act of impiety as well as of wanton destructiveness for any one to interfere with the order of things which we find established, and let us treat any attempt at interference with it as an overt act of war."

The great recognized powers of Europe were then England, France, Spain, and the Austrian empire. Russia was slowly coming to a knowledge of her own strength, and was beginning to assert her claim to a share in the arbitration of the balance of power. Spain had reached her zenith, and was distinctly going down. If Russia had not yet recognized her own strength, Spain, on the other hand, had decidedly outgrown and exhausted hers. Spain had, not long before, stretched her empire farther over the world than the empires of the Cæsars had ever reached, and, indeed, Spain may be said to have accomplished what Alexander the Great only wished for—the discovery of new worlds to con-

WHAT THE QUEEN CAME TO—ABROAD

quer. The decay of Spain's greatness as a conquering and a domineering power has been described by Macaulay in some of his most picturesque and characteristic pages as the result of her bad system of government at home. No one can deny that every word said by Macaulay about the evil systems of government into which the rulers of Spain caused their country to sink is well deserved. Spain's misgovernment of her Flemish subjects forced on that revolt of the Netherlands which was maintained by generation after generation, until the oppressed at last succeeded in making themselves free. Something like the same story might be told of other provinces where the Spanish rulers, by sheer misgovernment and oppression, made the yoke of Spain unbearable, and led to new disruptions of the Spanish empire.

But it is coming of late to be recognized that there is a natural principle of growth and decay in great states which seems to be almost a part of the physical system of nature. The life of a state would appear to have its allotted season of growth and decay like the life of a man. At all events it may be reasonably contended that the greatness of a state, its season of supremacy over its region of the world, must have its natural time of decay as it had its time of development, and that no state can overshadow all its neighbors for an indefinite lapse of time. No form of government, however enlightened, practical, and beneficent, could have made the Roman empire endure down to our own time, and although Spain might have lasted longer than she did if her system of government had been founded on better principles, it seems quite clear now that in Queen Anne's time Spain was sinking into the inevitable decrepitude of old age.

Holland was then one of the rising countries of

Europe, and as she had no pretension or desire to become one of the conquering states, she could safely look forward to a long life of quiet prosperity if only her neighbors would let her alone. Sweden had lately begun to distinguish herself in war, but her fitful, brilliant incursions into the battle-fields of Europe had only amazed and startled the world as the invasion of some Northern pirate fleet might have amazed and startled a French or English seaport. The Turk was still a trouble to Europe, but the days when it was feared that he might overrun half the continent had evidently passed away. Italy was divided among various lords and masters, and indeed her very name was only, as Metternich long after declared it to be, a geographical definition.

The growing greatness of France and the sinking condition of Spain were the facts which, in the mind of statesmanship at that time, seemed most seriously and immediately to threaten the balance of power in Europe. The statesmen of England were then, as at most other times, particularly anxious and watchful about the growth of the influence of France on the European continent. Every succeeding year of Spanish decay seemed only to offer new invitations and opportunities to France for the disturbance of the balance of power. We shall the better understand the feeling of England towards France at that time if we carry our recollections back to what we all know to have been the feeling of many English statesmen, only a few years ago, with regard to the growing power of Russia. There was then a nervous anxiety about every movement made by Russia. With certain of our statesmen it did not need evidence of actual preparations against any of England's Eastern possessions to make them convinced that Russia's very existence threatened dan-

WHAT THE QUEEN CAME TO—ABROAD

ger to England, and that it would be a part of the patriotic duty of Englishmen to make common cause with the very Turk himself, if only by such companionship we could check the ambition of the Muscovite power. The time may possibly come when readers of history will find it as hard to understand what business England had in promoting and taking part in the Crimean War as matter-of-fact readers find it now to understand what business England had, during the early years of Queen Anne's reign, to trouble herself about the attitude of France with regard to the vacancy in the succession to the crown of Spain.

The quarrel, as has been stated, was none of Queen Anne's seeking. Anne may be said to have inherited it just as she inherited the throne, for it would hardly have been possible for her under all the conditions to strike out a new policy of her own even if she had had the mind or the strength for a new policy. The war to which Anne succeeded began out of the rivalry between the aggressive policy of France and the defensive policy of other states on the European continent. Louis the Fourteenth was then King of France, and during his reign the kingdom over which he ruled had risen to such a position in letters and arts as it had never enjoyed before, and to such a place in arms as it never held again until the days of the Great Napoleon. The constant dread of other continental states was that France might be tempted at any moment to extend her territories this way or that, on one pretext or another, by the mere force of conquest. William the Third was naturally a close observer of the policy of France, and watched with anxious and jealous eye every movement on the part of Louis the Fourteenth which seemed to threaten fresh annexation. William was a shrewd and crafty politician as well as a soldier, and he did not scruple, on more occasions than one, to enter into terms with Louis, to "pack cards" with him, if we may adopt the language of Shakespeare's Mark Antony, for the purpose of making some arrangement which might at least postpone a threatening war, even though the arrangement were to be made at the expense of some smaller state.

There came a crisis, however, when William found it impossible any longer to deal with the policy of Louis by other means than the arbitration of war. Spain was then ruled by one of the weakest and least capable of monarchs or men, Charles the Second. The immediate trouble was that Charles was childless, and that in his condition of health it might be taken for granted that he must die without leaving any direct heir to follow him in the line of succession. In the year 1700 Charles died childless, and then came the momentous question— Who is to have the throne of Spain? No difficulty whatever arose in this instance from the lack or scarcity of claimants—the throne of Spain was not by any means going a-begging; the trouble was that there were too many claimants, and that each claimant had too many backers. One of the claimants was the Dauphin of France, another was the Emperor of Germany, and yet another was Joseph, the Electoral Prince of Bavaria. Now, in the case alike of the Dauphin and the Electoral Prince all right of succession to the throne of Spain had been formally renounced by the parents of both at the time of their marriage because, if such renunciation had not been made, the union of these pairs would have been regarded by all Europe as boding threats of intolerable disturbance to the balance of power. With regard to the family of the Emperor, there had been no such formal renunciation, but then the claim of the Emperor's family by its degree of relationship to the dead King of Spain was the weakest of the three, and in any case it must have been evident to all the world that the successor to the imperial throne of Germany would never be allowed to enter into peaceful possession of the Spanish throne as well. On the other hand, it was hardly in the nature of things that the heir to the monarchy of France could be quietly allowed to establish himself as King of Spain, even if there had been no formal renunciation of his claim at the time when his parents were married.

The two rising rival powers on the European continent were then the monarchy of France and the curiously constructed, partly federated, partly despotic empire of Germany. It was out of the question to suppose that the other states of Europe could look calmly on and see either France or Germany become owner of the vast territorial possessions of Spain. It might be said, indeed, that there were two states of Europe— England and Holland—which had but little direct concern in the disputed inheritance. The people of the United Provinces, as the Dutch and Flemish populations were then termed, were essentially a trading and a navigating people who had not long succeeded in establishing their independence, who had no ambition to extend their territory, were only anxious to be let alone and to follow the occupations in which they were becoming more and more successful, and who could have sailed the seas and sold their merchandise just as well though France or Germany became master of Spain. But the trouble with Holland was exactly that which has been concisely described by Schiller's Wilhelm Tell—one must be ever in trouble when one has bad neighbors. Holland was always, and not unnaturally, on the watch against encroachments from some of her neighbors, and she knew well enough that the stronger this or that neighbor became the more likely he would be to grasp at new acquisitions of territory. Holland, therefore, from the first showed herself most active in all the endeavors that were made to bring about something like a final and satisfactory settlement of the claims to the Spanish succession.

England, on the other hand, would appear to have but little direct interest in the dispute. Even if the heir to the King of France were to succeed at once to the crown of Spain, and thus in time become King of France and Spain together, it was hardly probable that his wildest schemes of aggression would lead him to contemplate the annexation of England. William might, of course, have kept to his island sovereignty, looked after the prosperity of his people and the strengthening of his dynasty, and left the continental powers to settle among themselves, by force of arms, the future ownership of Spain. But even if William had been endowed by nature with the temperament of a philosopher, it is not likely that he could have given full scope to the impulses of such a temperament at a time when the balance of power was still a dominating principle in the polities of Europe.

William, however, was not left to settle the question in his own mind by a statesman-like study of the possible effects which the crisis might bring with it to the balance of power. A sudden and apparently a spontaneous act of insult and defiance on the part of the King of France brought William at once to his feet and into the great quarrel. James the Second had been for a long time an exile in France, and his claims to the English succession as well as his personal bearing had made an impression on the mind of Louis the Fourteenth. When James came to die, the heart of Louis was touched, and in an impulse of something like Quixotic generosity he formally recognized James's son, the Old Pretender, as he was called in later days, as King of England. When the news of this audacious stroke of policy was brought to England, it created such a storm of anger all over the country that William would have had much difficulty in holding his people back from war, even if it had been his purpose to keep them within the lines of peace.

Of late years the English people had had rather too much of continental embroilments. William, who had warred against France up to the settlement of Ryswick, had since then received but slender encouragement to carry out the strong and enterprising policy which he believed best suited to maintain England's place among the great powers of Europe. Now he found, in a moment, that he could count on the full support of his people in a forward policy. The insult of the King of France, as it was then regarded by the vast majority of Englishmen, had done it all. The existing Parliament, which had been slow to vote the supplies William thought necessary to carry out his military plans, was dismissed and a new Parliament was summoned which showed itself ready to maintain him to the full in any course of action he might deem it statesman-like and patriotic to follow. Even before this had come about the English ambassador had been recalled from France, and the ambassador of King Louis dismissed from London. By the energy and the influence of William the alliance was restored, and England, the German empire, and the United Provinces of Holland pledged themselves to resist the aggressive policy of France and to prevent the kingdoms of France and Spain from being united under one sovereign. This was the Grand Alliance, the crowning work of William's ever-active life.

THE REIGN OF QUEEN ANNE

The reader who contemplates this particular chapter of history will see one fact at least clearly established amid all the confusion of claims to succession, and counter-claims, and all the rival and conflicting interests of dynasties and of systems. The political development of England had advanced one step beyond that of France. In France the recognized head of the state was able to pledge his people to the cause of divine right, while the ruler of England only occupied his throne by virtue of a principle of hereditary succession which recognized the right of the people to have something to say in the settlement of their monarchical line. England had, indeed, to go on a quest among the royal families of Europe in order to find the one which could claim the nearest relationship to some royal house of England, while at the same time disclaiming any title which identified it with the pretensions of the house of Stuart. The Bill of Rights and the Act of Settlement admitted and represented some claim on the part of the state and the people to institute a new line of succession, maintaining, when it had been instituted, the principle of hereditary descent. France still held to the divine right of kings—a right which was maintained until the great revolution went to work with a new experiment.

The European struggle which we know as the War of the Spanish Succession was, with her kingdom, the inheritance of Queen Anne. William did not live to carry it on. Seldom in the history of any country has an entirely inexperienced sovereign come in for so tremendous a crisis with the creation of which the new sovereign had absolutely nothing to do, and probably no other woman sovereign has ever come so suddenly into an inheritance of such portentous responsibility.

The relative value of the rival claims made to the

throne of Spain is a matter of but slight account to the readers of history now. There was so much of intermarrying among members of the continental houses that it was hardly possible for any sovereign to die childless without leaving his kingdom open to the competing claims of various aspirants, each of whom contended, with some plausible array of argument, that his birth brought him nearest in the order of divine right. None of the continental sovereigns, or of the statesmen who served them, thought for a moment of settling the question by any reference to the wishes or the interests of the Spanish people themselves. Nor was there any way of settling the controversy by an appeal to some international Areopagus. Strokes must arbitrate— the rival claimants must fight it out with such help as each of them could get from neighbors who had no direct and personal interests in the quarrel. No question of principle either in statesmanship or morals was concerned in the controversy, or could be invoked as a direct influence in its settlement. It was a dispute of grasping princes, to be settled on battle-fields and on seas by armies and fleets. Such was the war which was just breaking out when Queen Anne succeeded to the English throne.

Louis the Fourteenth was then at the height of his power. Under his rule, although certainly not because of any fostering qualities in him, France had reached the highest position in arms and in arts which she had yet attained in history. The age of Louis the Fourteenth was, on the whole, the greatest age of French literature. We cannot trace the sudden and splendid uprising of that literature to any inspiring influence which came from King Louis. It may well be doubted whether the birth and the growth of genius owe much, in any case, to the influence of a monarch, and the effect of royal patronage is shown quite as often in the encouragement of the art that is fictitious and fleeting as in the encouragement of the art that is genuine and destined to make its enduring mark. Perhaps we may take it for granted that true art will find its expression whether it be favored and patronized by royal influence or not; but in any case Louis the Fourteenth does not seem the kind of sovereign whose intellect and education would have enabled him to point with his sceptre at the right man to fill the foremost place in literature or in art.

Louis the Fourteenth was so fortunate as to live at a time when French literature and art commanded the admiration of the whole civilized world, and he had himself done much, in obeying the impulses of his own vainglorious ambition, to make France the dread and wonder of Europe in politics and in war. At the same time and by the very same qualities he had opened the way for the great troubles, domestic and foreign, which were to culminate in the French Revolution. By the revocation of the edict of Nantes he had compelled some of the best and bravest of his subjects to seek shelter in foreign lands and to add to the intellectual, industrial, and military strength of peoples who were afterwards to be the rivals of France. He was a narrow-minded bigot on all questions of religion, but the devotion to his own religion, which he professed and which he endeavored to enforce upon others, never restrained him from the indulgence of his own selfish and sensuous vices. The very defects, the very worst qualities of his character only helped the more to make his reign a subject of deep and inexhaustible interest for the students of history and of character, for the writers and the readers of romance. Here and there one may come on some episode or incident of his reign which has supplied matter for study, for speculation, and for psychological puzzle to all succeeding generations. Few historical mysteries have ever excited more curiosity, given occasion for more controversy, or started more plausible explanations than the story of the Iron Mask, for which George Agar Ellis, the English author and diplomatist, afterwards Lord Dover, appears to have been the first to find the true solution. Perhaps the highest praise that the critical historian can well give to Louis the Fourteenth—Louis the Great, as he was called—is that when we contrast him with his successor, Louis the Fifteenth, we are inclined to think that the figure of the elder ruler seems stately and kinglike in comparison, and the reign of the latter Louis seems an anticlimax when we study its history after that of his predecessor.

The most striking figure among continental sovereigns at the time which we are now describing was undoubtedly that of the Russian Czar. Peter the Great has been well described by the first Lord Lytton as one of the greatest sovereigns ever born to a throne. Julius Cæsar, Cromwell, Napoleon — these were not born to thrones; but Peter the Great began his career at the point where other conquerors have commonly reached their climax. The ambition of Peter was to make himself a great man and his realm a great country, and he accomplished both his objects. He was determined that Russia should become a naval power, and he had first to turn his attention to the means by which he could be enabled to extend her territory to the sea. Augustus found his city of brick and left it of marble; Peter the Great found a land-locked dominion and made a way for it to the sea. He devoted himself with indomitable energy and patience to the study and practice of mechanical arts which might help him in the accomplishment of his purposes. He travelled through foreign countries; he worked at ship-carpentering in the dockyards of Holland; he studied the building of vessels under the shadow of the Tower of London.

Bishop Burnet had some talks with Peter while the Czar was pursuing his practical studies in London, and seems to think him a sort of rough semi-savage. Indeed, the Bishop appears to have been rather at a loss to understand how Providence could have placed such a man at the head of a great and rising state. As sovereign of Russia he made his country for the first time an influence and a power in the politics of Europe, and beyond all question he laid the foundations of that vast military and maritime empire which counts for so much in the history of the modern world, and does not even yet suggest the limits of its possible development. The character of Peter was disfigured by almost savage defects of temper, by utter unscrupulousness, by sensuous vices, and by a cruelty which was sometimes implacable. He appears to have had in him something of the Oriental nature, the craft, the cruelty, the sudden contrasts of generosity and ferocity, of clemency and severity, of noble impulse and of selfish freak which we associate with the conventional portraiture of an Eastern despot. But whatever his personal defects, it is certain that the Czar Peter was one of the greatest men living at a time when there were many great men, and that he was creating a powerful and a developing state while other sovereigns were unconsciously doing their very worst to bring to ruin the fabric which had been bequeathed to them by their predecessors.

Charles the Twelfth of Sweden was in his meteoric course when Queen Anne came to the throne of England. Charles was one of the most brilliant and picturesque figures then to be seen on the battle-fields of

Europe. He was a very Quixote of national ambition and adventure. He amazed and even bewildered Europe by his genius and audacity. Statesmen and soldiers of the older school did not know where to look for him, or how to deal with him, when he suddenly flashed his search-light upon their political combinations and their territorial schemes. Blushing glory had not yet to hide Pultowa's day, as Johnson put it in those lines from his *Vanity of Human Wishes,* which will be remembered when the most elaborate essays of *The Rambler* have ceased to find even specialist readers.

The dominions of the German Emperor were made up of Austria itself and of the federated states, as they may be called, which belonged to the Germanic system. There were nine electoral princes, called Electors, who asserted and exercised the right to choose the Emperor of Germany. That empire still claimed to be the representative of the Holy Roman Empire, whose head was crowned at Rome by Pope John the Twelfth. The Elector of Brandenburg was now King of Prussia. The Germanic system may be described as made up of three estates—the electors, who chose the emperor; the nobles and bishops and governors, who constituted in a certain sense a House of Peers; and then something like a popular organization supposed to represent the interests and the feelings of the general community. Already the German empire, in its historic sense, was growing to be but the shadow of the Holy Roman Empire, and it could not have needed much foresight to discern that the electors of Brandenburg as kings of Prussia would come before long to contend for the leadership of the Germanic peoples. The Emperor of Germany was still, however, a sovereign whose power on the European continent might compete with that of France. The alliance which brought England, Germany, and the United Provinces into an engagement to resist to the uttermost the attempt of Louis the Fourteenth to make Spain a part of the French kingdom was one which even the ambition and arrogance of Louis himself could hardly have contemplated without some sense of grave responsibility. Louis was ready to brave all. His declaration that there are no more Pyrenees has become one of the famous sayings of history, but its fame is fully equalled by its fallacy, and the Pyrenees, crossed and recrossed since that time, are still the dividing-line between France and Spain.

Poland was still a kingdom—a kingdom troublesome to itself and to the world in general; a kingdom which under all its changes seemed ever to have been endowed by fatality with a constitution unsuited to its own conditions and the conditions of succeeding epochs. But Poland has a brave, gifted, and patriotic race for its people, and through its many changes has been able to win for itself the sympathy and good wishes of all lovers of liberty. For some time yet it is to appear and reappear as a nationality and a political force in the struggles of European dynasties and peoples. Its efforts to maintain its independence as a nation and a state are to be sung by poets and pictured by romancists from most of the civilized countries of the world, and the sword of many a foreign volunteer is to fight for its cause on all its battle-fields.

Thus may rapidly be described the principal actors and influences in the great struggle on which Europe was about to enter when Queen Anne announced to her Parliament her resolve that England should declare war against France.

CHAPTER IV

THOSE AROUND QUEEN ANNE

AMONG those who stood around the Queen at the time of her accession to the throne, the most conspicuous and greatest figure was that of John Churchill, then Earl and soon after Duke of Marlborough. Never was a man born into a time more peculiarly fitted to prepare for him a stage suited to the full development and display of his commanding qualities. Never was a man better gifted by nature with the faculties which enable him to find or make such a stage. In describing the character of Marlborough, the first difficulty is to know how to give the full measure of praise or blame without seeming to attempt the accomplishment of that task which is, in the language of Shakespeare, " to solder close impossibilities and make them kiss." The public and private faults of Marlborough, even if we tax them down to the most rigid limits that impartial history will admit, are such that they would seem to put the character of him who possessed them out of the reach of most men's sympathy. Yet, on the other hand, if we do the barest justice to the better parts of the man's nature, we must admit that he had qualities in him which would have gained affection and admiration from minds of the most diverse constitution, even if he had not been the greatest soldier, and in many qualities the greatest hero, of his time.

We can all remember the old story of the two knights

who fell into a fierce quarrel about the color of a certain shield, which the one declared to be white and the other maintained to be black. After the disputants had fought long and fiercely over this question, some friends at last intervened, and the argument was referred to the arbitration of the shield itself, when it was found, by the easiest inspection, that the shield was black on one side and white on the other. It might appear within the range of possibilities that the same dispute could long be maintained with perfect sincerity about the character of Marlborough, provided each disputant were so absorbed in his own view of the question as to look only on that side of the shield which had suggested his own conclusions. Concentrate your attention for a time on the dark side of Marlborough's character, and it may well appear all black—fasten your gaze upon the brighter side, and you may become satisfied that it is all white.

About Marlborough's genius there is, at all events, no possibility of dispute. He was the greatest European general of his time, and he was probably the greatest English general known to history up to our own time. It would be hardly too much to say that he combined in himself all the qualities of daring, foresight, energy, enterprise, imagination, minute power of observation, cool, calculating sagacity, and indomitable patience, which must be united in order to make a consummate military commander. The controlling power which he could exercise over the minds of men and over the hearts of women was, in itself, a sort of genius. Nature had given him appearance and manners which well fitted him for the task of attracting those who came within the range of his influence and moulding them to his will. He was singularly handsome of face and graceful of form—in any crowd of men, in any society, he would have been singled out in a moment as the most attractive figure. No stranger could come near him without feeling an instant desire to know who he was and to learn all about him. We read in classic legend that when Momus had racked his sarcastic brain in order to find some word of disparagement to say about Venus, he could think of no fault to find with the goddess but that her feet made too loud a sound when she walked. The most disparaging critics of Marlborough's physical charms seemed to find nothing worse to say of him than that his voice was sometimes untuneful in its tone.

Marlborough belonged to a Devonshire family, and started in life without much fortune to carry him on. He entered the army, and after a while found advancement at the court of James the Second—partly, it is painful and pitiful to relate, through the influence of his sister, Arabella Churchill, who had been mistress to the King when he was Duke of York. He served in one of the wars against the Dutch, and served for a time under Turenne himself, who saw almost at a glance the young man's genius for war. Returning to England, he began to rise steadily in the King's service. Meanwhile he had secretly married the beautiful and imperious Sarah Jennings, who was destined to exercise, through her influence over him and over Queen Anne, a directing power for a long time in the movement of English history. James the Second endeavored to induce Marlborough to become a Roman Catholic. Perhaps the young soldier saw, even at that time, that such a conversion would not be likely to bring him to the winning side; at any rate, he held to the newer order of ideas. Marlborough had clearly made up his mind, from the very first, that his mission in life was to secure a career for himself, and that no doubts or scruples were to interfere with that object. He had no hesitation about accepting the patronage of the Duke of York, although he knew by what influence that patronage had been secured. Unless the stories told of him from time to time, and believed by his frineds as well as by his enemies, were all untrue, Marlborough turned even his love affairs to practical account for the advancement of his own self-interest. As might easily be supposed, he was much admired by women, and he was not above accepting handsome presents of money from ladies who also honored him with other favors. It was said of him in his earlier days that he used to lay down as a maxim for the guidance of young lovers that a woman who is really fond of a man will be all the fonder of him if he consents to accept her money.

Marlborough held to James the Second as long as it seemed convenient to his own self-interest to act the part of a loyal and devoted follower. When William of Orange was about to invade England, with the object of dethroning James the Second, Marlborough was appointed to high command against the invader. Marlborough, however, saw that his hour had come, and he went straightway over to the service of William, and lent the help of his energy and his military genius to dethrone his former master. This was not the first act of treachery, as it was not the last, which Marlborough committed against the man who, for whatever reason, had taken earliest notice of him, had become his patron, and put him on his way to success at court and in camp. Marlborough devoted himself to the service of William with as much fidelity as his peculiar temperament allowed, the path to preferment was for a time clear before him, and no considerations of self-interest interposed to tempt him from the straight way. He had many opportunities under William of proving his great capacity as a soldier, and throughout the whole of his career he made it evident that he was no less a statesman than a soldier. His influence over the Princess Anne had always been very great, owing chiefly to the fact that his wife, Sarah Jennings, had obtained, and for a long time held, such a complete dominion over the mind and heart of Anne as one woman rarely obtains over the mind and heart of another.

King William appointed Marlborough to be governor over the young Duke of Gloucester, the only one of Anne's numerous progeny who gave any promise of living to maturity, and it is said that William went so far out of his ordinary way of precise and literal address as to speak to Marlborough on that occasion in the language of high compliment. The King told Marlborough that if he could make the young prince anything like Marlborough himself he would have fulfilled the highest wishes of the boy's mother and of the sovereign. Any hopes that were founded on the life of the poor young Duke of Gloucester were soon destined to be disappointed; the young prince, who had Marlborough for his governor and Bishop Burnet for his preceptor, was not allowed by the fates to have much opportunity of showing that he had benefited by so exceptional a course of education.

When Anne came to the throne she may fairly be described as under the absolute dominion of Marlborough and his wife, but of Marlborough chiefly through the medium of his masterful and far-reaching consort. Few chapters of personal history can be more curious or more interesting than that which tells of the strange supremacy so long exercised over the mind of Anne by Marlborough's wife. Whole volumes of correspondence preserve the story of this extraordinary friendship. On the marriage of Anne with Prince George of Denmark, Lady Churchill, as the future Duchess of Marlborough was then titled, was appointed a lady of her bedchamber. Throughout the whole of her life it was an inherent quality of Anne's nature that she must depend upon somebody, take her orders from somebody, have her path of life and even her ways of thinking pointed out to her by somebody, and for many years this occupation was uncompromisingly undertaken by Lady Churchill. There is something touching, something pathetic, in the affectation of mystery, often ridiculous enough in itself, with which these two women were pleased dramatically to enfold their close and constant correspondence. It was arranged that Anne should be known in this scheme of letter-writing by the name of Mrs. Morley, and Lady Churchill by that of Mrs. Freeman, and other eminent personages had their identity disguised to as little practical purpose by equally unpretending appellations.

In the *History of the Reign of Queen Anne,* by John Hill Burton, there is a sentence quoted from one of Anne's letters to Lady Churchill, written at a time when some difficulties arose which led Marlborough to threaten that he might have to resign his position in the Queen's service. "As for your poor, unfortunate Morley," Anne writes, "she could not bear it; for if ever you should forsake me I should have nothing more to do with the world, but make another abdication; for where is a crown when the support of it is gone?" In the same volume is a letter written by Anne to Lord Godolphin "at a point of time between her father's death and her own accession."

"*For the Lord Godolphin.*

"WINDSOR, *Tuesday night.*

"I can not lett your servant goe back without returning my thanks for the letter he brought me, & assureing you it is a very great satisfaction to me to find you agree wth Mrs. Morley conserning ye ill-natured, cruel proceedings of Mr. Caliban, wch vexes me more then you can emagin, & I am out of all patience when I think I must do soe monsterous a thing as not to put my lodgings in mourning for my father. I hope if you get a coppy of ye will Ld. Manchester says he will send over, you will be soe kind as to let me see it, & ever believe me your faithful servant."

Anne's spelling is somewhat peculiar, but it was not any worse than that of many men and women of her time who made profession of higher literary accomplishments than she ever claimed as her own. The reader will naturally be curious to know something of the identity of the person described as Mr. Caliban. At the time of her life, when the letter was written, Anne was in the habit of describing William the Third by that Shakespearean appellation. Indeed, we find in Coxe's *Life of Marlborough* that among her intimate friends she occasionally called the King the Monster, Caliban, or the Dutch Abortion. It appears, however, quite certain that the Caliban phrase, as applied to King William, was the boasted invention of Mrs. Freeman and was only adopted by the obedient Mrs. Morley.

Until her accession to the throne Anne led a quiet and almost secluded life, concerning herself but little with all that was going on in the great world around her, and content to be taught how she ought to think and feel by the clever and brilliant woman who exercised for many years an unqualified dominion over her. Now, if Marlborough had any one strong feeling suffusing and inspiring his whole nature outside his mere self-interest, his love of glory, and his desire to give his genius a fair field for its exercise, it was assuredly his devoted and passionate attachment to his wife. That splendid quality of patience which stood him in such good stead during the interruptions and delays put in his way by hostile fortune, and by the shortcomings of his allies and his supporters during his great campaigns, enabled him to bear the changeful temper and domineering ways of his wife without showing any sign of irritability or resentment. It has to be said in bare justice to Queen Anne that she must have had some capacity of her own which enabled her to comprehend the genius of Marlborough, quite independently of the influence exercised over her by Marlborough's wife, for it was not until after Anne came into the responsibility of royal position that Marlborough was enabled to prove himself equal to one of the most momentous tasks ever imposed upon a military commander.

Sidney, Lord Godolphin, was one of the most prominent and influential statesmen of the time, and he had the advantage of being in close alliance and friendship with Marlborough. Through the influence of Marlborough, Godolphin was appointed to the office of Lord High Treasurer, a function which has no exact equivalent in the political business of our modern days, but may be described as a sort of combination of the rank of prime-minister with the functions of Chancellor of the Exchequer. We shall, of course, meet with Godolphin again and again in the chapters of this history, and it is now only necessary to say of him that he was undoubtedly one of the most careful and capable managers of the public funds an English sovereign has ever appointed to office, and that in providing for the long and perilous war which had to be undertaken his financial skill combined the maximum of efficiency with the minimum of waste.

Marlborough and Godolphin were both members of the Tory party, but the word Tory, as it was understood in those days, would hardly serve as a description for

THOSE AROUND QUEEN ANNE

any Tory party in more modern times when political parties are created by principles and by interests which have nothing to do with the question of royal succession. Our modern ideas of a Tory would naturally represent him as a man who believed that the best interests of the country were served by intrusting the task of its government, as much as possible, to the hands of the aristocratic classes, and by resisting, as far as possible, the growth of democracy. Our typical Whig, on the other hand, if we take him as he began to show himself during the reign of George the Third, would be a man who believed that the object of a patriotic party was to introduce, as far as might seem expedient, the representative principle into the work of government, and to give the people in general some share in the making of the laws. We have outgrown of late the Whigs and the Tories even of George the Third's day, and the Whig may be said to have passed altogether into history. The Whig is now either a Liberal or a Radical. The Tory still retains his old name, unless he prefers to be called a Conservative, and although he has necessarily advanced with the times, he still keeps to his old business of resisting as long as he can the spread of the democratic movement. But the Whigs and Tories in the days of Marlborough and Godolphin had political purposes to occupy them which are unknown to our times. The Tory had in his heart a partiality for divine right and the Stuart dynasty, while the Whig looked forward to hereditary succession on the lines established by the reign of William the Third and the Act of Settlement.

In the Tory party at the time of Queen Anne's accession the two leading men were Robert Harley, afterwards Earl of Oxford, and Henry St. John, afterwards Viscount Bolingbroke. Harley was the man of capacity, Bolingbroke was the man of genius. If the enthusiastic eulogy bestowed by a poet could be taken as creating a picture which posterity might accept as a faithful likeness, then surely the praise bestowed by Alexander Pope would give Harley a place in history as a model of public and private virtue. Pope ascribes to Harley:

> "A soul supreme in each hard instance tried,
> Above all pain or passion, and all pride,"

and other lines to the same effect which have nevertheless not established themselves as the pronouncement of posterity. Pope poured forth raptures of admiration upon Bolingbroke. Down to very recent days there was hardly any line of English poetry more familiar in the mouths of men—the majority of whom, even when they quoted the line, had not the least idea of its personal application—than "the feast of reason and the flow of soul." It was St. John, the poet tells us, who "mingles with my friendly bowl" that feast of reason and flow of soul which until our own days, and quite lately, became too much the recognized property of after-dinner orators. Even an admiring poet, however, could hardly go too far in paying a tribute to the genius of Bolingbroke. Pope tells us how "nobly pensive St. John sat and thought." We do not now usually contemplate St. John as sitting and thinking in this nobly pensive mood. We think of him as the brilliant orator, the almost unrivalled parliamentary debater, the great prose writer, the fascinating man of fashion, the reckless libertine, the versatile political conspirator. In an age of commanding political figures his was one of the most commanding; in an age of great prose writers he wrote many pages which will live with the best.

THOSE AROUND QUEEN ANNE

The uncertain temper, the disturbed principles and practices of the time, can hardly find better illustration than in the story of a supposed discovery that was made shortly after the accession of Queen Anne. Some of those around the Queen put into circulation a report that a number of private papers had been found soon after the death of William the Third which showed that the late King had a plan—or it might be called a plot—in hand for the removal of Anne from her place in the dynasty, and even, it was said, for her imprisonment or banishment, and for placing the head of the Hanover family on the throne of England. This story found so many serious believers that at last it was thought necessary to make an official inquiry into the alleged facts. A commission was actually appointed, one of whose members was Marlborough himself, to search the whole of the late King's papers and to report to the Queen and to Parliament whether they contained any evidence of such a design. A careful search was made among all the letters and papers, of whatever kind, which William had left behind, and, of course, the result of the inquiry was that nothing could be discovered which gave any support, suggestion, or excuse for the diffusion of such extraordinary statements. Then the professed friends of the Queen, who had been helping to spread these utterly groundless reports, grew suddenly ashamed of the encouragement which they had given to the rumors, and went about emphatically disclaiming any belief in them, and protesting that even when they talked privately about the existence of this scheme they had only done so for the purpose of protesting their utter disbelief in it. On the other hand, there were found many persons, as there always will be found when such a controversy arises, who shook their heads gravely over the official report of the inquiry, and cautiously, but with persistency and with increasing emphasis, declared their sad suspicion that there was a great deal more in the matter than those in high places were willing to admit. They did their best to establish a belief that the official report had been nothing but a deliberate arrangement to avert a national scandal and to prevent the purpose of the late King from being made known to the country. A strong effort was made by some of those who accepted the report of the commission, and who had never believed in the whole story, to get some steps taken for bringing to public trial and punishment those who had had a prominent part in spreading abroad the story of the alleged scheme. Nothing came of it, however, and the controversy was allowed to pass away without recourse to any process of law.

There were times in Queen Anne's life when she seemed willing to believe in anything which told her that the late King had been filled with an unconquerable distrust and dislike of her, and had been, up to the last, quite capable of approving any scheme which might prevent her from maintaining her position on the throne of England. It was an age of conspiracy and counter-consipracy in political life at home and abroad, an age when families were divided against themselves by political passions and dynastic interest, and nobody could have known better than Queen Anne did how little even blood relationship, to say nothing of family connections, could be relied upon as a guarantee for enduring loyalty, political integrity, and personal affection.

The country was now on the eve of a great crisis. The Queen had announced to Parliament her determination to carry out the policy of William the Third, and her resolve to declare war against France. Her allies were to be the Emperor of Germany, with such of the electoral German states as were willing to become active supporters of the Emperor's policy, and the United Provinces of Holland. The Queen conferred on Marlborough the office of commander-in-chief over all the forces of England on land and sea. Marlborough was now, in fact, only at the opening of his great career. He had fought on many a battle-field before this time, and wherever he had found an opportunity of proving his military capacity he had given ample promise of a genius for command. Up to this time he had not had a chance of showing to his country and to the world that he possessed the qualities which would enable him to take rank among the greatest soldiers in history. He was now more than fifty years of age, and the Marlborough of immortal fame had yet to assert himself and to prove himself.

If the Grand Alliance had not been reconstructed by Anne, and if England had followed what would probably have been the policy of a later age, and allowed the dynastic quarrels of continental states to settle themselves without the intervention of English armies and fleets, the world might never have come to know that the foremost supporter of the new Queen was a soldier qualified to rank with the greatest military commanders in ancient or modern history. The woman born to be Queen was not much given to profound reflection, and had but little of the imaginative power which can foresee the greatness of a national crisis or comprehend the qualities of men near to her who are destined to make history. But Mrs. Morley was devoted to Mrs. Freeman, and she had probably some faint conception of the part which Mrs. Freeman's husband was to fill in the reign of Queen Anne. It may be said, while we are dealing with this part of our subject, that Sarah Jennings was for many generations believed to be the Atossa satirized by Alexander Pope in his *Moral Essays*. More recently a theory has been started that Pope did not intend his satirical poetry as the picture of Sarah Jennings, but as that of another woman who held a high rank about the same time. Unless, however, there are very convincing grounds for rejecting what may be called the contemporary belief as to the original of a satirical sketch, it is safer to assume that contemporary opinion guessed rightly, and to accept Atossa as Pope's pen-sketch of John Churchill's adored and domineering wife.

The coronation of Queen Anne took place in the year of her accession, and was attended with all the splendor of ceremonial and all the array of heraldic symbolism in its minutest details which, for many succeeding generations, have been considered essential components of a coronation. Westminster Hall, and the majestic Abbey which stands near it, were the principal scenes of the historic display. The Queen herself was in very weak health and had to be carried or supported during the greater part of the ceremonies. We shall not enter into much detail of description, but there are some parts of the day's pageantry which may have an awakened interest for readers of the present day. There were two accompaniments of this coronation which became for the first time a part of the ceremony. These were the parliamentary test and the coronation oath. They were introduced and adopted for the avowed purpose of proclaiming to the world that the Revolution had established new conditions under which, and under which alone, the sovereign of England could hold the throne and demand the allegiance of the English people. They constituted, in fact, a legal declaration that the old doctrine of divine right was done with forever, and that the sovereign of a plot to take up the challenger's glove, and thus at least testify to the world that there existed a rival claimant to the throne of England in the person of a still surviving representative of the royal Stuart line.

It might have seemed more in accordance with the fitness of things, or at all events with the artistic fitness of things, if such a challenge, supposing it to have been seriously planned at all, even for the sake of theatric effect, had been delivered on this occasion when the last of the Stuarts was seated on the throne, and arrangements had been made for the succession of a foreign family, rather than at the later day when the new dynasty was actually in possession. Queen Anne, however, does not seem to have been a sovereign with whom dramatic or romantic effects had much to do, and her coronation as that of avowedly the last of the Stuart sovereigns was allowed to pass off without a challenge.

CHAPTER V

DISSENT AND DEFOE

THE religious troubles which beset the Queen on her accession to power were not by any means fully represented in the declaration which contained her disavowal of all sympathy with certain beliefs and practices of the Church of Rome. There were questions of religious conformity which had nothing to do with the faith adopted by James the Second. Dissent among Protestants themselves was beginning to be a subject of most serious controversy, and drove many, who professed a horror of the spiritual servitude enjoined by the Church of Rome, into a constant clamor for the intervention of the criminal law in order to put down all freedom of private judgment among Protestant denominations. Not to speak for the moment of the fierce controversies concerning the maintenance or the suppression of Presbyterianism in the kingdom of Scotland, there was a storm arising against Protestant Nonconformists in England itself which might have aroused a feeling of satisfaction in the breast of the least vindictive Papist sufferer for his belief. An agitation was going on all through England which had for its object the most rigid exclusion from all public office of every one who not merely showed any lack of enthusiasm for the doctrines of the state Church, but who failed to make his full acceptance of all these doctrines known by a sufficient number of public and formal protestations in the proper places during certain specified terms of each year. It was not thought by any means enough that an aspirant to public office should have given no sign whatever of conscientious objection to any tenet of the state Church. It was insisted that unless he made known his absolute conformity by a certain number of public professions within a specified time, he ought not to be considered a fit person to be intrusted with the duties of any office held under the control of the established authorities.

Even so sound a churchman as Bishop Burnet was sometimes astonished, and often not a little amused, at the alarm and passion aroused in the minds of many respectable and intelligent Protestants by the existence and growth of dissenting denominations in England. Such persons were constantly asking whether, after all, it had really profited anything to get rid of the Pope, the Jesuits, and the Stuart dynasty if here at home in England men were allowed to go about and start new theories concerning ecclesiastical discipline, and even to hold meetings and conferences, and to preach sermons in support of heterodox and dissenting opinions. What was the use of the Reformation? it was asked. What was the good of establishing a state Church if men were to be allowed, without interference on the part of the law, to form themselves into Nonconformist congregations, to hold religious services of their own, to choose their pastors, and to give so-called religious instruction to their families without any regard for the authority of the state episcopate or the decisions of convocation?

Nothing could be more certain than the fact that dissent was growing and spreading day after day among English communities. Nothing, indeed, could have been more natural, among all the changing conditions of the time. Within the memory of living men not yet old there had been a king who professed the faith of the Church of Rome, followed by a king who professed the faith of the Church of England, and now by a queen who, while proclaiming her conformity with the doctrines of the English state Church, was believed to be secretly in sympathy with the dynastic claims of that Stuart family to which she herself belonged, and whose immediate and intimate friends were shrewdly suspected of participation in political schemes for a counter-revolution and for the restoration of the exiled princes. Every one must have seen that Marlborough was the devoted servant of James the Second until it suited his interests to go suddenly over and become the devoted servant of William the Third, and after he had made that remarkable change and had greatly profited by it he was still believed to be in constant communication with the representatives of the discarded dynasty.

On the other hand, these very fluctuations of opinion and of allegiance among those with whom dynastic interest or merely personal self-interest was the principal guiding force, only made the sincere among all denominations more devoted than ever to their own convictions, and more ready to take alarm at anything which boded the predominance of antagonistic ideas. The Dissenters and Nonconformists of all sects were beginning to revolt more and more against the rigid rule of the state Church. These Dissenters and Nonconformists were not content with holding their own opinions and keeping them quietly to themselves, but they must take to the convening of meetings for the diffusion of their heterodox views. There were associations which might almost be called public springing up everywhere for the teaching of dissenting doctrine and the enrolment of dissenting citizens. The growth of such organizations aroused alarm and wrath among the less tolerant of the churchmen, and a clamor was raised for the intervention of the crown and Parliament. What to do with the Dissenters became, in fact, the great question of the day among all zealous churchmen. It was insisted that they should not be allowed to go on as they were going, if the rule of the state Church were to be maintained, and zealous churchmen forgot all about the perils of Papistry when they contemplated the dangers of Dissent.

The crisis seemed to call for the right man, and some eager churchmen were allowed to believe, during a short space of time, that the right man had come to the front. It was certain at least that a man had made his appearance who professed his capacity to show the public the readiest and most masterful way of dealing with the Dissenters. This man was destined, for a time, to be the most-talked-of personage of his day, but even while his name was on the lips of every one, none could have predicted the real fame he was destined to win.

Daniel Defoe was an Englishman by birth and ancestry, despite the foreign suggestion conveyed by his name. The name of his father was, in fact, simply Foe, and the son Daniel had changed it into Defoe or De Foe more than twenty years after his birth. He was the son of a butcher in an obscure part of the city of London, but he obtained a good education at a school established for Dissenters, and when still a young man started in business as a maker and vender of stockings. Those were troublous times, and it is not surprising to learn that Daniel Defoe was believed to have been "out" in Monmouth's rebellion. He afterwards took service in King William's army, and appears to have travelled in France and Spain. He was concerned later in various business occupations and enterprises, and at one time he became bankrupt, but he seems conscientiously to have paid all his debts by slow degrees.

Even while engaged in his business projects Defoe's mind troubled itself constantly about political and religious questions, and he was a firm supporter of King William's policy. Defoe found a way of supporting that policy which was more practical and more wide-reaching than any casual interchange of argument with his daily companions in business could have been. He became a pamphleteer, and thus availed himself of the one department of the public press which was most effective in those days. He was soon known as a pamphleteer of especial vigor even in that age of vigorous prose and active pamphleteering. He seems from the very opening of this part of his career to have had a remarkable capacity for adapting himself to the level of any controversy in which he felt inclined to engage. His opinions were unquestionably genuine and were all his own, but he had the faculty, wanting to many a controversialist, of being able to enter thoroughly into the feelings of his antagonists, and thus to meet them with the kind of argument which it was most difficult for them either to refute or leave unnoticed. He always put forth his case in such a manner that it neither went over the heads of his opponents nor fell unnoticed at their feet. In fact, that power of imagination which enabled him later in some of his immortal works to picture scenes which he had never looked upon, and to describe with all semblance of reality troubles which he had never undergone, enabled him at the opening of his career as a writer to create for himself the form of attack likely to tell most heavily upon the peculiar forces which he had to encounter.

Defoe's early training and his ways of thought had made him a strong supporter of the claims set up by the dissenting bodies for the right to conduct their own form of worship according to their own conscience, and he could not see why a state Church, established by law in England, should have an autocratic power to dictate men's faith to them, when the very men who claimed for it such a right were foremost in their repudiation of the spiritual jurisdiction of Rome. The hostility which was growing so much against Dissenters, and especially among the influential, and what may be called the privileged classes, had become so strong that nothing short of some parliamentary action against Nonconformity could possibly satisfy it. Defoe had written poems with a political purpose. One of these, called "The Trueborn Englishman," was a pamphlet in verse in defence of the policy and the reign of William the Third. Defoe had not much of the poetic gift; the indescribable quality which, apart from mere skill in melody, distinguishes genuine poetry from even the finest prose, was not bestowed upon him. The main object of this rhymed pamphlet was to argue down the still popular feeling which made men hold aloof from complete loyalty to William simply because he was a foreigner. Defoe argued, with much common-sense and good-feeling, that every true-born Englishman ought to recognize the claims of the sovereign who had been called to the throne and whose policy was to make England prosperous and great even though a foreign country had given him birth. "The good of subjects is the end of kings," Defoe pointed out, and when this end is labored for and accomplished by a sovereign, he is then truly entitled to rank as an English monarch. The pamphlet gave great satisfaction to William, who showed his good-feeling towards Defoe in many ways, and the writer then seemed fairly on the road to advancement.

When King William died and Anne succeeded him, Defoe had a new political task to undertake. Before that he had had to champion the policy of a king against the opposition which proclaimed itself in consequence of William's foreign birth, training, and descent; now he had to champion the claims of the Dissenters against what was popularly believed to be the sentiment of the Queen. Anne was known to have strong convictions in favor of the claims made out by churchmen, clerical and lay, for the supremacy of that form of Protestantism which had been established as the religion of the state. Defoe hit upon a most effective method of vindicating the cause of the Dissenters and holding up to public condemnation those who were striving to bring all the powers of the law to bear against their demands for liberty of conscience. He issued a pamphlet called "The Shortest Way with the Dissenters." This famous pamphlet was a piece of the most elaborate and powerful satire. Defoe transformed himself, for the time, into a domineering and unyielding High Churchman, and he professed to advocate all the views of such a personage with uncompromising and unlimited conviction. His argument was that the Dissenters deserved no favor, and even deserved no toleration. He contended that whenever Dissenters had any power they invariably exerted it to suppress all liberty of conscience which was not that precise liberty of conscience suited to their own beliefs and their own interests. Every attempt that had been made by Presbyterianism in Scotland to vindicate its own claims he described as a deliberate attempt to crush out all freedom of religious thought and all unorthodox forms of religious worship.

It may, perhaps, be owned that the intolerance sometimes displayed by Presbyterians in Scotland lent more semblance of justification to this part of Defoe's argument than Defoe himself could have intended or would have admitted. Defoe had, of course, stood up stoutly in his own person before this as a defender of the moderation and tolerance shown by Scottish Presbyterianism when it had power to oppress the religious belief of those with whom it was not in agreement. But when Defoe set himself to present the case for the English state Church as an English churchman might have presented it, we can easily understand how he made himself, for the time, a representative of the extreme spirit of the churchman and allowed himself to argue down even his own genuine conviction. The spirit of the novelist was there as well as that of the mere satirist. If he had been putting himself, for artistic purposes, into the form of a religious hypocrite, he would no doubt have entered into the very spirit of a Tartufe. If he had been engaged in a vindication of Moll Flanders or Colonel Jack, he would not have hesitated to push his case beyond the bounds of reasonable and logical defence. So when he put himself into the shape of an intolerant High Churchman it was no part of his task to make the arguments of the High Churchman consistent with the arguments of Daniel Defoe.

The pamphlet begins with a studied moderation of tone and grows gradually more and more vehement, passionate, and arbitrary as the work proceeds. This was part of Defoe's plan. He makes his churchman, whose self-assumed task it is to set forth the shortest way with Dissenters, begin with an affectation of Christian-like forbearance, and then grow by degrees hotter and hotter as he expounds his views, until towards the end he loses his temper altogether and shows himself, what he is really intended to be, an overbearing and merciless tyrant. In this mood he replies to some possible objections which might be raised as to the cruelty of the measures by which he proposes to deal with Dissenters. He considerately admits that it may be cruelty to kill a snake or a toad in cold blood, but then he goes on to point out that " the poison of their nature makes it a charity to our neighbors to destroy these creatures—not for any personal injury received, but for prevention; not for the evil they have done, but the evil they may do." Such creatures as serpents, toads, and vipers, he goes on to say, " are noxious to the body and poison the sensitive life—these poison the soul, corrupt our posterity, ensnare our children, destroy the vitals of our happiness, our future felicity, and contaminate the whole mass." " If," he declares, " one severe law were made and punctually executed, that whoever was found at a conventicle should be banished the nation, and the preacher be hanged, we should soon see an end of the tale."

In this spirit and this tone Defoe set out his plan for dealing in the shortest way with Dissenters who would not accept the principle of absolute conformity. The pamphlet was a capital piece of satirical extravaganza. It illustrated the very extreme of the temper which would tolerate nothing in Protestantism that did not show a complete submission to the doctrines and rules of worship ordained by the state Church. The pamphlet was anonymous, and it was for a while accepted by many people as a sincere and deliberate exposition of the policy which its author believed to be called for by all who held that there was only one true way to maintain the Church in its proper position, and that that one way was the suppression of all independent belief and all nonconforming practices. Some of those who felt in sympathy with what they understood to be the author's exposition of his belief thought that perhaps he had gone a little too far in his controversial fervor, but they still sympathized with its general object, and were willing to overlook the occasional excesses into which he might have been tempted by his conscientious desire to secure the predominance of the Church. Many, of course, understood and appreciated the satire from the very first, and welcomed the pamphlet as a masterly *reductio ad absurdum* of the arguments by which too zealous churchmen had been endeavoring to force the Queen and the Parliament into a policy for the suppression of all dissent.

When the real meaning of the writer began to be universally understood and the pamphlet was recognized as an audacious satire, a positive storm of fury raged around his devoted head. The High-Church party in general regarded the pamphlet as a scandalous libel, and offered a large reward for the discovery and apprehension of the perpetrator. A motion was carried in the House of Commons that the book should be burned by the common hangman, and the government, yielding to the pressure from without and from within, issued a proclamation which is in every way worth reproduction as a piece of history illustrating the condition and temper of the times, and indeed is worthy of reproduction if only for its personal description of one of England's greatest authors. The proclamation set forth:

"Whereas Daniel De Foe alias De Fooe is charged with writing a scandalous and seditious pamphlet entitled 'The Shortest Way with the Dissenters.' He is a middle-sized spare man about forty years old, of a brown complexion, and dark brown colored hair, but wears a wig; a hooked nose, a sharp chin, gray eyes, and a large mole near his mouth; was born in London and for many years was a hose-factor in Freeman's yard in Cornhill, and now is owner of the Brick and Pantile work near Tilbury Fort in Essex. Whoever shall discover the said Daniel De Foe to one of her Majesty's principal secretaries of State or any of her Majesty's justices of peace so as he may be apprehended shall have a reward of fifty pounds to be paid upon such discovery."

There was not much chance of Defoe's trying to escape, even if he had been inclined to make any effort at escape, after such a description of his person, his occupation, and his whereabouts, and it seems only bare justice to the literary intelligence of the age to say that nobody who had any acquaintance with the pamphleteering issues of the day could have had the slightest doubt as to the identity of the author. Defoe was quickly and easily captured. He was put on his trial at the Old Bailey for a seditious libel, and as there was no possibility of his disclaiming the charge or offering any defence which could have availed him in the eyes of the law at such a time, he decided on taking the situation as he found it and merely pleading guilty. Perhaps he may have thought that this course would obtain for him some consideration from his judges, but if he had any such hope it was destined to instant disappointment. He was sentenced to stand three times in the pillory, and after that to be imprisoned until he should pay a large fine and find security to be of good behavior for seven years. "Thus," as he says himself, "was I a second time ruined, for by this affair I lost

DISSENT AND DEFOE

above three thousand five hundred pounds." Savage and brutal as was the treatment awarded to Defoe, he appears to have been treated with more leniency during his imprisonment than he might have been at a later period of English history. While he was a prisoner in Newgate he was allowed to publish poems and pamphlets, and to prepare for the issue of a periodical, a sort of newspaper, the contents of which were written solely by himself, and which he continued to issue two or three times a week for many years after he had been set at liberty. Defoe was kept in prison for more than a year.

Anne was by no means wanting in feelings of humanity, and she could hardly have had much sympathy with the kind of policy which had found its illustration in the treatment inflicted on Defoe. There were some men in the land, even then, who had courage enough to plead for a mitigation of his term of imprisonment, and influence enough to commend their views to the notice of the Queen's ministers. William Penn, the famous Quaker, the founder of the State of Pennsylvania, was then at the height of his renown. He had accomplished his great work in the spread of Christian doctrine, he had settled that establishment in the New World which would in itself have made his name immortal, and he occupied himself earnestly in attempting to obtain a mitigation of Defoe's sentence. John Hill Burton, in his *Reign of Queen Anne,* publishes some documents which have a curious interest, and have given rise to some conflicting explanations in connection with Penn's humane efforts for the release of Defoe. One of these is a private letter from Godolphin to the Earl of Nottingham, one of the Secretaries of State, which notes the fact that "Mr. William Penn came to tell me he had acquainted my

Lord Privy Seal that Defoe was ready to make oath to your lordship of all that he knew, and to give an account of all his accomplices in whatsoever he has been concerned, provided by so doing he may be screened from the punishment of the pillory, and not produced as an evidence against any person whatsoever. And upon my acquainting the Queen with this just now at noon, her Majesty was pleased to tell me she had received the same account from my Lord Privy Seal, and seemed to think this, if there were no other, occasion for the cabinet council to reach here to-morrow, and has commanded me to tell you so."

Burton is inclined to believe that Defoe was really willing to give an account of all his accomplices, provided he might be relieved from the punishment of the pillory and not produced as a public witness against his friends. Godolphin's document, he thinks, "must touch the fame of Defoe in the eyes of all who may not believe that the chief advisers of the sovereign had conspired with her to blacken it." "One can imagine," he says, "a touch of comic risibility gleaming in Defoe's thoughts when he succeeded in sending the sternly earnest Quaker on such an errand." Then he goes on to say: "There will be the less to surprise us in this affair when we make better acquaintance with Defoe, and perhaps find that, whatever wealth of virtues he possessed, scrupulosity as a public man was not among them." Most readers, however, will be rather inclined to believe that Godolphin was willing to get out of a troublesome business as soon and easily as possible, and that he somewhat exaggerated the nature of the suggestion which Penn described himself as authorized to make on the part of Defoe. The word of William Penn is wholly beyond doubt, and there is certainly no reason to believe that Defoe could possibly be guilty of the mean and craven suggestion described in Godolphin's letter.

Nothing came of Penn's interference at that time. Defoe was kept in prison for more than a year, and then Harley, who had become Secretary of State, used his influence with the Queen to obtain the prisoner's liberation. Anne was not inclined to keep up the rigor of Defoe's punishment any longer, and it appears she was so greatly touched by the condition of distress in which Defoe's wife was placed that she sent her a gift of money, and after some further delay ordered the remission of the fine and gave back to liberty the author of the pamphlet which had created such a political convulsion. We learn on Defoe's own authority that he was afterwards employed by Harley and by Godolphin in the service of the Queen, and we know that in 1706 he was sent by Godolphin, with the approval of the Queen, to occupy himself in Scotland for the promotion of the parliamentary union. Defoe never rose to his full fame during the reign of Queen Anne. The production of *Robinson Crusoe* was wanting to the literary glory of that reign, so rich in masterpieces of prose and poetry.

The effort made by William Penn to obtain Defoe's exemption from the disgraceful punishment decreed for him is an appropriate illustration of Penn's whole career, and indeed of the work which Penn's co-religionists appear always to have marked out for themselves. The Quakers are hardly to be classed among the dissenting bodies of Queen Anne's reign. Theirs was the very dissidence of dissent. It cannot be said that their hand was against that of every other community in the religious world, but it may almost be said that the hand of every other religious community was against them. They only saved themselves from the worst of persecution by that course of non-resistance, or, at all events, passive resistance, which their religious principles prescribed for them. It was hardly possible, even in the days of roughest religious controversy, to keep inflicting bodily punishment on men who were pledged never to defend themselves by force of arms. The Quakers carried out the principles of Christianity, according to their own definitions of those principles, with a rigid fidelity which might often have put the disciples of other Christian sects to shame. They strove with undismayed perseverance to maintain peace among men, to treat all men as their equals and their brothers where justice had to be administered and where charity could find work to do. The story of Penn's life belongs to earlier days than those of Queen Anne. His best work had been done, and his fame as a philanthropist had been secured before the opportunity came for him to intervene on behalf of Daniel Defoe, in the futile hope of saving him from the ignominy which, after all, only inflicted disgrace upon the age, and could not inflict any dishonor on Defoe. There is, however, a peculiar fitness in the historical chance which associates, in such a manner, the names of Daniel Defoe and of William Penn.

CHAPTER VI

ON THE ROUGH EDGE OF BATTLE

WHILE the three dissenting bodies—the Presbyterians, the Baptists, and the Independents or the Congregationalists—are fighting their battles against the more aggressive of the churchmen, and the Quakers are standing aloof from each and all, the war has opened and is going on, and Marlborough is commander-in-chief of the allied forces in Holland. We must study the field and survey the forces arrayed on either side.

The position of Marlborough could not be better described than in the lines which Shakespeare has put into the mouth of Ulysses when he is addressing Agamemnon:

> " Thou great commander, nerve and bone of Greece,
> Heart of our numbers, soul and only spirit,
> In whom the tempers and the minds of all
> Should be shut up."

Ulysses, indeed, addresses Agamemnon in language of studied flattery, but the words which he uses might be employed to describe with literal accuracy the position of Marlborough at the head of his allied forces. Other words used by Ulysses in the same scene may be employed to illustrate, no less faithfully, some of the conditions which tended most to interfere with Marlborough's work and to delay the execution of his finest plans:

> " And look how many Grecian tents do stand
> Hollow upon this plain, so many hollow factions."

It is not too much to say that, while the avowed object of the allies was one and the same—the maintenance of the Spanish monarchy against the policy of Louis the Fourteenth, which demanded its absorption into his own possessions—each of the states forming the alliance had its own separate end to serve, and was unwilling to spend its resources for any purpose outside the range of its own immediate interests. England and France might be regarded as opponents brought face to face with each other by a direct and long-standing antagonism. These two states had been enemies in the open field again and again. England had won some of her greatest military triumphs on the soil of France, and had annexed French territory and proclaimed it part of the dominion of the English crown. France had old scores to pay off with England, and Louis the Fourteenth had come to understand only too clearly that his ambition could never have full satisfaction on the continent of Europe while England remained strong enough to assert the right of interfering with his aggressive schemes. These two opponents may be said to stand up to each other in the spirit described by the Homeric line in which one rival declares to another that either you must overthrow me or I will overthrow you. Agreements, and even alliances, between England and France had been tried from time to time, but no lasting principle of companionship could be found for such a rivalry. Therefore it might be safely taken for granted that England and France would have to fight out this contest to the bitter end, and that neither would swerve from any responsibility, or hold back from any expenditure, until the contest had been positively decided, and one or the other had to submit.

But the armies on both sides had taken the field under very different conditions. The foremost of England's allies was the Emperor of Germany, and the empire of Germany had become, by this time, something like the hereditary possession of the house of Hapsburg. The position of emperor was still, indeed, treated as elective, and whenever a vacancy took place, the electors assembled in due form in the historic chamber at Frankfort-on-the-Main and solemnly went through the ceremony of choosing the supreme representative of the German states. During many generations, and even during centuries, there had been no substantial opposition to the claims of the house of Hapsburg, and the German, or, as we may call him, the Austrian emperor was as certain of his succession as if the dignity had been one of hereditary descent. Readers may remember that there was a time in the history of the Caliphate when the principle of election was vaguely supposed to govern the succession, although, in point of fact, the right of hereditary descent was invariably recognized in the commanders of the faithful.

The electors of the empire at the time with which we are now dealing were nine in number. Three of these held their right as representatives of ecclesiastical power — the Archbishops of Mayence, Treves, and Cologne—and then there were the electors of Saxony, Bohemia, Brandenburg, Bavaria, the Palatinate, and the Duke of Hanover, whose family had by this time been chosen to succeed to the throne of England. Two of these electors—Cologne and Bavaria—had taken the side of France. The electors of Mayence and Treves maintained a neutral position, Brandenburg, the Palatinate, and Hanover sided with England and Holland against France. The electorate of Brandenburg had long been growing in strength and influence, and just before the opening of the war Frederick, the elector, demanded that the Emperor, in return for his promised support, should sustain his claim to be created a king. The Emperor and his ministers believed that it would not be for their advantage to resist the claim, because if they did so they might lose the powerful support of Brandenburg. Frederick, therefore, was made King of Prussia. This was the first recognition of that great German power which, during so many generations, disputed for supremacy with the empire of Austria, and achieved it... h within the memory of most of us as the result of the war of 1866, that seven weeks' war which ended in the defeat of Austria at Sadowa.

Frederick, the first King of Prussia, was the grandfather of Frederick the Great. The Elector of Saxony had become King of Poland, an electoral appointment also, and he had quite enough to do in trying to maintain his position by force of arms to prevent him from rendering any assistance to the alliance against France. Thus it will be easily seen that the German supporters of the Grand Alliance had interests of their own to consider which kept them from throwing themselves heart and soul into the policy represented by England and Holland. France was likely to continue a powerful and dangerous enemy in any case, all the more dangerous because she must be a neighbor as well as an enemy. Nothing short of her complete overthrow, which could hardly be counted upon in any scheme of human policy, could seem a sufficient guarantee to the German princes for a thorough adhesion to a course which, even if it secured the object of England and of Holland, might at any crisis, or after any settlement, leave these German princes open to France's future purposes of retaliation. The determination of England and Holland was that the King of France should not absorb into his dominions the kingdom of Spain; but even if their object were to be fully accomplished and the ambitious designs of Louis the Fourteenth in that direction were to be frustrated forever, France might still be left with ample power to revenge herself on some of the German states which had taken up arms against her.

Even as regarded England and Holland, although the main and avowed purpose of both was identical, it could not possibly be held that they had quite the same interest in opposing the projects of King Louis for the absorption of Spain. Let the war end as it might, Holland, like the German states, would be left with France a dangerous neighbor, while England might well regard herself as destined to hold her own under all conditions against the most ambitious and reckless of French sovereigns. Holland, moreover, had but little interest in warlike enterprise. Shipping, commerce, and handicrafts were her sources of prosperity, revenue, and renown. She was already one of the most active colonizing states in Europe, but she sought to carry out her schemes of colonization by her ships and her traders, and not by force of arms. She had been drawn into antagonism to France because unless the ambition of French sovereigns should receive some emphatic check, she could not count on being able to conduct in safety her work of commerce and of colonization. It will be seen during the course of this narrative that in the diversity of interests which inspired the Grand Alliance, even Holland often found herself reluctant or unable to lend all the help to Marlborough which was demanded by the simple and straightforward policy he had to carry out.

When the war began Leopold the First was the Emperor. He was then an old man, having occupied the imperial throne for not much less than half a century, and before the campaigns had come to their close he died. The imperial power passed to his son Joseph, a soldier and a man of genuine capacity, who was much esteemed by his own people for his high character and sincere regard for the interests of his subjects. Joseph's brother, Charles, was the man whom the Grand Alliance had chosen as the claimant best entitled to the succession in Spain.

Before the war had gone on very long the Grand Alliance received the accession of two other members. One of these was Victor Amadeus the Second, Duke of Savoy, who may be regarded as the founder of the present kingdom of Italy. Victor Amadeus had in his character much of the heroic temperament, the spirit of enterprise, and the gift of acquiring popularity among his subjects which the world has long been accustomed to associate with the princes of the house of Savoy. He had suffered so much from the intolerance and the arrogance of Louis the Fourteenth that he was almost literally driven to take up arms on the side of the Grand Alliance, although the interests of his people and his own inclinations might well have enabled a less overbearing and unscrupulous sovereign than Louis the Fourteenth to secure his co-operation for the armies of France. Louis had acted towards him, on more than one occasion, on the impulse of the same aggressive spirit which had dictated to him the ostentatious recognition of the exiled Stuart prince, and thus forced William the Third to take up arms against France.

The other ally who joined England and Holland about the same time as the Duke of Savoy was the King of Portugal. Bishop Burnet traces, in a few lines, the history of the earlier negotiations with the King of Portugal to induce him to enter into a treaty of alliance with England. The narrative would be interesting if only as an illustration of the fluctuations of principle and policy which were common among the sovereigns and ministers of continental states about the time when the Grand Alliance was in process of formation. The King of Portugal's ministers, Burnet tells us, " were in the French interests, but he himself inclined to the Austrian family. He for some time affected retirement, and avoided the giving audience to foreign ministers. He saw no good prospect from England; so, being pressed to an alliance with France, his ministers got leave from him to propose one on terms of such advantage to him that, as it was not expected they could be granted, so it was hoped this would run into a long negotiation. But the French were as liberal in making large promises as they were perfidious in not observing them; so the King of France agreed to all that was proposed, and signed a treaty pursuant to it, and published it to the world. Yet the King of Portugal denied that he had consented to any such project; and he was so hardly brought to sign the treaty that, when it was brought to him, he threw it down and kicked it about the room, as our envoy wrote over. In conclusion, however, he was prevailed on to sign it; but it was generally thought that when he should see a good fleet come from the allies he would observe this treaty with the French as they have done their treaties with all the rest of the world."

The general expectation was fully borne out by the result. Sir Paul Methuen, the English envoy at the court of Portugal, succeeded in prevailing on the King to cast in his lot with the states who were able to offer to him the most advantageous terms. The situation might be illustrated fairly enough in a few lines from Sheridan's immortal comedy, " The Critic." The scene is that in which Tilburina endeavors to win over her father the governor to her plans. She offers him "A retreat in Spain," to which he rejoins "Outlawry here." "A title," she suggests, and he replies indignantly, "Honor!" "A pension," she suggests, and his proud answer is "Conscience!" Then she comes to the point more effectively, and asks him what he thinks of "A thousand pounds," to which he replies: "Ha; thou hast touched me nearly!" Methuen, the English envoy, offered to the King of Portugal a commercial treaty with England, giving the wine of Portugal an immense advantage in the English market over the wine of France. This inducement touched the monarch and his ministers so very nearly that it may be said to have finished the negotiations.

The arrangement then made is famous in history as the Methuen treaty. That part of the bargain which had most interest for coming generations was the condition that the tax upon Portuguese wines imported into England should be one-third less than that imposed on wines coming from France, and in return for this concession Portugal was to import all her woollen goods from England. The treaty had a very decided effect on the English upper and middle classes. Up to that time the favorite drinks in England, among those who could afford to drink wines at all, were the clarets and burgundies of France; but the cheap admission of the stronger wine from Oporto, the wine which has always since been known in these countries as port, soon made it the habit and the delight of a large proportion of Englishmen and Scotchmen. The ancestors of the present generation continued for long years to indulge themselves freely in this powerful wine, and seeing that those who came to love it indulged in it quite as freely as they had allowed themselves to do in claret, the influence of the Methuen treaty had anything but a wholesome effect on the heads and the habits of Englishmen and Scotchmen. If there had been a British Anacreon at any time during the following half-century he must have sung the praises of good old port, and indeed the liquid may be said to have established itself in literature as well as in actual life among contemporary English institutions. It was recognized as a good old gentlemanly habit in the days of Dr. Johnson and in the days of the younger Pitt to be able to drink a quantity of port every day which would have proved utterly beyond the powers of a more recent generation. Even the medical faculty got into the way of prescribing a liberal allowance of port as an essential part of the true Briton's daily diet. On the other hand, it is only fair to say that the milder wines of France had still their champions. There are some famous lines which describe the effect of the new importation on the habits and nerves of the population of this island who lived on the north side of the Tweed. Often as the lines have been quoted, we cannot resist the temptation to quote them once more:

> " Firm and erect the Caledonian stood;
> Sweet was his mutton and his claret good.
> 'Thou shalt drink port,' the English statesman cried;
> He drank the poison, and his spirit died."

The treaty was afterwards modified and altered in several particulars from time to time, but it remained for Mr. Gladstone, within the memory of men now living, to give back to the wines of France their admission on cheaper terms into these countries, and thus to effect a genuine and a wholesome change in the daily habits of the wine-drinking population. The alliance between Great Britain and Portugal was more durable, however, than it could have been made by any conditions which merely dealt with the importation of wines. England proved the trusty friend of Portugal during many a change and on many a battle-field in days long after the War of the Spanish Succession had become merely a matter of history.

Louis of France had really no allies of any importance in this great war. The Elector of Bavaria had been brought over to the side of France, but even he had not committed himself to the alliance at the time when the war began. Another ally of Louis was the Bavarian Elector's brother, the Elector of Cologne, but the assistance which such a state could give in such a struggle brought little or no serious advantage with it. King Louis had some great soldiers in his army. One was his famous marshal, the Duke of Vendôme, the extraordinary soldier whom Macaulay has described in some vigorous and vivacious passages. "This man," says Macaulay, "was distinguished by the filthiness of his person, by the brutality of his demeanor, by the gross buffoonery of his conversation, and by the impudence with which he abandoned himself to the most nauseous of all vices. His sluggishness was almost incredible. Even when engaged in a campaign he often passed whole days in his bed. His strange torpidity had been the cause of some of the most serious disasters which the armies of the house of Bourbon had sustained. But when he was roused by any great emergency his resources, his energy, and his presence of mind were such as had been found in no French general since the death of Luxembourg. . . ."

Another of Louis's great commanders was the Duke of Berwick, the illegitimate son of James the Second, last Stuart King of England, by Arabella Churchill, Marlborough's sister. It was a strange stroke of fate which thus brought Marlborough into antagonism with the son of his own sister, but the son of James the Second was undoubtedly in his fitting place when he led a French army against the soldiers of the new dynasty in England. Berwick was in his way a great soldier. As a commander he was cool, calculating, cautious; he was not made up of surprising contrasts and paradoxical qualities like Vendôme; he had not Vendôme's brilliant flashes of military genius and moods of overwhelming energy, but he proved himself a commander who could put to trial even the foremost of the generals whom England sent to meet him on the battle-field.

France had some obvious advantages for the coming struggle. She was, as a whole, obedient to one supreme will. Louis the Fourteenth was a despotic monarch, and under him despotic monarchy had become an almost absolute power. In all that great region which acknowledged his control King Louis had only to issue his commands and he had no fear of divided counsels among the generals and the forces to whom he issued them. He had a large standing army, well accustomed to war, an army which of late years had grown habituated to victory. Nothing is more difficult than to obtain a trustworthy estimate as to the number of troops which the belligerents on either side could bring into the field, but so far as one can form an opinion it would appear that France could put at the disposal of King Louis a larger force than the members of the Grand Alliance, taken together, could set in opposition to him. The few allies who had been induced to pledge themselves to his support counted for almost nothing in the great approaching campaign, and whether they stood by him or deserted him, or actually turned against him, could have made but little difference in the ultimate fortunes of the war. England, on the other hand, could not yet feel herself secure against the chance of a movement in Scotland to restore the Stuart dynasty. "Ere the king's crown go down there are heads to be broke," are the words which Walter Scott put into the mouth of Claverhouse, whom he pictured in his last efforts to restore the fortunes of the Stuarts, and the words might well have applied to the desperate resolve of many adherents to the fallen dynasty in the early days of Queen Anne and in days much later still. The condition of Scotland at the time when the armies of the Grand Alliance were taking the field was still far from satisfactory to the English government, and no one could venture to say what the result might be if a French force were to effect a landing at some seaport north of the Tweed.

But the intolerant policy of Louis had created a movement among the populations who inhabited the regions of the Cevennes mountains which threatened a serious trouble to his plans at a moment singularly inopportune for him. The Cevennes mountains stretch for a certain distance almost side by side with the Rhône, and then turn towards the Pyrenees, which, though not of great height there, are rugged and steep and had at that time much marsh and much forest spreading towards the Mediterranean. This extensive country seemed as if it were marked out by nature as a region in which a fighting and desperate population, even though small in numbers, could hold out long against the forces of a well-disciplined army, no matter what its superior strength. The population of the Cevennes mountain district had suffered much by the revocation of the edict of Nantes, for it was a strongly Protestant population, and was not in the least disposed to give in to the decree of barbarous intolerance which King Louis had proclaimed. The inhabitants of this region belonged for the most part to a simple and sturdy peasantry, who had all the faith of fanaticism in their resentment of the outrageous policy put in force against them, and they soon found leaders capable of inspiring and guiding their desperate resistance.

Almost immediately after war had been proclaimed between England and France, a rising, which was begun at first by a very small number of men, broke out into organized resistance to the persecuting policy of King Louis. Bishop Burnet describes the rising as an "unlooked-for accident," but to those who can survey the events from the clearer point of view which later years command, it would seem by no means an accident or anything unlooked for, but the natural and very justifiable result of the policy which the French King had consented to put in force. "When it first broke out," says Burnet, "it was looked on as the effect of oppression and despair, which would quickly end in a scene of blood; but it had a much longer continuance than was expected, and it had a considerable effect on the affairs of France; for an army of ten or twelve thousand men, who were designed either for Italy or Spain, was employed without any immediate success in reducing them." In a later passage of his history, Burnet tells us that "The rising in the Cevennes had not been yet subdued, though mareschal Montravel was sent with an army to reduce or destroy them; he committed great barbarities, not only on those he found in arms, but on whole villages, because they, as he was informed, favored them: they came often down out of their hills in parties, ravaging the country, and they engaged the king's troops with much resolution, and sometimes with great advantage; they seemed resolved to accept of nothing less than the restoring their edicts to them; for a connivance at their own way of worship

was offered them; they had many among them who
seemed qualified in a very singular manner to be the
teachers of the rest; they had a great measure of zeal
without any learning; they scarcely had any education
at all."

The good Bishop Burnet does not seem to have
been very enthusiastic in the cause of men who might
well be regarded as his own co-religionists. He appears to have been rather surprised that they could not
see their way to come to terms when what he describes
as " a connivance at their own way of worship " was
generously tendered to them on the part of King Louis.
The remainder of this passage from Bishop Burnet is
well worthy of a place here, for it illustrates very effectively the condition of the times and the spirit which
animated the men of the Cevennes mountains. " I
spoke with the person who, by the Queen's order, sent one
among them to know the state of their affairs; I read
some of the letters, which he brought from them, full
of a sublime zeal and piety "—the Bishop seems by this
time to become awake to the deeper realities of the
rising—" expressing a courage and confidence that
could not be daunted; one instance of this was, that
they all agreed, that if any of them was so wounded in
an engagement with the enemy, that he could not be
brought off, he should be shot dead, rather than be left
alive to fall into the enemies' hands; it was not possible
then to form a judgment of that insurrection, the reports about it were so various and uncertain, it being
as much magnified by some, as it was undervalued by
others; the whole number that they could reckon on
was four thousand men, but they had not arms and
clothes for half that number, so they used these by
turns, while the rest were left at home, to follow their
labor; they put the country all about them in a great

fright, and to a vast expense; while no intelligence could be had of their designs, and they broke out in so many different places, that all who lay within their reach were in a perpetual agitation; it was a lamentable thing that they lay so far within the country, that it was not possible to send supplies to them unless the Duke of Savoy should be in a condition to break into Dauphiny; and therefore advices were sent them, to accept of such terms as could be had, and to reserve themselves for better times." We can judge from this passage that Queen Anne's advisers were willing to make the best use they could of the Cevennes insurgents, but the insurgents do not seem to have been inclined to adopt the prudential advice offered to them, and to reserve themselves for better times.

The rising came to be known as the rebellion of the Camisards, or wearers of the shirt *camisa,* a kind of blouse or smock-frock which most of them wore in the first instance as a mere matter of accident or convenience, which became adopted as an easy means of recognition by sympathizers during the progress of the struggle, and afterwards was accepted as the recognized uniform and emblem of the whole insurrection. They had some resolute and capable leaders, the most distinguished among whom was Jean Cavalier. We shall hear more of the insurrection and of this leader before long; at present it is only necessary to describe its origin and its purposes in order to call attention to one serious trouble which beset the King of France at the very opening of the war, a trouble which, like many others of his reign, he would never have had to encounter if he had not yielded himself wholly to that policy of persecution which his favorites pressed upon him. It is a fact worth noticing in further illustration of this point that the command of the English and Portuguese forces sent by the Grand Alliance to the west of Europe was given to a French Protestant, the Earl of Galway, who had renounced his allegiance to the French sovereign in consequence of the persecuting policy exercised over the Protestants of France, had accepted a commission from King William, and now, honored with an Irish peerage, was to render brilliant service to the cause of the allies against Louis the Fourteenth.

On the other hand, the German Emperor was weakened to a great extent by the effects of a like policy of persecution. The provinces of Hungary and Transylvania had long been disaffected towards the imperial rule by the fact that the Protestant populations, who resented bitterly the manner in which they had been oppressed because of their religion, were always looking out for any alliance which might give them a chance of rising against the imperial rule, and were positively craving for any opportunity of accomplishing a complete separation from Austria. Nor can it be forgotten that England, by her treatment of the Catholics in Ireland, had driven the Irish people into sympathy with the Stuart cause, and by her treatment of the Scottish Presbyterians was at that very time arousing the sentiment in Scotland which made that country a favorable arena for any attempt at a restoration of the exiled dynasty. More than one English historical writer has deduced an obvious lesson as to the political consequences of religious persecution from the manner in which France was weakened by her treatment of the Huguenots after the revocation of the edict of Nantes, and the German empire was enfeebled by its treatment of the Protestants in Hungary. But these writers have failed to draw any moral from the fact that England herself was suffering because of the manner in which she had oppressed the Catholics in Ireland and the Presbyterians in Scotland. The truth is, that in those times there was not much to choose, so far as the policy of religious persecution was concerned, between one state and another, between one sovereign and his rival.

CHAPTER VII

"THE CAMPAIGN"—BLENHEIM

THE story of the war has to divide itself into two parts—the operations in the Low Countries and Germany, and those which were carried on in the southwest of the European continent. The Dutch people had of their own free will, and on the inspiration of their best national advisers, agreed to place their forces under the command of the Duke of Marlborough. They had recognized from the first the great military and political capacity of Marlborough, who had, indeed, made himself well known and very popular among the Dutch people, and they saw the immense advantage of having the full control of the armies operating in that part of Europe placed in the hands of one leader, especially when that leader was endowed with such gifts for the conduct of a war as they could not but acknowledge to be the possession of Marlborough. As the war went on it brought out a whole group of generals whose names have taken an enduring place in history. Marlborough himself, Prince Eugene of Savoy, Peterborough, and many others on the side of the Grand Alliance; Vendôme, Berwick, and others on the side of France. It was a war of navies as well as of armies, and on the sea the Grand Alliance naturally made a splendid show, the feats of Rooke alone having raised monuments of English victory which are holding their firm place up to the present hour. No such war was ever seen in

"THE CAMPAIGN"—BLENHEIM

Europe from that time until the outbreak of the French Revolution, when the policy of European states, in endeavoring to overbear the national impulse of the French people, opened a field for the genius of the First Napoleon.

The War of the Succession proved itself a test for the national endurance and resolve of peoples, alike for the genius of commanders and the discipline of armies. It was a struggle in which the survival of the fittest was amply, and we might almost say scientifically, illustrated and demonstrated. It exhibited a series of campaigns under the most varying conditions, and the lessons to be learned from all the wars of former and succeeding days might be studied in the history of that one tremendous struggle. Many of the predictions which were most confidently made at the opening of the campaign were falsified before it had nearly come to a close. In quarters where weakness of resistance had been generally taken for granted an unconquerable resolve to hold out to the very last compelled universal recognition. On the other hand, the very difficulties at the outset considered most formidable gave way with a suddenness which reduced to mere confusion all previous calculations. The war was great as a magnificent military pageant, but it can hardly be called great in its abiding results. When all was done it left the political arrangements of the European continent very much as it had found them. England, of course, although she took the leading part in the struggle, was safe enough in her insular position and in the strength of her armies and her fleets not to be exposed to the risk of any lasting disadvantage from the greatest successes her enemies could obtain in the field. She had a stronghold to which, at the worst, she could always retire and bid defiance to the vengeful malice of her bitterest foes. The armies which could not stand against Marlborough and his English troops on the continental battle-fields were not likely to have any chance of doing better if they were to attempt an invasion of England. Even if we leave England out of the calculation, it must be observed that France and the empire found themselves after the close of the war in very much the same condition as before its opening. It was reserved for other events and for a much later time to call into existence that newer German empire which superseded Austria as the representative of the German-speaking populations, and to create that kingdom of Italy which was welcomed with so much enthusiasm by modern civilization.

The force which England sent to serve under Marlborough in that part of the campaign which was to be conducted in the Low Countries was to consist of forty thousand men. A separate force was to be sent by England to Portugal, and forty thousand men were voted for the navy. The Emperor, and the German states which acted on his side, were to furnish one hundred and twenty thousand men. England had to make great efforts in order to obtain the requisite number of troops for her army, and the statute-book for this part of Queen Anne's reign bears testimony still to the new measures which had to be adopted in order to tempt recruits to enter the military service. The armies of France were understood to bring into the field a number much larger than those provided by England and her allies. The object of Marlborough was to capture at once as many as possible of the strong places which France had obtained by former campaigns in the region of the Low Countries and Germany, and thus to secure a vantage ground as a starting-point for his movements, and at the same time to

"THE CAMPAIGN"—BLENHEIM

establish a safe barrier between the operations of his Dutch allies and the operations of their French enemies. His policy was to make a sudden rush at the opening of the war, and thus at once to impress the enemy with a recognition of his military energy and power, to upset all the calculations which his enemies had formed as to their means of directing the campaign, and to keep the Dutch forces perfectly free for the arrangement and development of their own movements.

In the history of the war we shall find that there were two distinct orders of generalship. One class of leaders relied mainly on slow and steady movement, on the old familiar Fabian policy of patient endurance, waiting for the right opportunity to strike a heavy blow, and holding out against all difficulties and disasters; the other a policy of sudden rush, bewildering the antagonist by its unlooked-for impulse and energy. In times within the recollection of living men we have seen how in two great campaigns the Prussian generalship, first displayed against the Austrians, and not long afterwards against the French, succeeded in thus upsetting all the preliminary calculations of the enemy, and making the first blow struck in the campaign an omen of the final and decisive victory. The generalship of Marlborough shone with equal brilliancy in each mode of warfare. Marlborough was great alike in a plan of sudden, unforeseen rush, and in slow, steady, patient movement. He was always open to the suggestions and the advice of those who acted in alliance with him, and if he saw any plan which he believed to be superior to his own, he was ready to adopt it; he entered fully into its spirit, and carried it out to better effect than its authors could themselves have done. But it need hardly be said that throughout the whole of his campaigns he very seldom met with instances of this kind, and after a prompt but full consideration of all the plans he almost always saw that his own was best adapted for its purpose. Like Clive, at his council of war, he gave every suggestion its due consideration, and then quietly adopted the advice of his own judgment and acted upon it. We shall see during the course of the war that he could show under the most adverse conditions that sublime patience, that slow, unconquerable power of mere endurance which a great soldier of modern times—General Grant, afterwards President of the United States—once described to the author of these volumes as the most essential quality for successful command.

By a series of sudden and daring movements Marlborough captured a number of the French strongholds, and thus made the ground which they had occupied a most convenient theatre for the exercise of his own operations. The capture of some of these towns and strong places was accompanied by picturesque incidents of bravery which have won a place never to be forgotten in the history of modern warfare. Marlborough himself on one occasion escaped by the merest chance, and, by a curious stroke of good fortune, the fate of falling into the hands of his French enemies. For a time the appalling news spread through the Dutch people in the Low Countries that the commander-in-chief had been taken prisoner by the French, and the consternation spread by this report was only outdone by the exultation which followed the certain and prompt news that he and his allies had been saved from such a disaster.

Marlborough was, indeed, an innovator on the old-fashioned forms of campaigning which had for some time prevailed on the continent of Europe. The slow and steady etiquette—for it may almost be called so—which had governed the plans of regular campaign was totally upset, was put to complete confusion and disorder by the daring inspiration of Marlborough's military genius. On the other hand, the enemies who had begun to look for sudden movements and surprises and were trying to shape their own plans in order to counteract such a policy, found their calculations often reduced to bewildering nothingness when it suited Marlborough to remain quiet and motionless until some special opportunity, on which he had been carefully calculating, afforded him the means of making the decisive stroke which it had been his object all through to accomplish. Thus the French commanders began to have the conviction borne in upon them that there was no counting on Marlborough, that when they had made all their plans to resist some sudden onward movement their hopes were utterly disappointed, and Marlborough frustrated all their arrangements by a course of deliberation and delay, and then made his sudden stroke from some direction which no foresight of theirs had led them to anticipate and guard against. With the capture by storm of Liège, then a city nominally independent but garrisoned by the French, the English commander completed his plan for clearing and securing an advantageous basis of operations for himself and his Dutch allies.

The lower valley of the Rhine was now one of the frontiers of what may be called Marlborough's camping-ground. This was the first genuine discomfiture which the French had received for many years in their movements of aggression on the field of continental warfare, and the news was received with unbounded exultation in England. It was for that successful enterprise that Marlborough received his dukedom, and Queen Anne herself attended a solemn ceremonial in St. Paul's to celebrate the victory. The desire, and the obvious policy, of Marlborough were that he should follow up his advantage by a series of bold movements, and that he should make an attack on the city of Antwerp itself. But he was greatly hampered in the execution of his plans by the delays in council and the difficulties put in the way of his prompt action by his Dutch allies. The generals of the Dutch forces were accompanied by a number of delegates from the central authorities of the United Provinces, whose business it was to consult with the commanding officers on every military plan, and to insist that their own suggestions and their own advice should be listened to before any active step was taken. In point of fact, Marlborough found himself thus accompanied everywhere by what may be called a civilian council of war, and the civilian council appears to have been actuated by a business-like anxiety to consider the cost and the risk of every movement before giving it approval. Such a course of proceeding might have been highly reasonable and prudent in the commercial transactions of life, and a cautious trader might fairly have been allowed to satisfy himself that the possible profits of an undertaking would be worth the certain risk and expense, before committing himself to its execution. Even in ordinary commercial transactions, however, it might easily happen that the too slow and cautious speculator would find the possible opportunity secured in advance by some more enterprising rival, and in the business of war the more successful rival is not likely to be content with merely securing the gain for himself, but will aim at the complete destruction of his opponent. Marlborough was to a great extent dependent on his Dutch allies for supplies and for forces, and he had to know, over and over again, that while the chances of this or that plan were the subject of slow and steady discussion, the opportunity for carrying it out was passing away, and encouragement was given to the enemy to make a forward movement of his own on the delaying English and Dutch allies.

A large part of what is now the kingdom of Belgium was at this time still under the dominion of Spain, and so far as regards the purposes of the war might be considered in the enemy's country. The capture of Antwerp would have made Marlborough master of a splendid field for the operation of his further plans, but owing to the hampering influence of his allies he found that it would be hopeless for him to undertake such an enterprise at that time, and he had therefore to content himself with obtaining possession of Bonn, on the Rhine, and thus securing still further his expanded vantage ground. Meanwhile there had been some spirited fighting in north Italy, and a victory won at Cremona over the French forces had made the empire safe for a time against any invasion of the armies of King Louis from that quarter. The victory of Cremona was won by Prince Eugene of Savoy, who commanded the allied armies in the northern parts of Italy. Up to this time Marlborough and Eugene had never met, but from this time Marlborough began to see in Eugene the promise of a military co-operation and comradeship which might well be worth cultivating, and a confidential communication set in between the two generals whose names were destined to be afterwards linked together in fame. Even with such a distance between them, Marlborough could follow the movements of Prince Eugene's game.

Prince Eugene, " der edel Ritter " of German song, was one of the heroic soldiers of the war. His name will always be associated with that of Marlborough. As we have already said, he was a younger son of the house of Savoy. He was the youngest son of the Prince of Savoy-Carignan, and his mother was a niece of Cardinal Mazarin. From his birth he thus may be said to have combined two nationalities, for he was born in Paris, he was brought up in the court of Louis the Fourteenth, and he was intended for the priesthood; but he had no calling whatever for the clerical profession, and even in his boyish studies showed already his taste for a military life and his determination to be a soldier. Indeed, if destiny ever had marked out a young man for the business of the camp and the battle-field, Eugene of Savoy may be said to have had his destiny thus forcast for him. After the death of his father some estrangement arose between Louis the Fourteenth and the widow of the Savoy prince. In those days and in that sphere it was no uncommon thing that the favored courtier of one week should be the discredited exile of the next, and Eugene's mother was banished from the court. King Louis refused the application which Eugene had made for a commission in the royal army, spoke slightingly of him as a little abbé, and made it only too clear to him that he must expect no toleration from the court of France. Eugene from that time ceased to regard himself as a Frenchman, renounced his allegiance to the King of France, and took service under the Emperor. He got his first taste of warfare in an expedition against the Turks, in which he displayed all the courage and ability that his most admiring comrades of former days could have expected of him. When the Emperor was engaged in war against Louis the Fourteenth in Italy, Prince Eugene had opportunities of paying off some of his old scores against the Grand Monarch, and at a later day he won European renown by the defeats which he inflicted on the Turks in Hungary, defeats which may be said to have formed a decisive chapter in the history of Turkish aggression. His success in this campaign gave him the foremost position among the commanders in the imperial service.

When the War of the Spanish Succession began Eugene was put in command of the imperial forces, and the conditions of the campaign brought him into co-operation with Marlborough. Between Marlborough and Eugene a friendship soon sprang up which only deepened as time went on. The two men were not, by any means, alike in character or in temperament. Eugene had the single-mindedness and the romantic nature of the knight-errant. Marlborough, with many noble qualities, was capable of almost any act of treachery where he saw his way to secure some prize and believed the prize to be worth the temporary sacrifice of principle and honor. The two men differed from each other as much in military disposition as in personal character. Eugene was all compact of headlong courage and almost heedless impetuosity. His motto was "Ever forward." His men would have followed him anywhere, and it has to be said that he would have led them anywhere, no matter how impossible the success of the enterprise might be, if the passion took him for the rush of an onward movement. He had none of Marlborough's superb patience, none of his calm, steady foresight, none of his comprehensive, calculating power. Eugene, in fact, was a splendid leader of cavalry, a knight without fear and without reproach, but Marlborough was one of the greatest commanders whose names live in history. The two men, however, were thoroughly in sympathy. Eugene appreciated the supreme qualities of Marlborough, and

Marlborough understood Eugene's noble nature and the extent and the limits of his military capacity.

Marlborough always said that there was nothing that he could not trust to Eugene, and nothing that Eugene could not do if he only got a fair opportunity. During many stages of the campaign they were divided from each other by wide distances and were often compelled to act as if in absolute independence. But whenever it was possible for them to keep in touch with each other they did thus keep in touch, and the genius of Marlborough was enabled at once to direct the energies, and to profit by the suggestions, of Eugene.

A serious crisis intervened for the time in the plans of Marlborough. Owing to the continuous obstacles interposed in his way by the slowness, the unwillingness, and the incessant councillings of his Dutch allies, he found it impossible to carry out his enterprise for the capture of Antwerp. The armies of the allies in other parts of the continental field of campaign had received some serious checks from the French, which even the brilliant success of Prince Eugene at Cremona had not done much to counterbalance. King Louis could only see that Marlborough was not keeping up his sudden forward movement; he had yet no means of divining that the delay was owing entirely to the slowness and hesitation of the Dutch commissioners, and he seems to have taken it for granted that the delay denoted some hesitation on the part of Marlborough himself. The result was that Louis began to feel greatly encouraged as to the prospects of the campaign, and was forming schemes in his mind for a forward and daring movement on the part of the main French army. Marlborough probably guessed by instinct that King Louis was meditating some decisive movement which for the moment he could do nothing to prevent or even discourage. At one time he felt so disgusted by the enforced inaction to which he saw himself doomed, for the moment, that he was actually making up his mind to resign his command and to leave the Grand Alliance to try what it could do without him. He went so far as to let the home government know that he was unwilling to assume the responsibility any further, and it required all the assurances and the pressure of Godolphin to prevail on him not to resign his command. Marlborough had great faith in the judgment and resource of Godolphin, and so long as he could feel assured that ' might rely upon the home government for full support in any enterprise he might decide upon, he was not the man to give way before adverse conditions.

Marlborough's hands were very full about this time. He was the political as well as the military adviser of the English government, of the Emperor, and of the United Provinces. He was unceasingly engaged in efforts to bring about a better understanding between the Emperor and the Protestants of Hungary. He was doing all he could to stimulate and make use of the rising in the Cevennes. Marlborough hated nothing so much as the writing of letters, and only the pressure of actual necessity could compel him to send home despatches sufficiently long for the information of Queen Anne's ministers. Yet it should be said that even in his seasons of greatest stress he could always find time to write love-letters to the imperious wife whom he adored, and to assure her that in the midst of all his battles, his sieges, and his various other troubles, he was always her devoted admirer and her faithful servant.

The rising in the Cevennes had assumed very serious proportions. The efforts of Louis to put down the movement by mere slaughter and cruelty had proved wholly ineffectual. Jean Cavalier and his Camisards were not men to be crushed into submission. They had risen in rebellion for a cause which was much dearer to them than life. In an appeal which they addressed to the governments of England and of Holland they set forth their purposes and their resolves in the most straightforward and manly terms. "We are ourselves," they said, "not in rebellion against our lawful prince, but merely to defend a right of nature. We follow but the dictates of our conscience. We are not to be frightened by numbers, however superior to our own. We desire to harm no persons who do not strive to harm us. But we shall not hesitate to make just reprisals against our persecutors as we are sanctioned in doing by the common laws of nations, by the common practice, and also by the Word of God." Sometimes it may be admitted the reprisals which they did attempt and carry out were undoubtedly cruel and severe, but they were driven to positive desperation by the savage cruelties inflicted on them and on all around who encouraged and supported, or were believed to encourage and support, them. Their course, in fact, was clear. They were determined that so long as any of them remained alive to fight for their cause, they would fight for it to the bitter end. It became evident that nothing but a war of extermination could bring the rising to a close. Jean Cavalier showed the true spirit of a gallant and unconquerable soldier.

Louis at last sent against them one of his greatest military commanders, Marshal Villars; but Villars, who was a man of keen judgment, and, on the whole, of enlightened views, soon saw that the only way to success must lie in keeping up the fight until the last of the Camisards had been done to death; he knew well what such a policy as this must cost his royal master, and he was not the man to enter on it except as the last possible resource. He saw and thoroughly appreciated the military genius of Cavalier, and he ventured on his own account to make overtures which showed his willingness to enter into conditions that might lead to a lasting peace. He offered to open negotiations with Cavalier. The result was that arrangements were made by which, under certain conditions, something like liberty of conscience was guaranteed to the rebels, with a free pardon to all of them who were willing to accept the terms, and immunity for the region from the oppressive taxation until that part of the country should have had some breathing time to recover from the cruel effects of the previous devastation. Cavalier accepted the conditions, although he had much difficulty in prevailing upon some of his followers to be guided by him and to act upon his decision, so deeply rooted was the terror with which the hitherto remorseless policy of Louis had filled their minds and hearts. Cavalier, however, was influential enough to have his way with the main body of the insurgents, and the result was that, although the rebellion still held out for a time, it greatly lost its force, and after a while the large majority of the inhabitants were enabled to return to their industrial occupations and to live in peace. It must be added that in some instances the terms of the treaty were carried out by the French government in a grudging and a niggardly spirit, and that a large emigration from the oppressed district set in.

For the time the struggle was over, and Cavalier accepted service under the government of Queen Anne. He was despatched into Spain, and in command of a gallant band of his Camisards he bore a brave part afterwards in the memorable battle of Almanza. Cavalier himself, leading a desperate charge, was severely wounded, and was left for dead on the battle-field. He recovered, and was made a general in the English army, and in the service of England he continued until his death. When peace was restored he was appointed governor of Jersey and afterwards of the Isle of Wight, and died quietly in Chelsea, in the May of 1740. We are anticipating time and events in order to complete at once the story of this brave and noble career.

For the present we must turn to the position of Marlborough as he found himself after he had made up his mind to go on with his command to the last. In the mean time Prince Eugene and his forces had come into Bavaria, and Marlborough was thus enabled to enter into frequent communication with the gallant Prince of Savoy. The two commanders met for the first time in the duchy of Würtemberg, and there they spent some days together and arranged their plans for an active and decisive co-operation.

King Louis, as we have already said, had become inspired by the resolve to make a supreme effort which should utterly confound the whole policy of the English and the Dutch. His project was to invade the empire itself, and to make a forward movement which was to end in nothing less than the siege and capture of the Emperor's capital, Vienna. Marlborough seems to have divined his purpose by one of those instinctive impulses of military genius and inspiration which did him such splendid service during the whole of his career. Louis put into the field all the forces he could command, but he kept on sending separate armies on different expeditions, threatening this or that member of the Grand Alliance, in order to divert attention from

"THE CAMPAIGN"—BLENHEIM

the master-stroke of military enterprise which it was
his purpose and his hope to direct to a complete success. Marlborough thoroughly appreciated the plan.
It was just such a plan as he himself, under like conditions, would have made up his mind to put into
action. He felt sure that he understood the King's
intentions, and that he knew the best way to frustrate
them. In the famous words which Grattan applied to
Edmund Burke, "He saw everything — he foresaw
everything." He determined to force the French into
a great pitched battle, and to upset all their calculations by a signal victory.

The policy of the French had, up to this time, been
to evade anything like a decisive encounter on a grand
scale, to play a sort of waiting game, and to take all
the advantage they possibly could from the difficulties
put in Marlborough's way by the slowness of his allies
and by the manner in which the forces of the Grand
Alliance were compelled to act on so many and so
widely separated fields. Marlborough forced the counsels and the hands of his Dutch allies. He suddenly
crossed the Neckar, and directed his movements right
through Germany towards the Danube, formed a junction with the army of the Emperor under the Prince
of Baden, stormed the heights which were guarded by
some of the French allies, crossed the Danube itself,
and made his way into Bavaria. There he encountered
the French forces, strengthened by the coming of Marshal Tallard on the scene to the assistance of the Bavarian troops. Marlborough effected a junction with
the force commanded by Prince Eugene. Marshal
Tallard had at his back an army of more than thirty
thousand men, who, when joined with the troops under
the command of the Bavarian prince, numbered about
sixty thousand, and thus the forces of King Louis were

strengthened so far as to give them an advantage in numbers over those of the Grand Alliance. The allied armies now had at that place and time a number of about fifty-two thousand fighting men, but Tallard was strongly intrenched, and in the matter of artillery was much stronger than his opponents.

The French were still anxious to avoid, at all events to postpone, a great engagement, which it was Marlborough's determination to force on them at once. This resolve was Marlborough's own policy altogether. There were some of the officers, even under his own command, who tried to persuade him that his policy was not only dangerous but desperate. The mind of Marlborough was clearly made up. He assured them that a great engagement was necessary to their united purpose; that he could trust to the bravery and energy of the allied troops to carry all before them, and that now was the time and in front of them lay the field where the great battle must be fought, and, as he felt convinced, could actually be won. Night was approaching, and Marlborough spent part of that night in prayer and the remaining hours in close counsel with Prince Eugene. When the first rays of light began to show themselves in the summer sky on the morning of August 13th the English commander gave the signal for a forward movement. The scene of action enclosed the little village of Blenheim, the name of which is destined to be as famous in history as that of Waterloo.

The village of Blenheim stands on the north bank of the Danube, which is there broad, deep, and very rapid; at a point not far below the village a small stream, the Nebel, runs into the great river. The land there was at that time almost all swampy, but crossed by some well-wooded hills. Prince Eugene, in accordance

"THE CAMPAIGN"—BLENHEIM

with the directions of Marlborough, made the first movement. Marlborough was at the centre of the English forces. The first business of the English commander was to accomplish the crossing of the Nebel streamlet. Tallard seems to have taken the enemies' movements rather too easily and confidently. He probably thought either that they could not succeed in crossing the stream, or that if they did cross it and get into the marshy and hilly regions beyond, they would become so much disordered by the effort that to crush them in their disarray would be an easy piece of work for him. Tallard as a soldier belonged rather to the old school; he was a believer in a deliberate and methodical policy, governed by ancient and well-established rules, and did not count on the perfect order which the troops of Marlborough had learned to maintain even in the fiercest rush of a sudden onward movement. On the right of Marlborough's centre one force of the allies had made an attack, and were encountered, delayed, and actually driven back for a time by the impetuous rush of the Irish brigade. This Irish brigade was made up of a large number of exiles from Ireland, who had been trained on many battle-fields and had taken service under the King of France. During generations in the past and for some time to come, there was hardly a battle fought between an army of England and an army of France in which the French cause was not brilliantly sustained by a regiment of Irishmen, whom the policy of successive English governments had driven from the service of England, and had forced to take arms on the side of England's great enemy.

The news was soon brought to Marlborough that the line of the English troops had been broken by the bold rush of the Irish brigade, and that there was even a possibility of all communication with the troops under Prince Eugene being cut off. This was just the crisis to call into action the genius of a commander like Marlborough, if, indeed, any other commander of that age could be said to be like Marlborough. Marlborough took the field at once, drove back the Irish brigade, and before the evening had far advanced the whole of his cavalry had been brought across the stream. Marlborough ordered a general advance of his main body against the lines of the defending French. Then the great battle took place, and it did not last long. The French were completely defeated, and Marshal Tallard himself was made a prisoner while endeavoring to find shelter in Blenheim. Marlborough behaved with gracious courtesy to the distinguished prisoner, put his own carriage at Tallard's disposal, and saw that the French marshal was secured against all danger. Then he found time to write the despatch which is still preserved and makes a part of English history. The despatch was dated August 13, 1704. These were its words: "I have not time to say more, but to beg you will give my duty to the Queen, and let her know Her Army has had a Glorious Victory. Monsr. Tallard and two other Generals are in my Coach, and I am following the rest. The bearer, my Aide-de-Camp, Coll. Parke, will give Her an account of what has pass'd. I shall doe," he thus wrote, in his old-fashioned spelling, " it in a day or two by another more att large." The despatch was signed "Marlborough."

The village of Blenheim itself had still to be captured by the forces of the allies. Blenheim had been occupied by some French battalions, and these were as yet in possession of the place. It was not a fortified place; was not a stronghold in any sense of the word. It was a convenient possession for the French commander as a starting-point for the conduct of his operations, and if he could only have cleared Marlborough and Eugene out of the field, it would have been a convenient place to return to, and would have served as the scene of new preparations. The French troops who fell back upon it, and occupied it after the defeat of the main army, soon found that it was impossible to hold it as a place of arms. They had the English army in front and the Danube behind. Many tried to swim the river, and lost their lives in the attempt. Marlborough's troops kept up a continual firing on the French troops who were thus beleaguered, and gave them little opportunity of escape. The French behaved bravely, and many of the officers and men were well inclined to stand the final assault of the allied forces and give up their lives rather than yield the place. More prudent counsels, however, prevailed—to hold out would have led to a mere slaughter. The capture of the place was inevitable; further resistance only meant the futile destruction of brave men in masses. The surrender was made, and the battle was over. According to the most accurate accounts which can be obtained, Marlborough and his allies had about fifty-two thousand men in the field, while the French had somewhat more than sixty thousand. The loss of the English and their allies in killed, wounded, and missing was about eleven thousand, and that of the French amounted to more than forty thousand, killed or taken prisoners, to say nothing of the large numbers who were not likely to answer any roll-call, but were wandering as stragglers and fugitives over the face of the country.

Bishop Burnet's concise account of the great battle is of the highest value, because it is taken, for the most part, at first hand and on the best authority. "I will not," says the Bishop, modestly, " venture on a particular relation of that great day." But then he goes on to say that he has " seen a copious account of it, prepared by the duke of Marlborough's orders, that will be printed sometime or other; but there are some passages in it, which make him not think it fit to be published presently. He told me he never saw more evident characters of a special providence than appeared that day; a signal one related to his own person; a cannon-ball went into the ground so near him, that he was sometime quite covered with the cloud of dust and earth that it raised about him." Then the Bishop proceeds, as he says, to sum up the action in a few words:

" Our men quickly passed the brook, the French making no opposition. This was a fatal error, and was laid wholly to Tallard's charge. The action that followed was for some time very hot, many fell on both sides; ten battalions of the French stood their ground, but were in a manner mowed down in their ranks; upon that the horse ran many of them into the Danube, most of these perished; Tallard himself was taken prisoner. The rest of his troops were posted in the village of Blenheim; these, seeing all lost, and that some bodies were advancing upon them, which seemed to them to be thicker than indeed they were, and apprehending that it was impossible to break through, they did not attempt it, though brave men might have made their way. Instead of that, when our men came up to set fire to the village, the Earl of Orkney first beating a parley, they hearkened to it very easily, and were all made prisoners of war; there were about thirteen hundred officers and twelve thousand common soldiers, who laid down their arms, and were now in our hands. Thus all Tallard's army was either killed in the action, drowned in the Danube, or become prisoners by capitulation. Things went not so easily on prince Eugene's side, where the elector and Marsin commanded; he was repulsed in three attacks, but carried the fourth, and broke in; and so he was master of their camp, cannon, and baggage. The enemy retired in some order, and he pursued them as far as men wearied with an action of about six hours, in an extremely hot day, could go. Thus we gained an entire victory. In this action there were on our side about twelve thousand killed and wounded; but the French and the elector lost about forty thousand, killed, wounded, and taken."

Bishop Burnet seems to have been inclined to disparage the spirit with which the French who occupied the village of Blenheim were disposed to encounter their enemies. Many accounts of that part of the day's events given by observers on the English side bear willing and generous testimony to the courage displayed by the French and to the fact that the French officers in command had some difficulty in prevailing on their men not to struggle on to the very last. It is even stated that one French regiment burned its colors when the order for surrender was given. Nothing seems to be more certain than the fact that any further resistance would have been utterly futile and that Blenheim would have been taken all the same, no matter how those who defended it were captured or were slain.

Thus ended the first great battle between the armies led by Marlborough and the forces of King Louis. The glory of the victory was essentially Marlborough's own. The great commander was, indeed, splendidly seconded by Prince Eugene—" Great praise the Duke of Marlborough won and our good Prince Eugene," as the words go in Southey's rather feeble poem—and he was supported by the indomitable bravery of the troops who acted under his orders. But not merely was the plan of the battle his own, but the plans which brought about the battle and forced it on the enemy. Indeed, the whole policy which made that particular region a field of battle, and thus shattered the enterprise which King Louis had hoped to carry out, was the creation of Marlborough's own genius. To win a chance of putting his policy to any test, he had to surmount difficulties created by his own allies, which were hardly less formidable and less obstructive at one time than any that could have been thrown across his path by his embattled enemies.

The news of this great victory was received in England with a very natural outburst of exultation. The estate of Woodstock, where Blenheim Palace was afterwards built, was bestowed upon Marlborough in grateful recognition of his services. The Emperor expressed a strong desire to confer upon Marlborough some signal and special honor in acknowledgment of the work he had done, and offered to create him a prince of the German empire. Marlborough declined to accept this dignity until he should have entered into communication with Queen Anne, and obtained her permission for one of her subjects in command of her army to become a prince of a foreign state. The Queen graciously accorded her permission. Marlborough thereupon obtained the privilege, extraordinary for an English subject, of becoming a prince of a foreign empire, and not long after the Emperor made him a gift of the province of Mindelsheim, in Bavaria, as the principality which was to enable him to sustain his new title. At home the building of the palace of Blenheim was begun on the royal manor of Woodstock. It was to be the possession of him and his heirs, and a perpetual monument of the gratitude felt for him by the Queen

"THE CAMPAIGN"—BLENHEIM

and the country. Another honor, too, awaited him which is likely to be remembered through all history. An outburst of versified glorification in honor of Marlborough's name and services came from many English writers, but the English ministers, anticipating correctly the decision of time, did not consider any of these rhythmical laudations quite equal to the occasion. Godolphin, who was then what we should now call the prime-minister, was not quite the man to discover, by his own literary judgment, the fitting English laureate for such a triumph, but he consulted with some of his friends who knew rather more about poets and poetry than he did. He was advised to apply to a rising poet and essayist named Joseph Addison, then about thirty years of age, and at his request Addison was prevailed upon to attempt a poetic celebration of the victory. This he did in the famous poem called "The Campaign," some lines of which have since become the subject of incessant quotation. This poem shows how, at the crisis of the battle, " great Marlborough's mighty soul was proved," how he

> "Inspired repulsed battalions to engage,
> And taught the doubtful battle where to rage;"

how,

> "Calm and serene he drives the furious blast;
> And, pleased the Almighty's orders to perform,
> Rides in the whirlwind and directs the storm."

This passage is by far the finest and the most characteristic of the whole poem, and gives it, indeed, its title to immortality. Perhaps it is not too much to say that Addison's own fame and the greatest part of his career began with this poetic tribute, which recognized so thoroughly the master qualities of the great commander who had then, for the first time, given full proof of his genius for command.

CHAPTER VIII

PETERBOROUGH IN SPAIN

THE military and naval operations in and around Spain must form a chapter in this story quite distinct from that which describes the operations of Marlborough in the Low Countries and in Germany. Although the object of both campaigns was the same, yet owing to the difference of locality and conditions, the movements were carried on in absolute independence of each other, and it was, in fact, as if England had been engaged in two separate wars for distinct purposes in two different quarters of the globe. The command of the English expedition to Spain was given to the Duke of Ormond, a man who had shown courage and soldierly energy in former campaigns, but had none of the qualities which make a great general. There was, as a matter of course, a contingent of Dutch allies who had a general of their own nationality. The jealousies between the Dutch and the other troops, the difficulties about agreeing quickly upon any plan of combined action, which it had taken all the authority and all the patience of Marlborough to deal with on his fields of campaign, proved entirely too much for Ormond's management. The task which the allied forces had to undertake would not have been easy for any commander.

The allied forces were understood to be acting in the interests of Spain, and in order to rescue that country from being converted into a mere province or vassal of the French monarchy. But the population of Spain could hardly be called a declared party to the dispute of the rival princes who claimed the succession, and of the foreign states which supported one claim and opposed the other. Then, again, the armies and fleets of England and Holland had to begin their work of pacification by capturing Spanish towns and landing troops on the Spanish coast. To the mind of the ordinary Spaniard it might well have seemed that a foreign army of occupation was the army of an enemy, no matter what might be the name and title, no matter what might be the friendly or hostile professions of the sovereign who gave it orders to establish itself on Spanish soil. In fact, the war, like most wars in those times, was made in the interests of princes and dynasties only, and had as little to do with the condition and the sympathies of the population of Spain as with those of the population of England.

The troops of the Duke of Ormond made their appearance off Cadiz in August, 1702. One or two small towns were captured, but the Duke of Ormond proved himself utterly unequal to the occasion. Macaulay tells us what came of these captures. "No discipline was kept; the soldiers were suffered to rob and insult those whom it was most desirable to conciliate. Churches were robbed; images were pulled down; nuns were violated. The officers shared the spoil instead of punishing the spoilers." Cadiz was not taken, and after a few weeks of this worse than futile and absolutely disgraceful work it was decided by the allied commanders that the enterprise should be abandoned. Still, however, the whole enterprise was not abandoned without at least one exploit, although the exploit did not tend much to the advantage of the general policy or to the national glory of the allies. When the fleet was on its way back to England, and was off the coast of Portugal, the Duke of Ormond received news that the treasure-ships from America had arrived within European waters, and were making for the harbor of Vigo in order to escape the armament of the allies. The treasure-ships, which were said to be carrying a cargo of more than three millions in gold and silver, had actually got into Vigo Harbor. Here the blundering regulations of the Spanish authorities suddenly came to the help of those whom we may fairly call the invaders. It was one of the laws governing Spanish trade that the treasure-ships should unload nowhere but at Cadiz. A long delay, therefore, took place while the defenders of Vigo were striving to communicate with the central authorities and to obtain permission for the landing of the precious cargoes at Vigo. In the mean time the English fleet were able to settle the whole question. Some attempt was made to defend Vigo, but the troops of Ormond captured the forts, a large part of the treasure was sunk forever in the waters of the harbor, and the victors were only able to secure a portion of the spoil. As Macaulay tells us, "When all the galleons had been captured or destroyed, came an order in due form allowing them to unload." Never was there a more curious illustration of the effect which mere routine, in the business of administration, can sometimes work. If the central authorities had only sent their permission a little earlier for the unloading of the treasure-ships at Vigo, their whole cargoes might easily have been landed and removed to a place of security before the fleet of the allies had come up. The allies got some solid plunder out of their expedition, and had the satisfaction of knowing that the Spanish authorities got nothing whatever.

PETERBOROUGH IN SPAIN

That ended the attempt upon the Spanish coast for the year. But in the following year, the alliance with Portugal being now secured, a new attempt was made, and this time Sir George Rooke had command of an expedition which was destined to leave a lasting monument of its success in history. Sir George Rooke made an ineffectual attempt on Barcelona, and then suddenly attacked Gibraltar. Rooke disembarked some of his troops on the narrow link of land which connects the rock and the fortress with the inhabited shore. The attack was wholly unexpected. It was a saint's day, August 3, 1704, and many of the defenders of the fortress had gone to attend religious services a little way off. A body of English sailors accomplished the remarkable feat of clambering by a path, which to observers from a distance might have seemed impossible even for the agility of a goat, to the very top of the rock, and there they hoisted the English flag. The few defenders of the garrison who were left to look after its safety had nothing for it but to capitulate, and the fortress of Gibraltar thus suddenly became a part of the dominions of the English crown, and has remained an English fortress to this day.

Bishop Burnet's cool and matter-of-fact comments on this capture have a certain curious interest even now for the reader. The Bishop certainly does not seem to have shared in the general enthusiasm of his country. "It has been much questioned," Burnet says, "by men who understand these matters well, whether our possessing ourselves of Gibraltar, and our maintaining ourselves in it so long, was to our advantage or not. It has certainly put us to a great charge, and we have lost many men in it; but it seems the Spaniards, who should know the importance of the place best, think it so valuable, that they have been at a much greater charge, and have lost many more men, while they have endeavored to recover it, than the taking or keeping it has cost us. And it is certain that in war, whatsoever loss on one side occasions a greater loss of men, or of treasure, to the other, must be reckoned a loss only to the side that suffers most."

England, however, did not regard the capture of Gibraltar in this easy mood of methodical calculation. The old saying which couples lightly won with lightly lost does not apply to the occupation of Gibraltar. The capture of the fortress had been made with all the ease and the light suddenness which might belong to some military feat in melodrama, or even in comic opera. But England seemed only to grow more and more resolute in her determination to hold on to her prize in each succeeding generation. The sovereign who followed Queen Anne on the English throne was at one time well inclined to enter into arrangements with Spain for the restoration of Gibraltar. But his ministers understood too well the strength of public feeling to give any countenance to such a proposal, and the King had to back out of his suggestion very quickly, and try as best he could to convey the idea that he really had nothing of the kind in his mind, or that if he had, it was only his fun. Since that time no English statesman in office has ever entertained the idea of giving back the fortress of Gibraltar, and only the other day a commission was appointed by the English government for the purpose of ascertaining whether the defences of the rock and the fortress were still strong enough to defy any attack from a possible enemy, whether the enemy might come from within or without the country to which Gibraltar once belonged.

In 1705, after the fortress of Gibraltar had maintained with triumph a siege by the combined forces of

PETERBOROUGH IN SPAIN

France and Spain, in which the defeated besiegers suffered a severe loss of men and the English defenders lost very few, the government of Queen Anne thought the time had come to open an effective campaign on a large scale in Spain. Queen Anne's advisers were probably inspired as much by the victories which Sir George Rooke had so suddenly and easily accomplished as by the comparative failure of the expedition under the Duke of Ormond. This time they made up their minds that something more definite must be done. They had reason to believe that the provinces of Catalonia and Valencia were but little inclined to favor the cause of the claimant, whose relationship with King Louis seemed only too clearly to indicate a policy which must reduce the whole of Spain into the condition of a French province forever. The first object of the new expedition, so far as the ministers of Queen Anne could plan it, was to obtain possession of the great commercial city of Barcelona, the capital of Catalonia, and then to capture also some of the other seaport towns on the Spanish coast, and thus make sure of a convenient field of operations for a systematic invasion of Spain. The first movement for the carrying out of this plan was to find the man who could most safely be intrusted with its conduct, and Queen Anne's ministers had not much difficulty in making their choice.

Charles Mordaunt, afterwards Earl of Peterborough, was one of the most brilliant and adventurous figures in that age of brilliant adventure. During his youthful days he had served in the fleet and afterwards had been engaged in exploring enterprises of various kinds in the wild regions of Barbary. It was not uncommon in those days for young men of family to try their fortune and test their capacity in both the fighting professions, and Charles Mordaunt soon changed his naval career for the life of a soldier. He was born not long before the Restoration, and as a young peer he had opposed in the House of Lords much of the religious policy of James the Second. This course of action brought him so much into disfavor with the King and the King's court that he found it prudent to take refuge for a time in Holland, and while there he came into close association with William the Third. It is believed that he was among the most earnest of those who urged on William the advisability of putting himself forward as the representative of the rising opposition to the Stuart dynasty, and even as the invader of England for the rescue of the English people from the Stuart dominion. It is believed that he was the first Englishman of recognized rank who strove to persuade William that the enterprise had every chance of being crowned with complete success. Most assuredly it was an undertaking which would have suited thoroughly with the whole spirit of Mordaunt's character and with his genius for adventure, and nothing could well have seemed more delightful to such a man than to risk his life on so perilous an undertaking.

When the revolution had been accomplished, and William was on the throne of England, Mordaunt was made Earl of Monmouth, and held office as First Lord of the Treasury. He did not, however, get on very well with the new sovereign, and, indeed, any rule which seemed likely to bring about a steady progress in peaceful and practical government would not have much fascination for a man of his restless and ardent temperament. He was suspected and accused of encouraging plots against the new sovereign, and he not only lost his high public offices, but was actually committed as a prisoner to the Tower of London. In those days a change like that was not uncommon for a public man. The uncertainty which seemed to attend each new system of government, the absence of any clearly recognized constitutional principles applicable to all governments, and the fluctuation of opinions from this side to that, will explain many of the sudden changes in the career of men who can hardly be suspected of conscious duplicity or of mere self-seeking motives. There was no conclusive evidence to be brought against Charles Mordaunt, and he was soon released from his imprisonment, which must probably have appeared to him only one other incident in his life of continuous adventure. When he found that he had nothing else to do he was in the habit of starting out as a traveller to any part of Europe whither his restless temperament directed him, and perhaps it might be said of him, without extravagance of statement, that the only thing that his untiring activity would not allow him to do was to keep quiet and do nothing. He was very winning in manners, and, although his figure and personal appearance had not the grace and beauty which belonged to Marlborough, he was always a great favorite with women, and in the midst of all his enterprises he could find time to pay devoted attention to a charming woman. Swift, in some animated lines, tells of Mordaunt that " In journeys he outrides the post "; that " he travels not, but runs a race."

As a leader of men he had hardly a rival in those days, and the soldiers who served under him were so readily filled with his own enthusiasm that they only wanted his word of command to undertake any enterprise, no matter how difficult, no matter how dangerous, no matter how seemingly hopeless, if he would lead the way. The qualities of a really great commander for a long undertaking and over a wide field of action he could not be said to possess. He had all the quickness of conception, all the sudden impulses of energy and daring which often made so telling, so practical, and so successful a part of Marlborough's plans. But then these were only a part, and an occasional part, of Marlborough's military qualities, and Charles Mordaunt had none of Marlborough's patience, none of that cool, calculating foresight which enabled Marlborough to make arrangements for the far future, and to wait resolute and motionless until the opportunity should arise for making the right movement at the right moment. Macaulay says of Mordaunt that he was, " if not the greatest, yet assuredly the most extraordinary character of that age, the King of Sweden himself not even excepted." Macaulay goes on to say that he might be described as a " polite, learned, and amorous Charles the Twelfth." Macaulay describes him as "a kind friend, a generous enemy, and in deportment a thorough gentleman," as " in truth, the last of the knights-errant, brave to temerity, liberal to profusion, courteous in his dealings with enemies, the protector of the oppressed, the adorer of women." But the same historian does not fail to tell us that Mordaunt's " splendid talents and virtues were rendered almost useless to his country by his levity, his restlessness, his irritability, his morbid craving for novelty and excitement."

Before Queen Anne came to the throne Mordaunt had already become Earl of Peterborough on the death of his uncle, and on Anne's accession he at once began to take a public part in life again. Marlborough had a high opinion of Peterborough's military capacity, and, indeed, it was one of Marlborough's valuable gifts as a great commander that he had an instinctive appreciation of the high qualities of other men. It was believed at the time that Marlborough's personal recommendation secured for Peterborough the important post which was given to him and proved so well suited to his peculiar genius—the command of the Queen's forces in Spain. No other part of that immense enterprise could have been so admirably adapted for the full development of Peterborough's romantic energy as the field which was assigned to him in Spain. The very atmosphere of the region must have been congenial to him. He was a Don Quixote of a later day, made happy by conditions which allowed his knight-errant spirit to find opportunities for genuine chivalry in a service to which he had become devoted, and in enterprises which made romance itself a living reality.

The position assigned to Peterborough in this new Spanish expedition was one which gave him full command over the military force, and so much of control over the fleet that, so long as he was actually on board a vessel, he was to have a divided authority with the British admiral, Sir Cloudesley Shovel. The military force was not very great, amounting only to about five thousand men, of whom two-thirds were English and the remainder were supplied by the Dutch allies. The fleet first made for Lisbon, and by the time it had arrived there Peterborough found that he was miserably provided with food or with stores of any kind, and that the government had given him the disposal of very little money with which to supply all that was wanting. Peterborough's first act when he discovered the defective condition of his fleet was peculiarly characteristic. At his own cost, or at all events at his own risk and responsibility, he supplied his ships and his men with all that was needed to keep them in good condition for the work they had to undertake. He was, fortunately, enabled also to increase his military strength by two cavalry regiments put at his disposal by the Earl of Galway, the French Protestant soldier who has been already mentioned as engaged in Portugal on the side of the Grand Alliance. The Archduke Charles himself had been serving with Galway, and he now took a part in the movement conducted by Peterborough. Bishop Burnet always speaks deferentially of the Archduke Charles as the King of Spain. Of course the Archduke Charles was the claimant whom the Grand Alliance proposed to put upon the throne of Spain, and already recognized by the allies as king.

The design of Peterborough was not to linger over the capture of Barcelona, but to make a bold attempt and move directly on Madrid itself. The Archduke Charles and the Prince of Hesse were strongly in favor of the attempt on Barcelona, and both these princes were opposed to Peterborough's daring project, which appeared to them to be surrounded by insuperable difficulties. Peterborough was convinced that, if he accomplished his bold and thorough design, he could, by seizing on the capital, which was only one hundred and fifty miles away, bring the war to a close by that one decisive stroke. On the other hand, his belief was that the army at his command was not strong enough in numbers to effect the capture of Barcelona without a very heavy loss of men, and that, in fact, he should be only wasting his strength upon an enterprise which, even if successful, might fail to have any conclusive influence on the fortunes of the war. Barcelona was defended on one side by the sea and on the other side by the fortifications of Monjuich. These fortifications were so strong that Peterborough did not see how it would be possible even to attempt their investment without a much larger force than he had at his disposal. The idea entertained by some of his allies that there would be a general rising of the Catalonian populations in favor of the invasion found no confirmation in the events which were passing under Peterborough's eyes. Only a few hundreds of the Catalonian peasantry, furnished with such poor weapons as they could bring to the service, had come to the aid of the allies, and the task of providing them with mere food threatened to be a severe trial on Peterborough's resources.

The usual councils of war, the familiar arguments and delays, interfered with Peterborough's plans. Burnet says that King Charles, as he somewhat prematurely describes him, spoke on one occasion for several hours in the exposition and enforcement of his views. At last Peterborough became disgusted with the whole business, and seems to have made up his mind that, as he could not, under the conditions, attempt to carry out his own enterprise, it would be better to abandon the siege altogether and try some other plan. For this suggestion he was severely blamed by some of his comrades in arms, and it is curious to read by the light of subsequent history that there were those among them who did not hesitate to accuse him of what they believed to be a want of daring and of enterprise. While the Archduke Charles and the Prince of Hesse kept on still urging him to attempt the capture of Barcelona, they do not appear to have been able even to suggest any plan by means of which the venture might be safely attempted. Weeks were wasted in this futile discussion. With the instructions which were given to him, Peterborough did not see his way to carry out his own original project in defiance of some of his allies. He, therefore, conceived a new and daring project of his own, and by the sheer force of his military genius and energy he carried it to success. He outdid the most venturesome of his allies in this sudden project, risked everything in an enterprise much more audacious than anything which they had contemplated, and carried out his purpose. He accomplished by storm what they had only proposed to execute by a regular siege.

The citadel of Monjuich had practical command of Barcelona. It was for this reason splendidly fortified, and was garrisoned by some of the best officers and men in the Spanish service. It stood upon one of a range of hills the most distant from the allies, and it would have required for them a march of nearly ten miles if they did not mean to announce at once to the occupying garrison the real purpose of a forward movement on their part. For this very reason the occupying forces believed themselves to be perfectly safe from any attempt at a sudden attack, and were, therefore, likely to be off their guard if an audacious scheme of the kind should be attempted. This very fact only gave a new impulse to the daring spirit of Peterborough, who at once realized the possibility of its existence, and found in it a new inspiration for the design he had just conceived. At the dead hour of night he paid a visit to the Prince of Hesse and told him that he was resolved to make a decisive attempt upon the citadel. He gave the Prince of Hesse his choice to join in the attack or to remain behind, telling him at the same time that, happen what might, his mind was fully made up, and that the Prince must soon see whether British officers and men were quite the laggards and weaklings he had seemed inclined to believe them. Under these conditions there was nothing for the Prince, who was a thoroughly brave man, but to take his chance in the enterprise, and without further altercation Peterborough was allowed to have his way. Peterborough had only about one thousand five hundred English soldiers to follow him into the assault, and about one thousand more had been stationed as a reserve force under the command of Stanhope, the distinguished soldier and diplomatist of those days. Peterborough and his small band of followers made a circuitous march, and came to a halt only under the walls of Monjuich. Then there came to pass exactly what Peterborough had counted on as the first result of his appearance under the walls, and exactly what he hoped and expected to see. The defenders of the fortress, surprised by the audacious attempt, advanced into the outer ditch of defence to meet their assailants, and the English troops, prepared by Peterborough for such a movement, rushed upon their enemies, and after a desperate struggle completely defeated and scattered the Spaniards, and occupied this first line of defence. The Spanish troops in the garrison were so bewildered by the attack that Peterborough was able, almost with a single stroke, to become master of all the outworks.

At this critical moment an unexpected accident came in his way. News was suddenly brought to him that a large force was already on the march from Barcelona to the aid of the garrison of Monjuich. Peterborough at once left his place, and rode out some distance in order to ascertain, if possible, whether there was any truth in the alarming report. During his short absence something happened which might not unreasonably have been looked for under such critical conditions. A sort of panic seized upon Peterborough's troops. They became bewildered by the absence of their leader; they had heard the story of forces coming to the rescue of the garrison, and in their sudden confusion they were actually preparing to evacuate the outworks altogether and fall back on their reserves. Peterborough returned just in time, and, like some hero of romance, he retrieved by his own presence and daring the fortunes of that eventful night. He rallied in a moment the men who were abandoning their position, he inspired them with new courage by his voice and his leadership, and he led them back to their former position before the enemy had time to take advantage of their confusion and their retreat. Some of us still living can well remember the occasion during the great civil war in the United States of America when the sudden return of General Sheridan rallied a dispersing army and led it back to the scene of battle and to a complete victory. The troops under Stanhope soon came to the rescue. The Spanish force, which had, too late, been marching out of Barcelona to the relief of the garrison, fell back, and almost in another moment the capture of Monjuich was completely accomplished. The Prince of Hesse was one of the first victims. He was killed by a shot during the assault, but the assault itself was a complete success, and with the capture of Monjuich there was nothing left for Barcelona but to capitulate to the victorious English commander.

Peterborough made good use of his victory. He was now occupying the capital of the province, and he at once issued a decree restoring and guaranteeing to the population of that province all the ancient rights and liberties of which they had once been in possession. He thus succeeded in obtaining their cordial support for the cause of which he was then the living and conquering representative. There had been many jealousies among some of the Spanish provinces, and the Catalonians felt in especial a strong resentment of the superior position given to the inhabitants of Castille, who were, in fact, the somewhat arrogant and overmastering race in Spain, proud of their ancient descent, of their historical position and dignities, and looking on themselves as the ruling people of the country. Thus Peterborough won for himself by one successful stroke the allegiance and support of all that region, and many of its towns threw open their gates and welcomed the sympathetic conqueror. The Spanish government sent an army of more than seven thousand men to recapture one of those towns. Peterborough, with a force not a fifth of that number, succeeded in frustrating this attempt, and rendered it, in fact, a hopeless failure. Thereupon arose fresh difficulties with some of his companions. The Archduke Charles thought that enough had been done for fame, so far at least as the immediate enterprise was concerned, and strongly urged on the commander the prudence of returning to Barcelona and resting quietly there.

Peterborough, however, was not content. He knew that there was immediate work still to do. Like Charles the Twelfth, as described by Johnson, he thought nothing done while aught remained to do. He overruled all the counsellors who talked to him of prudence. In the heart of winter, in the midst of a mountainous country, where there were hardly any roads worthy of the name, with a force poorly armed and poorly provided in every way, and with the army of the retreating enemy still much stronger in numbers than his own, he kept on his energetic movement, and in the February of 1706 he made his way into Valencia. This was not enough for him. He learned there that a large body of Spanish troops was marching to the assistance of the retreating enemy. He still pushed on, and before his foes could have supposed that he was close on their quarters, he attacked the whole encampment, and killed, captured, or dispersed the new army which had been brought out against him. He returned to Valencia, bringing with him several hundred prisoners. Yet a little, and he was on his way to Madrid. Yet a little more, and the army of the invaders under Galway had made their entry into the Spanish capital, from which its royal occupant had fled in dismay, and there in the capital city the conquerors proclaimed the Archduke Charles as King of Spain. So splendid a success, accomplished by the indomitable energy and the military spirit of one man, has seldom been recorded in the history of war. Some words from Shakespeare might well be employed in description of Peterborough's success. He had wrestled well, and overthrown more than his enemies.

CHAPTER IX

EVENTS AND PARTIES AT HOME

ADDISON, in his poem, "The Campaign," to which some reference has already been made, likens the destructive work and the crash of the Blenheim battlefield to the tumult of a storm. "Such as of late o'er pale Britannia passed." Addison's allusion went home to the memory and heart of every one in England just then. On November 26, 1703, a tempest raged over a large part of Europe, and especially over England, which was long remembered as one of the destroying prodigies of all time. For generations after it was spoken of in England as the Great Storm, and was ranked as an event with the Great Fire and the Great Plague of London. No cause has ever been definitely assigned among the atmospheric, meteorological, or other conditions of the times for this terrible work of destruction, and, indeed, those who tell of its fury, and who saw with their own eyes the damage it was doing, did not trouble themselves much to make any careful inquiries into its origin, even if the scientific acquirements of the age had been qualified to lend much help towards the forming of a right conclusion. London, having then as now the largest population of any city in the civilized world, gave the most striking and most wide-spread evidences of the storm's destructive power. The river was swollen by inundations, and Westminster Hall was flooded through by the overflowing Thames. Whole fleets of merchant ships were torn from their anchorage and dashed ashore, and Queen Anne's navy suffered severely from the influence of the tempest. The spires and towers of churches were torn away and flung down in shapeless masses of ruined masonry. The Palace of St. James's underwent severe injury, and the chapel of King's College, Cambridge, was almost totally reduced to ruin. The Bishop of Bath and Wells was killed with his wife by the fall of a stack of chimneys.

John Evelyn, the author of the immortal *Diary*, saw and suffered by the tempest. "Methinks I still hear," he says, "sure I am that I still feel, the dismal groans of our forests when that dreadful hurricane subverted so many thousands of goodly oaks, prostrating the trees, laying them in ghastly postures, like whole regiments fallen in battle by the sword of the conqueror, and crushing all that grew beneath them." Then he goes on to tell of what happened in the Forest of Dean, in the New Forest of Hampshire, and in many other parks and groves. Evelyn introduces this description into his book, *Sylvia; or, a Discourse of Forest-trees,* and he pictures the work of the storm, as its effects made themselves especially appropriate to that subject. The Eddystone light-house was shattered to pieces, and those who occupied it at the time and had it in charge lost their lives with its fall. Vast numbers of cattle and sheep were destroyed, and it is believed that on land and sea more than eight thousand persons perished in and around this island. Britannia might well turn pale, in poetic metaphor at least, as Addison has described her, when she had to look on such a storm.

We have to turn for a while from the story of the war. The campaigns which were brought about by

EVENTS AND PARTIES AT HOME

the question of the Spanish succession lasted so long that they occupied by far the greater part of the reign of Queen Anne. Moreover, the vicissitudes of the war affected so often and so directly the fortunes of political parties at home, and the strife of these political parties had so close and immediate a bearing on the movements of the war, that it is not possible for the historian to make a separate chapter of the struggle on the continental battle-fields, and having followed it uninterruptedly to its conclusion, return to take up the thread of the domestic story just as if the one set of events had been wholly disconnected from the other. One who wrote of English history during the reign of Queen Victoria might very well treat the account of the Crimean war or of the Indian mutiny as a mere episode in his work, and, when he had brought each chapter of history to its conclusion, go quietly back to the movement of occurrences at home with the conviction that his reader's comprehension of the whole narrative and the bearing of one set of events on the other would in no wise be disturbed by the interruption; but it is not possible to follow such a course in dealing with the reign of Queen Anne and the events which marked, and made or marred, its satisfactory progress.

While Marlborough was leading the allies in the Low Countries and Germany; while Peterborough was carrying on his adventurous enterprises in Spain; while disaster to the arms of the allies was following victory, and victory was once again retrieving disaster, events were going on at home which had an abiding influence on the fortunes of England as a state, and yet were so dependent on the fortunes of the war, and had so much influence over those fortunes, that we cannot contemplate what was happening abroad and at home as separate parts of history. The two great parties into which English public life was then divided—the Tories and the Whigs—were profoundly influenced from time to time by the conditions of the continental campaign, and it would not always have been possible for the observer at home to predict, with any certainty, the course which this or that party might take in striving to influence the fortunes of the war.

The Tories were not in the beginning well disposed towards the whole policy of the war. They believed first of all in the divine right of kings. They had to recognize the force of circumstances which they could not hope to resist, and to accept the situation, as the modern phrase goes, or at least to put up with it as long as they saw no reasonable chance of converting it into other than it was. They had been compelled to go so far as to take up with the principle of hereditary succession and to try to regard it as a sort of divine right; but deep in the hearts of many influential Tories was the hope that, even yet, some interposition of Providence might restore the divine right to its old recognized place in the constitution of England. Many of the Tories were strongly disinclined towards a war with France, if only for the reason that the representatives of the Stuart dynasty had still their home in that country and were receiving the protection and even the recognition of Versailles. These, however, found themselves totally unable to resist the popular demand for war when Louis the Fourteenth made the political mistake of recognizing the exiled Stuarts as the rightful royal family of England. The war policy had to be adopted by the Tory party, and the great soldier of the day, who was leading the armies of England to victory on continental battlefields, was himself known to be a Tory in convictions and at heart. The Tories, therefore, had to make the war their own, and to proclaim their delight in every triumph which it accomplished.

One of the events of the time was a growing struggle between the House of Lords and the House of Commons. The hereditary chamber and the representative chamber might still be regarded as to a great extent rival powers in the state. The representative principle, although long established, at least in form, as the basis of the House of Commons, was still very new in its practical operation, and the period had only just begun when it was a settled condition of the constitutional system that the sovereign could no longer raise armies and dispose of the national funds without the consent and co-operation of the representative chamber. A conflict of authority had been making itself manifest between the principles of the present and the principles of the past, and this conflict found a remarkable illustration in the political events of the reign about the time at which we have arrived in this narrative.

A dispute, or, indeed, it might be called a quarrel, had been going on for some time between the two Houses of the English Parliament which involved a constitutional question of the highest importance to the state. The dispute had begun in the last Parliament elected under William the Third, and had continued in the first Parliament elected under Anne, but there had been for a while nothing more than the murmurings and grumblings which usually prelude a great storm. The whole dispute arose out of the election of a member of the House of Commons to represent the town of Aylesbury, in Buckinghamshire. It seemed to be a very small and trivial subject of dispute in the beginning. It might even have been regarded as involving nothing more than a merely personal claim and a demand for civil damages by an obscure citizen. The sheriff of the county of Buckinghamshire had issued his writ for the election of two burgesses to represent Aylesbury in the House of Commons. When the time for the election came, a man named Matthew Ashby tendered his vote for two candidates, and announced himself as a duly qualified voter. The official in charge declined to receive his vote, and Ashby straightway brought an action, which was tried at the next assizes, where he obtained a verdict with five pounds damages as compensation for the injury done to him by his exclusion from his right as a duly qualified voter. An appeal was made to the court of Queen's Bench, and the decision of that tribunal was a reversal of the verdict given at the assizes. It was declared that the man was not properly qualified to vote at the election. This judgment was founded on a resolution passed by the House of Commons before the action was brought, to the effect that the right of election for the borough of Aylesbury belonged only to inhabitants not receiving parochial alms. The plaintiff, in making out his case, described himself as "an inhabitant of that borough, not receiving alms," and went on to say that "the constables falsely and maliciously obstructed and hindered him from giving his vote at the election there." As the proceedings went on the evidence made it clear enough that the plaintiff in the action was certainly in such a condition as to excuse the constables if they mistook him for a person who actually received public alms. His occupation was that of an ostler, and he had been for a long time steeped in a condition of such utter poverty that if not actually in the receipt of alms at the time when he tendered his vote, he unquestionably came to be a recipient of parochial charity almost immediately after.

EVENTS AND PARTIES AT HOME

Here, then, had come up for the decision of the legal authorities what an eminent English judge of a later day sarcastically described as " a delightful point of law." A very different issue, however, presented itself for settlement along with this " delightful point of law." The case was carried out of the range of the ordinary law courts by a writ of error, and the judgment of the Queen's Bench was reversed by the House of Lords. The Lords, by their decision, affirmed that the constables at the Aylesbury election had no right to reject the vote of an inhabitant of the borough, otherwise duly qualified, who had not actually been in the receipt of public charity up to the time when he presented himself as a voter. This would seem to be a very reasonable decision on the part of the House of Lords, for if a man had not up to the time of tendering his vote been in the receipt of parochial alms, it could hardly be considered quite fair and reasonable that the constables should be allowed to act on a kind of prophetic inspiration, and to declare that, although the man had not been a pauper in the past, he was a sort of person very likely to become a pauper in the near future, and, therefore, ought not to be regarded as a qualified voter. Under such conditions the apothecary in " Romeo and Juliet," if it were possible for him to be a resident of Aylesbury, must have been in perpetual disqualification as a voter because of the *prima - facie* evidence that he must before long be a recipient of public charity.

The decision of the House of Lords raised a great constitutional question, during the discussion of which the personal solvency of the Aylesbury claimant soon passed out of public notice. That question was whether the House of Lords had any right to dictate the terms on which votes should be given for the election of members to the House of Commons. Of course there were legal conditions under which alone a man could be entitled to vote for the election of a member to the representative chamber, and over these distinctly legal conditions the House of Lords could not profess to exercise any power. But when some question arose as to the validity of a vote given for the election of a member to the House of Commons, was it for the House of Lords, the hereditary chamber, the parliamentary body which had nothing to do with the representative principle—was it for that House to decide a question which only affected the rights of the House of Commons? Other points of dispute soon began to show themselves in this complicating controversy. Several inhabitants of Aylesbury followed the example set them by Ashby, and brought actions against the local constables on the ground that these had unjustly disallowed their right to tender a vote at the election. The bewildering prospect seemed to be that everybody, in any part of the country, who believed he had a right to vote and whose vote had been disallowed by the local authorities, would straightway bring his action against these local authorities, and that the whole machinery of the law would be kept in lively motion for a long time to come in the vain effort to dispose of all this indefinite multiplication of claims.

Here again the House of Commons showed itself concerned about the maintenance of its own privileges and rights. The House of Commons particularly wanted to know who had any right to interfere with the manner in which its elections were conducted. It was especially the interest of the stronger party in the House to make such a demand, for if every claimant whose vote was disallowed could forthwith bring his action against the local authorities, a new terror would

EVENTS AND PARTIES AT HOME

be added to the electoral contest, and the candidate who had secured his triumphant majority would find a fresh campaign opening upon him the moment he had taken his seat in Parliament. The House of Commons then took the very decided step of committing for breach of privilege each of the luckless individuals who had brought actions against the constables for refusing to accept their votes. At the same time the House issued an address to the throne justifying the somewhat imperious course which it had taken against the men who brought these actions, on the ground that it is "the undoubted right and privilege of the Commons of England in Parliament assembled, to commit for breach of privilege; and that the commitments of this House are not examinable in any other court whatever." Then, as if to show how absolutely resolved they were to maintain what they considered to be their rights, the Commons actually ordered the committed claimants to be removed from Newgate and taken into the custody of the sergeant-at-arms. It appears that this order was for some reason or other put into execution at the mid-hour of night, thereby adding a stern gloom to the enforcement of the Commons' authority which might be worthy of a Turkish pasha or what Disraeli once called "the tyrant of a twopenny tragedy."

The Commons, however, went a step still farther. They appointed a committee to discover what persons had been engaged in soliciting or advising or prosecuting upon the writs of habeas corpus, or writs of error on the part of the persons committed for offending against the privileges of the representative chamber. The result of this inquiry was that three barristers-at-law and two attorneys-at-law were found to have given legal advice and assistance to the committed offenders, and the House directed the sergeant-at-arms to take into custody these professional gentlemen as aiders and abettors in the breach of privilege. The sergeant-at-arms actually arrested one of the three barristers, and held him in custody, but he reported that he was not able to find any of the other legal advisers. It now became the turn of the Peers to assert their rights and privileges. An order was issued by the Lords Spiritual and Temporal in Parliament assembled declaring that the legal gentlemen already mentioned "shall, and they have hereby, the protection and privilege of this House, in the advising, applying for, and prosecuting the said writs of error; and that all keepers of prisons and jailers, and all sergeants-at-arms and other persons whatsoever be—and they are hereby, for or in respect of any of the cases aforesaid—strictly prohibited from arresting, imprisoning, or otherwise detaining or molesting or charging the said persons, or any or either of them, as they and every of them will answer the contrary to this House."

Here was a very pretty quarrel, indeed, between the Lords and the Commons. A more distinct issue could hardly have been contrived by the perverse ingenuity of man, desirous to bring rival claims of authority into hostile and decisive action. The Commons proclaimed in substance to the Lords—We have a right to arrange all matters pertaining to our elections for ourselves, and if any one presumes to bring an action against one of our officials, we have a right to commit him to prison under the custody of our sergeant-at-arms. The House of Lords declared in reply—We are the highest court of law as well as a court of parliament, and we have a right to protect any person acting on the decree of a court of law which we have sanctioned from being taken into custody under your warrant and by your sergeant-at-arms. Nor did the Lords hesitate to show that they meant to be as good as their word in the assertion of their privileges. A few days after this warning had been given to the Commons, the sergeant-at-arms presented himself at the bar of the representative chamber to inform its members that a person had that morning brought him a writ of habeas corpus under the great seal, calling on him to hand over one of the persons in his custody in order that this person might be brought before the Lord Keeper of the Great Seal of England. The embarrassed sergeant-at-arms naturally desired to know which authority he was to recognize as supreme. He held in custody a certain person under an order of the House of Commons, and now behold! he was summoned to surrender his captive in obedience to an order from the House of Lords. The Commons were not long in deciding as to his course of action. A resolution was promptly passed "That the sergeant-at-arms attending this House do make no return of, or yield any obedience to, the said writ of habeas corpus; and for such his refusal, that he have the protection of the House of Commons."

Readers now would probably think that an opinion expressed by Chief-Justice Holt, one of the most eminent and enlightened lawyers of his time or of any time, fairly defined the limitations of the authority which the House of Commons claimed to exercise over the manner of their own elections. When the question was discussed before the court of Queen's Bench, the Lord Chief-Justice differed on this point from the three other judges who sat with him. These three judges held that an election to the House of Commons was a matter solely for the jurisdiction of the House of Commons. Lord Chief-Justice Holt declared that he saw a great difference between the election of a member to that House and the right to vote for a candidate at such an election. He admitted that the House of Commons alone had the right to judge whether an election had or had not been rightfully carried out, whether it was properly conducted without bribery, corruption, fraud, or violence, but he maintained that the right of voting in an election was quite a different matter and was, in fact, an original right founded on the man's legal qualification to vote. Such a qualification, he insisted, was made by act of Parliament, and, therefore, every question relating to the claim of the voter was the proper subject for the decision of a court of law.

The House of Commons still held to its former position, and acted on the principle that the question had now come to be strictly a question as to the right of the House of Lords to override the authority of the House of Commons in the election of its own members. The House of Commons insisted that any dispute as to the validity of the vote accepted by the officers whom the Commons had appointed to receive votes was a question which directly affected the right of the Commons to a full authority over the manner in which the elections to the representative chamber were to be conducted. The position of the Commons was that, if the House of Lords were to say, "We have the right to declare invalid a vote which you by your officers have accepted as valid," that would be in effect to claim a right which is as fatal to the privileges of the elected chamber as if the Lords were to assert a power of control over the validity of the whole election, and this is a power which belongs to the Commons and to the Commons alone. The Lords sent a message expressing a desire to hold a conference with the other

House in the Painted Chamber, in order that a good understanding might be arrived at between the two Houses, which the Lords declared they would always endeavor to preserve. "When either House of Parliament," the message went on to say, "shall have apprehended the proceedings of the other to be liable to exception, the ancient parliamentary method has been to ask a conference, it being ever supposed that when the matters are fairly laid open and debated, that which may have been amiss will be rectified, or else the House that made the objections will be satisfied that their complaint was well grounded."

The terms of the message seemed to announce and to invite a policy of conciliation. But then the Lords distinctly maintained the judicial claims of their House as rights which were in no wise affected by the existing dispute, and this was just the position which the House of Commons was not willing to recognize. The conference, therefore, did not seem likely to bring the two Houses to a better understanding. The Commons declared that they could not but see "how your lordships are contriving by all methods to bring the determination of liberty and property into the bottomless and insatiable gulf of your lordships' judicature, which would swallow up both the prerogatives of the crown and the rights and liberties of the people." Furthermore, the Commons went on to declare that "the bringing writs of habeas corpus upon the commitments of the Commons and a writ of error thereupon before the Lords, would bring all the privileges of the Commons to be determined by the judges and afterwards by the Lords upon such writs of error." Such writs of error, it was argued, would bring the liberty of every commoner in England to the arbitrary disposition of the Peers. "If a writ of error cannot be denied in any case and the Lords alone are to judge whether the case be proper for a writ of error, then all the Queen's revenues, all her prerogatives, and all the lives and liberties of the people of England will be in the hands of the Lords." "And by writs of error and appeals, as already exercised, they will have all our properties; by such newly invented actions they will have all our elections; and by such writs of habeas corpus and writs of error thereupon they will have all our privileges, liberties, and even lives at their determination." Finally, the Commons declared that "the novelty of those things and the infinite consequences of them is the greatest argument in the law that they are not of right."

The conference came to nothing, and as it did not seem probable that further consultation would lead to any better result, the Lords intimated that they had nothing more to say on the subject, and the friendly negotiations were broken off. The Lords issued an address to the Queen in which they set forth their own view of the whole case, and wound up with a prayer, "that no importunity of the House of Commons, nor any other consideration whatsoever, may prevail with your Majesty to suffer a stop to be put to the known course of justice, but that you will be pleased to give effectual orders for the immediate issuing of the writs of error." The Queen made a prompt reply. It was concise as well as prompt. It merely said: "My Lords, I should have granted the writs of error desired in this address. But finding an absolute necessity of putting an immediate end to the session, I am sensible there could have been no further proceeding in that matter." The Queen, therefore, left the controversy exactly as she found it. Acting, no doubt, under advice, she availed herself of the supposed necessity for bringing the session to a close in order to get rid of the immediate dispute, and leave it to settle itself by the course of events and the development of this or that competing power in the work of legislation.

Those who represented the claims of the House of Lords maintained, of course, that in the end there must be some law supreme over all the struggles of political parties. As an abstract proposition this is, no doubt, reasonable and clear. In point of fact, the right which the House of Commons exercised down to our own times in the hearing and decision of election petitions has for many years been transferred, with the approval of all intelligent men, to the legal tribunals of the country. At a time well within the memory of living men, the House of Commons had the right of hearing and deciding upon all petitions brought against the election of a member to sit in the representative chamber. The course which the House adopted was to refer each such petition for trial and decision to a committee of members elected by the House itself. When the question raised by any such petition represented a conflict between the two great political parties, it often happened that any one hearing the names of the committee who had been chosen by ballot read aloud in the House could have told at once which way the decision of the committee would go. It came to be in too many cases purely a question of party, and the grossest instances of bribery, corruption, or intimidation might be proved in vain if the majority of the committee happened to belong to that political party which would be likely to suffer if the prayer of the petition were granted. It may be admitted without hesitation that there was a great deal to be said for the case which the House of Lords endeavored to set up in the early days of Queen Anne.

Moreover, the advocates of the House of Lords argued at the time, and with only too much substantial reason for their argument, that the political party in power was in the habit of making its arrangements for elections to the House of Commons by appointing officials in each electoral district who would take good care not to disallow any votes which were given on the side of those who had appointed them, and to disallow as many as possible of those that were tendered on the opposite side.

On the other hand, it was already becoming evident to every thinking observer that the House of Commons was destined to be the real governing power of the state. The sovereign was to rule according to the advice of the ministers of the crown, and even already it was coming to be more and more clearly understood that the only real authority which the House of Lords could claim was the right to act as a sort of check in the last resort upon the action of the representative chamber, and thus to obtain time for a reconsideration of the particular question which a passing crisis might involve, and if necessary to compel a new appeal to the constituencies before that decision could be regarded as final. Even this power has been growing more limited in its actual operation, and its exercise has been gradually becoming a rarer event in constitutional history. Therefore, although the House of Commons may have shown a disposition, during the controversy which the Aylesbury election brought up, to strain its constitutional right beyond its natural province, yet it will now readily be admitted by all that the whole question of popular election to the representative chamber was a singularly ill-chosen subject as an occasion for the House of Lords to bring to a test the extent of its constitutional power in the business of government. The advisers of Queen Anne could not help seeing that the occasion was peculiarly ill suited for such a trial of strength, and the Queen, no doubt, was led to believe that the easiest way out of the difficulty was to bring the parliamentary session to a close and leave it to the growth of events and the lapse of time to develop a state of affairs which might ultimately settle the whole embarrassing controversy. Some such controversy has, indeed, been renewed again and again, even in our own times, but the obvious effect of years and of political change has unquestionably been to extend the governing powers of the Commons and to restrict, more and more, the right of control which public opinion could allow to the House of Lords. Perhaps the whole controversy arising out of the Aylesbury election could not be more fairly summed up than by the judgment that while the House of Lords may have been technically in the right, the House of Commons was acting, unconsciously perhaps, in the true spirit of the constitution, and that a decisive struggle between the two authorities could only lead to the triumph of that one which based its claims on the principle of popular representation.

Perhaps this is the right time at which to tell the story of that new arrangement instituted by the sovereign which called into existence the system known ever since by the name of Queen Anne's bounty. The Queen's bounty was, in fact, the application of the "first-fruits" and the tenths of benefices to the increase of the small livings which were held by so many clergymen of the Church of England. The existence of the fund, thus for the first time devoted to this purpose, carries us a long way back in history. When the religion of Rome prevailed throughout England there was an arrangement that the whole income of a benefice during its first year, and a tithe or tenth part of it during each succeeding year, was claimed and made over to the Vatican as England's contribution towards the maintenance of the papal revenues. During the reign of Henry the Eighth, when the Protestant Church was established in England, the grant was withheld from the Church of Rome, but for a while without any definite application of it to any other purpose. After a time this revenue was settled by Parliament as part of the regular income of the crown, and this was declared to be a perpetual arrangement. The bishops were supposed to be the distributors of the fund, and it was distributed, for the most part, among persons who enjoyed the favor of the king or of the bishops, without any special reference to charitable purposes or even to the benefit of ill-paid clergymen. Bishop Burnet tells us that during the reign of Charles the Second " it went chiefly among his women and his natural children." Bishop Burnet goes on to say: " When I wrote the history of the Reformation I considered this matter so particularly, that I saw here was a proper fund for providing better subsistence to the poor clergy; we having among us some hundreds of cures that have not of certain provision, twenty pounds a-year; and some thousands that have not fifty." The Bishop justly observes: " It is a crying scandal that at the restauration of King Charles the Second, the bishops and other dignitaries who raised much above a million in fines, yet did so little this way."

Bishop Burnet, it will be seen, evidently regards himself as the author of the reform which was carried out by Queen Anne. We are not inclined to dispute his claim to its authorship, which, indeed, he distinctly asserted at a time when some public contradiction must have been called forth by his statement, if there were any likelihood that his modest claim could have been effectively disputed. His own account is well worth quotation. "I laid the matter before the late king, when there was a prospect of peace, as a proper expression both of his thankfulness to Almighty God, and of his care of the church; I hoped that this might have gained the hearts of the clergy: it might at least have put a stop to a groundless clamour raised against him, that he was an enemy of the clergy, which began to have a very ill effect on all his affairs. He entertained this so well, that he ordered me to speak to his ministers about it; they all approved it, the lord Somers and the lord Halifax did it in a most particular manner; but the earl of Sunderland obtained an assignation, upon two dioceses, for two thousand pounds a-year for two lives; so that nothing was to be hoped for after that. I laid this matter very fully before the present queen, in the king's time, and had spoken often of it to the lord Godolphin."

In November, 1703, the measure was introduced to the House of Commons, with a special message from the Queen containing an expression of her strong desire that the bill should be passed into law. The preamble of this measure set forth that "Whereas a sufficient settled provision for the clergy, in many parts of this realm, hath never yet been made, by reason whereof divers mean and stipendiary preachers are in many places entertained to serve the cures and officials there, who depending for their necessary maintenance on the good will and liking of their hearers, have been and are hereby under temptation of too much complying and suiting their doctrines and teaching to the humours rather than the good of their hearers, which hath been a great occasion of faction and schism and contempt of the ministry." Then the preamble goes on to say that " your Majesty, taking into your princely and serious consideration the mean and insufficient maintenance belonging to the clergy in divers parts of this your kingdom, has been most graciously pleased out of your most religious and tender concern for the Church of England—whereof your Majesty is the only supreme head on earth—and for the poor clergy thereof—not only to remit the arrears of your tenths due from your poor clergy, but also to declare unto your most dutiful and loyal Commons your royal pleasure and pious desire that the whole revenue arising from the first-fruits and tenths of the clergy might be settled for a perpetual augmentation of the maintenance of the said clergy in places where the same is not already sufficiently provided for."

An act of Parliament was passed accordingly, and the institution which we know as Queen Anne's bounty became a part of the system by which the state Church is conducted. There were difficulties in the way of making a practical arrangement which prevented the Queen's sincere and high-minded purpose from being carried into full effect during her own lifetime. Nobody can pretend to say that even at the present time the distribution of the Church revenues is so reasonably and beneficently adjusted as to make fair provision for the maintenance of large numbers of the clergy, or that the distribution of the Church revenues has approached within measurable distance of perfection. It still happens that in numberless instances throughout England the hardest working, the most highly gifted, and the most thoroughly devoted clergymen of the state Church find the poorest earthly reward for their services as pastors and as religious teachers. But it is beyond question that the principle of a great reform was established by the legislation of Queen Anne's reign, and that Anne herself was deeply and sincerely interested in the settlement. We may give to Bishop Burnet the full credit for having originated the idea, but it must be owned that Queen Anne appreciated and welcomed his suggestions, and took care that they should be carried as far as possible into effect. Perhaps the popular name given to the new arrangement and still retained in ordinary speech is in itself the most appropriate tribute which could be paid to the sovereign who saw it carried into law, and Queen Anne's bounty becomes a goodly epitaph.

CHAPTER X

THE UNION WITH SCOTLAND

ONE of the greatest events of Queen Anne's reign was the accomplishment of the union between England and Scotland. This event had been a long time in contemplation and under discussion. When the union of the two crowns was definitely accomplished, after the formal and, as it proved, the final abolition of the Stuart dynasty, the legislative union of the two countries, being, as they were, geographically only one country, naturally came up for consideration as a necessary step towards the establishment of the imperial system. William the Third had taken the project in hand and given it his full approval and recommendation. One of the last acts of King William was to commend the legislative union in a message to the House of Commons. It was on February 23, in that year of 1702, which was destined so soon to see the close of his great career, and at a moment when the shadow of death was already on him, that he urged upon the House of Commons the imperative necessity of a complete union between the northern and southern divisions of the island. In this message William declared his full conviction "that nothing can more contribute to the present and future security and happiness of England and Scotland than a firm and entire union between them." William went on to say that he "would esteem it a peculiar felicity if during system accorded to the joint-stock companies of England. Englishmen, on the other hand, were jealous of the more energetic and far-reaching enterprises of their Scotch rivals, and the idea widely prevailed that Scotland was unduly favored to the restriction and disadvantage of England. The same kind of feeling began to exist between England and Scotland which already existed in both countries with regard to such a foreign state as Holland, for example, and the question was even raised whether the rivalries of trade between the two parts of the island might not sooner or later lead to actual war between England and Scotland. At that time the idea of a system of genuine and general free-trade had not come up as an accepted influence in European affairs, and men only saw in the successful undertakings of one part of the country an exclusion and hinderance to the trading efforts of the other. Many authorized conferences were held between English and Scotch commissioners for the purpose of arranging some system of common legislation which might make a constitutional union possible without undue restriction to the trading projects of either community. Time after time these consultations came to nothing or were abruptly broken off by what seemed to be the impossibility of any satisfactory arrangement.

It so happened, however, that one of the most adventurous and in the end disastrous speculations in that day of speculations had a direct and unexpected influence in promoting the legislative union between England and Scotland. This was the famous Darien Company, an enterprise which might be regarded in some sense as a precursor of John Law's famous Mississippi scheme, the South Sea Bubble of a later day. The Estates of Scotland passed an act a few years before Queen Anne's accession which was described as an act for company trading to Africa and the Indies, and aroused but little attention at the time of its passage. The schemes which were afterwards developed by this company were the outcome mainly of the enterprising spirit of William Paterson. Paterson was a man of unquestionable ability as a financier. He was a Scotchman by birth, but had settled in London at an early period of his life and made himself conspicuous there. He will always be remembered in history as the founder of the Bank of England, although some of his later projects brought him to be classed with John Law, the promoter of the South Sea Bubble. He had passed some years of his early life in the West Indies, and his name was well known in the financial circles of Hamburg, Amsterdam, and Berlin. He amassed a large fortune by his commercial dealings in London. He was one of the first directors of that Bank of England which he may fairly be said to have created. He was unquestionably a man of much foresight and sound judgment in finance, despite the one great failure which he brought upon himself and upon others, and he had clearly defined ideas of free-trade long before the genuine principle of free-trade came to be recognized as a principle of statesmanship.

Paterson was the guiding spirit of the new undertaking, and by his direction it took the form of a great colonization scheme. He laid his plans fully before the leading financiers of Edinburgh and Scotland generally, but under his guidance the company was to begin its operations in London. The directors of the company were to found a new colony in some suitable land of rich soil accessible to all the world, and this new colony was to invite all the communities of the earth to an equality of trade in buying and selling, import and export. The colony was to work the land they possessed to the fullest extent in the production of everything which the soil was especially qualified to bring forth, and were thus, in fact, to call into being a new world of productions especially commending themselves to the wants of the exhausted Old World. The ports of the new colony were to be unrestricted by any of the special arrangements which were unwisely believed to protect the ports of civilized nations in those days, when it was thought to be for the benefit of a community that only privileged and friendly traders should be allowed to enter its harbors. Paterson fixed upon the region of Darien, in the isthmus of Panama, as the home of his new colony.

The isthmus of Panama, which, it need hardly be said, is the connecting link between North and South America, has had more than once since the days of Paterson the disadvantage of being associated with a doubtful or disastrous game of speculation. The new colony advertised itself and its objects with splendid audacity. It offered itself as buyer and seller to the whole trading world. It said in so many words: We, the Scottish owners of this new colony, have got goods of priceless value to sell which can only be produced from a soil like ours, by such skill as we are able to bring to the work, and by the liberal use of that capital which we possess, and of which we know how to dispose in the best manner for the due development of such productions. That was the spirit of its invitation to the buyers; but then, on the other hand, it also issued its invitation to the sellers. It invited all the peoples who had anything rich and rare for sale to come to the new colony, where they were assured that they could find eager purchasers of everything worth buying and with plenty of capital to meet all demands.

In our modern days, when even the most restrictive duties on import and export trade are but light compared with those which had to be endured by former generations of traders, it may not seem easy to realize the temptation which Paterson's new scheme offered to the speculators of his time. But it is certain that the idea of forming a new colony which was free to trade with all the world and with which all the world was free to trade, had a strong fascination even for shrewd and practical men in the days when Paterson started his project. Great wars had been going on in Europe, and it has always been found that great wars foster the spirit of speculation. The New World was beginning to be regarded as a region of unlimited and indefinite promise to men possessed of courage enough to risk much in the hope of making a fortune. Paterson himself had courage enough to throw in his own lot with the fortunes of his colony. He went out to Darien and did his best to make the project successful.

Now, the project was in the mean time regarded with great jealousy by many English trading companies. Perhaps the very jealousy with which it was regarded was only a new tribute to its pretensions and a new argument furnished to its promoters with which to make good the reasonableness of their advertisements. The great English companies, they might have said, are jealous of this Scottish company because it is developing a magnificent idea, and is certain to make the fortunes of all who are wise enough, and lucky enough, to have shares in it. The English companies were full of complaint because of the fact that the Estates of Scotland had thus been allowed by their

THE UNION WITH SCOTLAND

own authority to confer such privileges upon a merely Scottish company, and, on the other hand, patriotic Scotchmen asked, What would be likely to become of Scottish enterprises if there were a legislative union with a people who would want to secure every great financial enterprise for themselves and to shut out their Scottish rivals from their fair share of commercial and trading profits? For a time, therefore, the floating of the Darien company seemed only to raise new difficulties in the way of that legislative union which King William had recommended and so many enlightened public men on both sides of the border sincerely desired. At one time the feeling ran so high that the English subscribers to the company, by a sort of common consent, refused to pay up the instalments on their shares; the shares were, consequently, forfeited, and the Scottish owners, who were now left to run all the risks and enjoy all the profits of the undertaking, were allowed to pursue the venture for themselves.

The company, however, did not prosper. The hopes which its projectors had of securing a great trading monopoly for themselves were destined to a speedy blight. The first trouble came from the fact that Spain, even in her decaying days, still asserted an absolute claim over undefined and illimitable territory in the New World. The region of Panama on which the new colony was settled might, up to that time, have been absolutely regarded as no man's land, but it stood in the close neighborhood of recognized Spanish possessions, and it soon became apparent that Spain would assert her claims, whether well founded or ill founded, and that the colonists would have to fight for their holding or give it up. A Spanish fleet appeared off the coast, and a Spanish army was on the march to attack Darien.

The colonists made one gallant attempt to maintain their territory. A small but most resolute force, suddenly summoned to arms by the authorities of the new colony crossed the isthmus, encountered the Spanish troops, who were utterly unprepared for any such attack and never supposed that an attempt of the kind would be made. The audacious assailants completely dispersed the soldiers of the Spanish monarchy. There was wild exultation in the new colony, a medal was struck in commemoration of the victory, and when the news reached Edinburgh, in due course, it was celebrated by a somewhat tumultuous demonstration which much alarmed the more peaceful and less enterprising citizens.

In the mean time it should be said that the representatives of King William the Third at foreign courts took good care to display no sympathy whatever with the doings of the Darien colonists, and, indeed, did their very best to make it known that these enterprising colonists were regarded in England as men in opposition to the policy of the King and as no better than adventurers, freebooters, and pirates. All this was not very likely to invite the world in general to any enthusiastic rivalry of trading with the new colony. Even the victory obtained over the Spanish force, however glorious a performance for the victors, did not seem just the kind of event to encourage peaceful trading, and to mark out the spot on which it took place as the most favorable scene for the quiet making of enormous fortunes. The new colonists, it was plain, would have to maintain their title by force of arms for some time to come, and the immediate question in the minds of outside observers was whether the Darien company would have to encounter a war with Spain or a war with England. The colony itself

THE UNION WITH SCOTLAND

was suffering from disease and something like starvation. The climate of Darien was utterly unsuited to many or most of the Scotch colonists who were trying to settle there, and the whole foundation of the scheme was laid on the assumption that the colonists would be free to do a roaring trade in a region especially adapted by kindly nature for such a purpose. The project soon came to complete disaster. The colonists had to surrender the territory on which they had settled to the peremptory demand of Spain in March, 1700. Paterson and some others had escaped before the final disaster, and Paterson continued to be an energetic promoter of financial schemes for many years after. But the Darien enterprise had come to an end, and its fate served, as we have already said, to form an effective argument in favor of the legislative union between England and Scotland.

It was evident that the energy of the Scottish trading spirit and the trade competition between England and Scotland could not long go on without bringing the two countries into frequent and dangerous dispute, unless a common Parliament were invested with equal dominion over both communities. The views of Bishop Burnet on this subject may be studied with much interest, if only because they are those of a contemporary observer who must have had ample opportunity of conversing with most of the leading men in England having to do with the working of the union project. "I cannot, upon such a signal occasion," the Bishop observes, with his usual gravity, "restrain myself from making some reflections on the directions of Providence in this matter. It is certain the design on Darien, the great charge it put the nation to, and the total miscarriage of that project, made the trading part of that kingdom see the impossibility of undertaking any great design in trade; and that made them the more readily concur in carrying on the union. The wiser men of that nation had observed long that Scotland lay at the mercy of the ministry, and that every new set of ministers made use of their power to enrich themselves and their creatures at the cost of the public; that the judges, being made by them, were in such a dependence, that since there are no juries allowed in Scotland in civil matters, the whole property of the kingdom was in their hands, and by their means in the hands of the ministers; they had also observed how ineffectual it had been to complain of them at court; it put those who ventured on it to a vast charge, to no other purpose but to expose them the more to the fury of the ministry. The poor noblemen, and the poor boroughs made a great majority in their parliament, and were easily to be purchased by the court; so they saw no hopes of a remedy to such a mischief but by an incorporating union with England. These thoughts were much quickened by the prospect of recovering what they had lost in that ill-concerted undertaking of Darien; and this was so universal and so operative, that the design on Darien, which the jacobites had set on foot, and prosecuted with so much fury, and with bad intentions, did now engage many to promote the Union, who, without that consideration, would have been at least neutral, if not backward in it." Paterson himself became, after his return home, one of the most earnest advocates of the projected union, and was, indeed, one of the first Scottish members elected, when the time came, to the united Parliament.

Such were the conditions under which William the Third sent his last message to his House of Commons, the message recommending the legislative union be-

THE UNION WITH SCOTLAND

tween England and Scotland. When Queen Anne came to the throne she was advised to appoint under her sign-manual a royal commission on the part of England to treat with commissioners from the Scottish Estates on the subject of the proposed union between the two divisions of her kingdom. Once again the difficulty created by the supposed rivalry of trading interests threatened to obstruct any satisfactory settlement. The Scottish commission was appointed, and the commissioners put forward, as what may be called a basis of negotiations, their national claim for " such an union as entitles the subjects of both kingdoms to a mutual communication of trade privileges and advantages." The English commissioners accepted the basis of negotiation, but they qualified their acceptance by a very important condition. Their declaration set forth that while the English commissioners recognized the communication of trade and other privileges to be the necessary result of a complete legislative union, " yet in the method of proceeding they must first settle with your lordships the terms and conditions of this communication of trade and other privileges." In effect, by these words the English commissioners stated that they would cheerfully accept the principle laid down by the Scottish commissioners, provided only it was made clear to them that the definition of that principle in the minds of the Scottish commissioners was precisely identical with its definition in the minds of the English commissioners. " We are quite in agreement so far as words go, but had we not better find out clearly whether we attach exactly the same meaning to the words, before we commit our agreement to the articles of a treaty?"—such was, in substance, the meaning of the English commissioners' reservation.

This course of procedure naturally brought the discussion to a point, and the Scottish commissioners found it necessary to put their meaning into words which admitted of no misunderstanding. They set forth four conditions. The first was "That there be a free trade between the two kingdoms, without any imposition or distinction." The second, "That both kingdoms be under the same regulations, and liable to equal impositions for exportation and importation, and that a book of rates be adjusted for both." The third article required "That the subjects of both kingdoms and their seamen and shipping, have equal freedom of trade and commerce to and from the plantations, and be under the same regulation." The fourth clause addressed itself even more directly and positively to some questions of recent dispute. Its stipulation was "That the Acts of Navigation, and all other Acts in either kingdom, in so far as contrary to or inconsistent with any of the above-mentioned proposals, be rescinded."

The English commissioners spent a week in considering these clearly defined conditions, and then proceeded to set forth their own ideas of free-trade in relation to the first article. They declared it as their opinion "that there be a free trade between the two kingdoms for the native commodities of the growth, product, and manufactures of the respective countries, with an exception to wool, sheep, and sheep-fells, and without any distinction or imposition other than equal duties upon the home consumption." The meaning of this opinion cannot probably be more clearly deduced than as we find it in the comment of John Hill Burton, the Scottish historian, who says that it "implied an exclusion on importation of foreign merchandise into England in Scots vessels, restricted the importation of Scots produce to the market for home consumption, and made important exceptions to the articles of home produce that might be imported." Then the English commissioners took up the third article, and on this they declared " that the plantations are the property of Englishmen, and that this trade is of so great a consequence, and so beneficial, as not to be communicated, as is proposed, till all other particulars which shall be thought necessary to this union be adjusted." It may, perhaps, be as well to explain that the commissioners use the word communicated in the sense of making common to both countries. Furthermore, the English commissioners declared that with the exception of some rather unimportant commodities, " as the case now stands by law, no European goods can be carried to the English Plantations but what have been first landed in England." And they add that the product of the plantations cannot " be carried to other parts of Europe till it has been first landed in England."

After some further delay and discussion the commissioners, English and Scotch, held a full and, as it turned out, a very friendly conference on the trade questions, and an agreement was come to by the court " That there be a free trade between all the subjects of the Island of Great Britain, without any distinction, in the same manner as is now practised from one part of England to another; and that the masters, mariners, and goods be under the same securities and penalties in the coasting trade," and, furthermore, " That both kingdoms be under the same regulations and prohibitions, and liable to equal impositions for exportation and importation; and that a book of rates be adjusted for both," and " That the subjects of both kingdoms, and their seamen and shipping, have equal freedom of trade and commerce to and from the plantations, under such and the same regulations and restrictions as are and will be necessary for preserving the said trade to Great Britain."

We need not follow out the further progress of these conferences through all their details. The events of the time were unquestionably leading, or forcing, both sides on to an agreement. The outbreak of war on the continent, and the part which England had to take in it, made it clear to all minds capable of calm and judicious observation that a legislative union of both parts of the kingdom would be the only possible security against the uprising of events which might force the North and the South into actual war. There was nothing like a real and general opposition, so far as England was concerned, to such a settlement of the question. Queen Anne herself was very anxious that nothing should be done which might affect in any way the supremacy of the English Church at home, and she appeared during one part of the discussion to be afraid that something of the kind might be the result of an immediate compromise. But it was hardly within the range of probability that any danger of that sort could be seriously threatened, and the general feeling of England was undoubtedly in favor of an amicable and final arrangement.

In Scotland there was for a time much opposition to the proposed union. There was a strong feeling that a legislative union would lead to the dethronement of Edinburgh as a capital, and that the representatives of Scotland would lose their importance and their power when once Westminster had become the legislative centre for the two kingdoms. Then, of course, there existed in Scotland the not unnatural or even unreasonable dread that the result of an act of union might imperil the independent constitution of the Scotch Church. In order to meet this difficulty, a distinct and definite understanding had to be arrived at that the legislative union should make no change in the condition of either Church. This was an agreement of absolutely vital importance, for it was made quite certain that under no conditions would the majority of the Scottish people consent to any union which might affect the independence and the constitution of the Church of Scotland. To this end the English Parliament and the Estates of Scotland passed definite acts declaring that each state should be free to maintain its own Church in its existing form and conditions. In other words, it was made clear by preliminary enactments that while there was to be only one crown, one Parliament, and one kingdom, there were to be two absolutely independent Churches. There were agreements also fixing the proportion of taxation to which Scotland, according to her means, should be held liable, and ordering that the proportion of Scottish representatives in the English Parliament should be fixed on reasonable terms. These terms were rather favorable than otherwise to the Scottish people, for it was felt that the growing population and the growing activity of trade and commerce in Scotland could not be adequately represented if the number of Scottish representatives in the Parliament of Westminster were to be estimated by a merely arithmetical proportion to the existing conditions.

Another question of great importance which had to be settled as essential to any act of union had to do with the laws and administration of justice in Scotland. The Scottish system of law differed in many momentous characteristics from the system existing in England. This question was settled, as it could only be settled, by an agreement that the Scottish system should remain as it was, absolutely independent of that which existed in England. The law of Scotland, with regard to marriage and the legitimacy of children, differed materially from that of England, and it was felt to be out of the question that Scotland could be induced to submit to any serious change in the long-established principles taken from the old Roman law which regulated her institutions. When this agreement had been arrived at there was little trouble in coming to an understanding upon other subjects. It had to be settled, for instance, what the national flag of the new and united kingdom should be, and the final agreement was that the crosses of St. George and St. Andrew should be borne by the national banner for the future. The ensign which we now know as the Union Jack was the historical creation of this agreement.

Queen Anne delivered an address to both Houses of the English Parliament. The royal address declared that " You have now an opportunity before you of putting the last hand to a happy union of the two kingdoms, which, I hope, will be a lasting blessing to the whole island, a great addition to its wealth and power, and a firm security to the Protestant religion. The advantages that will accrue to us all from an union are so apparent, that I will add no more, but that I shall look upon it as a particular happiness if this great work, which has been so often attempted without success, can be brought to perfection in my reign." After some discussion in both Houses, and after several divisions had been taken in the House of Lords, which only served to show that there was a strong majority in favor of the measure, the act was passed, and on March 6, 1707, the Queen came to the House of Lords and delivered her royal assent to the union of England and Scotland.

THE UNION WITH SCOTLAND

In an interesting and well-prepared volume by Edward E. Morris, which forms one of the series called *Epochs of Modern History,* and describes "The Age of Anne," the author calls attention to the fact that the conditions under which the union between England and Scotland was effected differed essentially from those under which, at the opening of the next century, the act of union between England and Ireland was passed into law. He shows the injustice in the Irish act of union which "consisted in the fact that the dominant Church in Ireland was not the Church of the people, a very large majority of whom were Roman Catholics." He points out as "a fact that requires notice that whilst the Scotch do not desire a repeal, the Irish as a nation do." This is, indeed, a fact of which history has been compelled since the passing of the Irish act to take account more and more seriously with each succeeding year. In Scotland the religion of the people was protected by special enactment, whereas in Ireland the Church of a small minority was made by law a dominant establishment.

More than a quarter of a century had to pass after the Irish act of union before the first Roman Catholic representative of Ireland was allowed by legislation to take a seat in the House of Commons. Even then that tardy measure of religious equality was only accepted by the Parliament at Westminster because Sir Robert Peel, a genuine statesman, had become convinced that unless it were passed he must have to encounter a civil war, and the great Duke of Wellington emphatically declared that he would not accept the responsibility of further resistance to the national demand of Ireland. There was, therefore, no gratitude felt or professed by the Irish people for the concession of Catholic emancipation, on the plain ground that the concession had been made, not to the demands of justice or generosity, but as an alternative which the ruling English statesmen preferred to the certainty of civil war. For more than another generation after the passing of the act of Catholic emancipation, the Protestant state Church was still maintained as an establishment in a country where at least five out of six of the inhabitants were Roman Catholics by religion. Mr. Gladstone completed the work of religious equality which Sir Robert Peel had begun.

It will be seen that, without any reference to other national sentiments or national claims, the act of union between Great Britain and Ireland differed in one of its essential conditions from the act of union between England and Scotland. No surprise can be felt by any reasonable man that on this ground alone the union was utterly unwelcome to Ireland, while it was cordially accepted by Scotland. It is certain that the union between England and Scotland was welcomed and accepted by the one part of the island as well as by the other, and has proved thus far a complete success. Even if the growth of new conditions, and the development of that principle of local government which is becoming more and more recognized as the essential part of every system of federation including different nationalities in one state system, should lead to some further modification of the terms under which England and Scotland are to remain in imperial union, that fact would not in the least degree affect the judgment of history on the working of the measure passed in the reign of Queen Anne. The act of union between England and Scotland must always be regarded as one of the greatest and most successful events which mark with honor the momentous history of that reign.

CHAPTER XI

"THE TRIVIAL ROUND—THE COMMON TASK"

WHILE the armies of Queen Anne are engaged on the battle-fields of the Low Countries of Germany and of Spain, and the controversies of religious denominations and political parties are going on at home, it may be a convenient time for us to endeavor to form some idea as to the manner in which the trivial round and the common task of life went on in England for the ordinary citizen. So far as regards the methods and the rate of passenger traffic in these countries, life was going on in the days of Queen Anne very much as it had gone on in the days of Elizabeth or in those of King John, or, indeed, for that matter, in the days of Julius Cæsar. What sails and horses could do for travellers was done, and there was nothing more, just then, to be done. But our ancestors who lived under Queen Anne were already beginning to enjoy the advantages of a regular system of postal communication. Of course there could be no quicker means of transmission at that time than during any former age since anything like civilization had set in. When Marlborough could put such a pressure on himself as to overcome his inherent dislike of formal letter-writing, and pen a despatch from the battle-field for the instruction of the government at home, his despatch travelled at just the same rate of speed and by much the same methods of conveyance as one of Julius

THE REIGN OF QUEEN ANNE

Cæsar's despatches might have done from Gaul or from Britain to Rome. But in Queen Anne's days there was at least a regulated system for such communication all over the kingdom, over the greater part of the European continent, and even across the ocean to some of England's distant colonies. A citizen of London was then well aware that on certain days of the week he could send a letter to this or that part of the continent, or farther off still, with a reasonable hope of its reaching its address.

In our modern days we are apt to regard the penny post as an institution deriving its existence from the inventiveness and the practical methods of Rowland Hill. But while we do unquestionably owe what may be called the national penny post, that is, the penny post circulating through all parts of the kingdom, to Rowland Hill's reform, it is certain that there was a penny post existing in the days of Queen Anne, although the range of its operation was practically limited to the metropolitan district. There was, in fact, a postal delivery every two hours to or from any part of the city or suburbs of London at the cost of one penny for each letter. This post was started somewhere about the opening of Charles the Second's reign. It was in the first instance only a private institution, or, more properly, a private speculation, and after a while it was annexed by the government and incorporated with the ordinary postal system. In Mr. John Ashton's interesting and instructive work, *Social Life in the Reign of Queen Anne,* we can read a full and explicit account of the keen and personal disputations which took place as to the actual authorship of the penny-postal system. We need not, however, enter into any discussion here with regard to the identity of the original inventor. There are few inventions known to modern

"THE TRIVIAL ROUND—THE COMMON TASK"

civilization which have not been closely accompanied by some controversy as to rival claims of authorship. It is enough for our purpose to know that the penny post, within its prescribed limits, was an institution in full existence and recognition at the opening of Queen Anne's reign.

When a letter had to travel beyond the metropolitan limits the charge was twopence a sheet for eighty miles, all letters travelling more than that distance having to pay threepence for a single sheet, and sixpence for a double letter, or twelvepence if the ponderous missive was swelled to greater dimensions. A single letter went to Dublin for sixpence, a double letter for one shilling, and one and sixpence an ounce was charged for any communication of greater bulk or weight. The cost of foreign postage might be regarded as comparatively cheap. A single-sheet letter could be sent to the West Indies for one and threepence, and a double letter for two and sixpence, but letters coming from the West Indies to England had to pay one and sixpence or three shillings each, or, if bulky enough to be rated according to mere weight, six shillings for each ounce. There were separate days assigned for the sending of letters to foreign countries, and, indeed, to any places outside the metropolitan range. On Monday letters went out to Spain, Italy, Germany, Flanders, and some of the North countries, and also to some parts of England. Tuesday was devoted to Germany, Holland, Sweden, Denmark, and also to North Britain, Ireland, and Wales. Wednesday occupied itself exclusively with the postal service of Kent and the Downs. Thursday sent out letters to Spain, Italy, and all parts of North Britain and England. Friday's missives ranged over Italy, Germany, Flanders, Holland, Sweden, Denmark, and also the much-favored Kent and the Downs. Saturday gave itself up to the service merely of England, Scotland, Ireland, and Wales.

Now, if we consider for even a moment, we shall see that the Londoner of those days or the resident of any part of Great Britain and Ireland must have found his work of letter-writing embarrassed and bewildered by a variety of considerations and calculations wholly unknown to our happier days. Leaving out of the question altogether the cost of mere postage, and the heavy tax thus imposed on those who were anxious to communicate with their friends abroad, we shall find that the effort to keep in recollection the particular days when the latest news from home could be conveyed to friends abroad must have brought a serious and continuous perplexity into the perturbed mind of the faithful correspondent. Now, when we write a letter and address it to its destination, we have nothing to do but simply to drop it into the post, and we know that as a matter of course it will be carried on its way by the next, and, for the time, the only channel of transport. But in the days of Queen Anne the dweller in England who was anxious to send news of himself to a friend in Spain or Italy, and who missed his Monday post, had the discomfort of knowing that his letter could not begin to go on its way before the following Thursday. Many a man who was, like most of us, not particularly tenacious in his memory of dates, must have despatched his letter just too late for Spain and Italy, and might have found something of peculiar interest to write about during the two or three following days if he had remembered in time that Monday and Thursday were the only parts of the week directly applicable to his purpose. In point of fact, the nearest parts of the European continent, and, for that

"THE TRIVIAL ROUND—THE COMMON TASK"

matter, a large portion of the British counties as well, were under the same conditions with regard to postage as those which now apply to America and Australasia and other regions beyond the ocean.

Most of us, even in these present days of almost incessant postal transit everywhere, must have been sometimes a little perplexed by the trouble of remembering the precise days when the latest post can be secured for America or for Australia. If we just bring our minds to a comprehension of the mental trouble which must have been created when the same consideration had to come up with regard to Ireland, Scotland, Wales, and even to many parts of England itself, we shall begin to understand that the work of correspondence with one's friends was a troublesome business in those days for even the easiest letter-writer. Enterprise, however, was not wanting in the steady-going years of Queen Anne's postal system. We read that one adventurous personage set up in London a postal institution all of his own device—a system by which letters were to be conveyed through all parts of the London district by messengers on foot at the reduced charge of one halfpenny for the single sheet. The post-office authorities were not disposed to put up with audacious rivalry, and they took steps to restrain this reckless innovator from his interference with their monopoly. The authorities, in fact, went so far as to issue through the columns of the *Gazette,* then as now the official organ of the government, a solemn proclamation against these amateur rivals of the regular postal system.

The proclamation set forth that, " Whereas Charles Povey and divers Traders and Shopkeepers in and about the Cities of London and Westminster, Borough of Southwark and Parts adjacent, and several Persons ringing Bells about the Streets of the said Cities and Borough have set up, employ'd, and for some time continued a Foot Post for Collecting and Delivering Letters within the said Cities and Borough and Parts adjoining for Hire under the Name of the Halfpenny Carriage, Contrary to the Known Laws of the Kingdom, and to the great Prejudice of her Majesty's Revenues arising by Posts."

The postmaster-general directed informations to be laid against these offenders for the recovery of one hundred pounds from each one of them for such an act, the fine to be renewed for every week's continuance of these doings, and also five pounds for every offence in the collecting and delivering of letters for hire under such conditions. The halfpenny post struggled on for a little against the resolute intervention of the postmaster-general, but competition was not likely to be profitable under these difficulties, and the public had soon to confine itself to the authorized plans and charges for the delivery of its correspondence.

The cost of communication through the medium of the government post-office naturally induced a considerable proportion of the letter-writing class to hunt up their influential and privileged friends, in order to obtain the benefit of the franking system—the system which allowed members of either House of Parliament, and others in office or authority, to secure a free passage through the post for any letters which they might honor by their signature on the outside. The practice of franking did not then, it is only fair to say, make anything like the exorbitant demands on the postal revenue which became a peculiarity of later days, and went on increasing steadily until the early years of Queen Victoria's reign. The fact is that the habit of letter-writing had not become, even for business men, anything like so engrossing a part of each day's work as it grew to be in times more near to our own. During Queen Anne's reign letter-writing for the great bulk of the population entered but little into the ordinary occupations and enjoyments of existence. Public men, officials, and persons largely engaged in commerce or business of any kind were necessarily in the habit of writing letters every day; but in ordinary life the penning and despatching of a letter was quite an event, and the majority of the population hardly ever went to the trouble of writing letters at all. Indeed, it may be very safely affirmed that the majority of the population did not write letters, for the very good reason that they did not know how to write. England was yet a long way from the busy times and the educational zeal which set up the system of Board Schools. In the matter of popular education the England of Queen Anne was far behind the Scotland of the same reign, and still farther behind the greater number of the German states.

The London Exchange was already the centre of the country's financial business, and was a centre for the financial business of many other countries as well. Dutch, German, and Italian traders and traffickers were conspicuous figures at this great market-place of speculation. The business of speculation itself was beginning in Queen Anne's time to be a trade and traffic all of its own. A statue of Charles the Second ornamented the centre of the Exchange, although the real life of that quarter, as we now understand it, had not begun its movement in the days of the Merry Monarch. A contemporary writer quoted by Mr. Ashton describes it as " a vast heap of Stones," and he goes on to tell us that " the Noise in it is like that of Bees; a strange Humming or Buzzing, of walking tongues and feet; it is a kind of a still Roaring, or loud Whisper." Then he describes it as "the great Exchange of all Discourses," and he affirms, very correctly, no doubt, that "no Business whatsoever but is here on Foot." Hereupon the writer becomes somewhat sarcastic, and he informs his readers that "all things are sold here, and Honesty by Inch of Candle; but woe be to the Purchaser, for it will never thrive with him."

All manner of salesmen crowded round the place, and at the entrance to the front portico nostrums of every kind were advertised by placards and commended in loud voices by the venders, and the credulous could buy at varying rates any species of drug which they were led to believe of service to humanity in the removal of every bodily infirmity and even the unlimited prolongation of life. Crowds of merely curious citizens and strangers always gathered around at Exchange hours, and many of these brought their wives, daughters, or sweethearts to enjoy the sights, and all the shops in the neighborhood did a roaring trade. The names of some of the well-known bankers of that time are identified with great financial business even in our own day. The millionaires, the multi-millionaires, of our present era, were unknown figures in the reign of Queen Anne. The greatest fortune amassed in trade or commerce, or accomplished by successful speculation at that time, would seem but very modest wealth if compared with the vast sums of money realized by the successful projector or speculator of a more recent day. The great private companies, or trusts, as they would be called in the United States, were the creation of an age nearer to our own and of business developments which had not blossomed into full existence, had hardly, indeed, come into existence

"THE TRIVIAL ROUND—THE COMMON TASK"

at all during the period pictured in Mr. Ashton's volumes.

Education, as we have said, had not spread itself in Queen Anne's days, or even in days much later, among that vast proportion of the population where the parents of the children could not afford to pay for their teaching, or did not regard book-learning as a thing worth paying for or worth the trouble of daily attendance. But it has to be stated that Queen Anne's times saw the systematic beginning of the charity school institution, which did something towards that work of free education now put within the reach even of the very poorest by our modern creation of Board Schools. Some of the famous schools existing in our own time were recognized institutions in London then. The Westminster School, the Merchant Taylors, Greyfriars, Christ's Hospital, and many others were flourishing. Among the classes which were above the restrictions of mere poverty, a classical education, as we still term it, and more especially the teaching of Latin, obtained much favor with parents. It was regarded as an essential part of every gentleman's education that he should be compelled in his scholastic days to go through a certain study of Latin and the Latin authors, with at least an infusion of the literature of classic Greece. The famous saying of Prince Bismarck, that it was better for a man to have forgotten Latin and Greek than never to have learned anything of them, appears to have been the central theory of education when Anne was Queen of England. The modern languages —at least French, Italian, and German—were special studies which were only insisted upon when they were regarded as likely to be of direct and practical advantage in the student's future course of life.

The education of girls seldom went beyond French,

a little music, skill in dancing, the use of the needle, and, of course, reading and writing of English without, however, any very pedantic attention to precision in the perplexing work of spelling. On the other hand, greater pains were probably taken at that time than in our own for the training of every girl to be an accomplished housewife, and to regard the cooking of dainty dishes as one of the accomplishments necessary to a well-brought-up young lady. The age undoubtedly produced many highly cultured women in England, but the general ideas as to the mental education of a woman were entirely different from those which dictated the mental education of a man, and that a sister should read and study the books which were thought essential for the proper bringing up of her brother was no more held in favor than the idea that she ought to learn as well as he how to swim and how to handle the rapier. Well-bred parents during the reign of Queen Anne would have been as much surprised to hear of a girl studying Latin as they would have been to hear of the same girl learning how to take her part in open-air contests of skill with her brother and his school-boy friends.

The club was now becoming a favorite social institution, although it was not yet anything like the widespread organization which has interwoven itself so universally into the social and political life of all civilized countries at the present time. The October Club was, for a while, the principal and the most prosperous institution of the kind in the reign of Anne. This was the club of the high Tories, who then regarded themselves as especially representing the gentlemen and the gentleman-like traditions of England. The country party met in social and political converse there, and the name of the club was taken from the good old

October ale which was popularly and traditionally supposed to be the favorite beverage of all sound country Tories. In one of his letters to Stella, Swift tells that " We are plagued here with an October club; that is, a set of above a hundred Parliament men of the Country, who drink October beer at home and meet every evening at a tavern near the Parliament, to consult affairs, and drive things on to extremes against the Whigs, to call the old ministry to account," and he adds that " The ministry seems not to regard them, yet one of them in confidence told me that there must be something thought on to settle things better."

We can, perhaps, without difficulty, form a kind of comparison between the October Club and certain political institutions of a time nearer to our own, although the party organizations of a more recent date have quite outgrown the idea of holding their meetings within the walls of an ordinary Westminster tavern, and must have their own private edifices of vast extent, solid structure, and imposing frontage. The Calves' Head Club will, perhaps, assist us to carry on the comparison. This club was the centre of opposition to Toryism, and it was described and denounced by Tory pamphleteers of that day as a downright republican institution, or even worse, which was accustomed to celebrate with musical rejoicing the anniversary of the day on which Charles the First was done to death. Some of these pamphleteers point, as conclusive evidence of the truth of their charges, to the fact that the members of the Calves' Head Club consisted in great part of Independents and Anabaptists and other Nonconformists. In other words, the Calves' Head Club was described by its enemies in very much the same spirit as that in which one of the earlier Radical clubs might have been shown up by a Tory zealot in the days before the representative system had yet expanded into something like household suffrage.

The Kit Cat Club was one of the most famous clubs of the time. It was called from the mutton-pies then known as Kit' Cats, although why they were thus designated is not quite certain. It succeeded in establishing a distinct reputation of its own, and we need not trouble ourselves now by any revival of the controversy about the derivation of its whimsical title. So far as it was a political organization it may be set down as belonging to the Whig party, but it was especially the meeting-place of wits and humorists and literary men of all political orders and shades. Its leading members had the honor of having their portraits painted by Sir Godfrey Kneller in three-quarter lengths, and for a time all sketches in such form obtained the generic name of Kit Cats. The drinking-glasses used by the club were adorned by mottoes taken from verses written by Sir Samuel Garth, author of *The Dispensary,* and Sir Richard Blackmore wrote, in 1708, a poem called "The Kit Cats." This club held its meetings at a tavern in King Street, Westminster. The Beef Steak Club and the Saturday Club held a leading place among the social gatherings of the day. Swift often speaks of the Saturday Club; he tells Stella that "I dined with lord-treasurer, and shall again to-morrow, which is his day when all the ministers dine with him."

The club-house in Queen Anne's reign, if we can call that a club which seldom aspired to meet in a building of its own, seems always to have been the meeting-place of men who gathered together for some special purpose, to promote political objects, or to discuss art and literature, or to bring together a number of kindred spirits for the sake of mere social companionship and hilarity. The club-rooms of modern times where men go to write their letters and read the newspapers, and are not supposed to enter of necessity into friendly relationship or even into casual conversation with other members whom they happen to meet there, do not seem to have flourished much during the reign of Queen Anne. Then, as now, there were certain clubs which, apart from any question of political organization, were supposed to confer distinction on every one who was fortunate enough to be received as a member. At that time, as in our own, a young man's chances of finding a favorable reception in good society of this or that political order, or of no political order in particular, might be greatly advanced by the mere fact that he belonged to some club of high and established reputation.

The coffee-houses and chocolate-houses were a special feature of London social life in Queen Anne's reign, and the names and the ways of some of them have found an abiding place in literature. The coffee-house was not a novelty at that time, but in Queen Anne's reign it reached its highest popularity. It must not be supposed that the coffee-houses served out to their customers no drinks stronger than coffee; for some of them had the reputation of recognizing no scrupulous teetotal restrictions as to the character of the potations they were willing to supply to all who entered the premises. In general, however, the coffee-house was used as a place for the sipping of coffee and the hearing of news. Certain of these houses had a distinct political character, and Defoe tells us that a Whig would no more go to the Cocoa Tree Chocolate-house than a Tory would be seen at the Coffee-house of St. James. Button's has won a distinct fame of its own because it was so much frequented by Addison and his friends. It stood in Russell Street, Covent Garden. The lion's head which was used there as a letter-box has been mentioned in many a brilliant paper of that time, and, after various removals, when Button's Coffee-house was taken down, came into possession of the Bedford family and was preserved as a relic. The names of Garraway's, of Lloyd's, and some others are still remembered by every one, and represent important institutions which have long outgrown the original purpose of the founders. The coffee-house of the better order was, indeed, a sort of club without the exclusiveness belonging to actual enrolment as a member.

There was a certain exclusiveness maintained, in fact, although not in name, by the character which each of the important coffee-houses gradually came to acquire. One, as we have said, became the resort of Tories in general, and after a while few but Tories ever cared to cross its threshold. Another was frequented by leading Whigs, and visitors who were not Whigs soon found themselves out of place there, and ceased to enter it. A third was recognized as the haunt of literary men and wits, and although mere strangers, whether residents of London or visitors from the country, were glad to look in for the sake of seeing distinguished men and the chance of hearing good things said, and were proud to be able to talk to their friends about all they had seen and all they had heard, and perhaps a good deal that they had not seen or heard, yet they did not feel themselves quite at home in such a place, and were regarded as mere outsiders even by themselves. It often happened that when a man of political or literary distinction gave a dinner to some of his friends in the coffee-house which he especially patronized, the host entertained his guests with wine supplied from his own cellar, and the proprietor of the coffee-house received a small payment for his acquiescence in this foreign importation. The coffee-house, in fact, held a place between the club and the tavern. It was more free and easy than the club, but anybody, however eminent his name or exalted his class, might go there without causing any of the scandal which would have been certain to arise if he were seen to enter an ordinary tavern. The coffee-house was one of the characteristic institutions of the age, and the literature of Queen Anne's reign pays ample tribute to its peculiarities, its popularity, and its influence on the manners of the time.

Queen Anne was not a patroness of the drama, and appears even to have had a conscientious objection to giving it any encouragement by her own presence within the walls of a theatre. But she showed a close and keen interest in the dramatic performances of her time, at least so far as that interest could be manifested by frequent, and, no doubt, well-meant endeavors to make the manners of the theatre conform with her own ideas of decorum and propriety. Again and again she issued manifestations of her royal will that certain freedoms of speech, of gesture, or of costume on the stage or behind the scenes should be modified in accordance with seemliness and modesty. The good Queen, although she never entered a play-house, evidently kept herself well informed about all that was going on in the London theatres, and was ready at any moment to interpose by royal admonition when she had reason to believe that something was said or done which it would have offended her eyes to see and her ears to hear. One of these proclamations, which is prefixed Anne R., admonishes that "We have already given Orders to the Master of Our Revels, and also to Both the Companies of Comedians, Acting in Drury Lane and Lincoln's Inn Fields, to take Special Care, that Nothing be Acted in either of the Theatres contrary to Religion or Good Manners, upon Pain of our High Displeasure, and, being Silenc'd from further Acting; And being further desirous to Reform all other indecencies, and Abuses of the Stage which have occasion'd great Disorders, and Justly give Offence; Our Will and Pleasure therefore is, and We do hereby strictly Command, That no Person of what Quality soever, Presume to go Behind the Scenes, or come upon the Stage, either before, or during the Acting of any Play. That no Woman be Allow'd or Presume to wear a Vizard Mask in either of the Theatres, and that no Person come into either House without paying the Prices Establish'd for their Respective Places." It concludes by threatening severe penalties for any infraction of these orders.

On January 20, 1704, the House of Lords returned thanks to the Queen for her determination to restrain the play-houses from immorality and indecent behavior. Another proclamation issued not long after in the same year takes notice that complaints have been made to her Majesty "of many indecent prophane and immoral Expressions that are usually spoken by Players and Mountebanks contrary to Religion and Good Manners," and requiring that the Master of the Revels shall take care to have all plays and other performances brought, fairly written, to him at his office in Somerset House, to be corrected by him before they shall be set on the stage, under severe penalties in case of neglect of this revision. The same orders were specially applied to all companies of strolling actors, all mountebanks, and keepers of puppet shows, and announced that, without the revision and

"THE TRIVIAL ROUND—THE COMMON TASK"

the permission of the Master of the Revels, these exhibitions, too, would be subject to penalties, no matter what other licenses they might profess to have. The Queen even issued orders to regulate the conduct of the lackeys and footmen sent by persons of rank to keep places for them until their arrival at the theatre, inasmuch as it appeared that the conduct of these lackeys and footmen sometimes caused much offence to the regular frequenters of the theatre.

Some of us can well remember that her late Majesty Queen Victoria, on more than one occasion, published a letter with her own signature condemning certain performances, chiefly acrobatic exhibitions and such like, because they brought with them danger to the lives of the acrobats, and led to accidents which ended in the death of women taking part in such performances. But Queen Victoria never seems to have had occasion to proscribe any of the ordinary performances at a theatre, and no doubt felt that she could safely trust to the care of the Lord Chamberlain, who held office under the authority of the court. Perhaps the modern reader might be inclined to wonder why Queen Anne, when she interfered so often with the practices of the theatres, did not feel it necessary to issue any orders against the representation of certain pieces, the scenes and dialogue of which contained so much that in modern days would have been regarded as intolerable by any audience.

Queen Anne, however, could only act according to her lights, and according to the manners of her age; and some of the most popular and successful plays of that time, written by authors of established renown, contained scenes and dialogues which a barn-door company of strolling actors would not venture to produce before any audience of our time. Indeed, the good Queen Anne, when, on rare occasions, she had plays performed in her own Palace of St. James, was content to authorize and look upon such pieces as Dryden's "All for Love, or the World well Lost," which would certainly startle a modern audience out of its propriety. The fact is worthy of notice merely as an illustration of the different ideas as to dramatic seemliness which prevail in different ages, for there can be no question as to the purity of Queen Anne's mind, and her rigorous resolve to encourage or tolerate nothing which seemed to her likely to contaminate the morals of the performers or the spectators. It has also to be borne in mind that the comedies of the Restoration were many of them so grossly indecent, in purpose as well as in language, that the new order of things, introduced under Queen Anne's authority, must have seemed like the work of a complete moral reformation.

London, during Queen Anne's reign, had three great theatres generally open throughout the season. There were, indeed, four or five theatres altogether, but all these seldom invited audiences at one time. Drury Lane, the Queen's Theatre, in the Haymarket, Dorset Gardens, and the house in Lincoln's Inn Fields were those which especially commanded public attention. The Italian opera was then an institution of recent origin, and was the object of much satirical criticism among writers of the day who regarded it as rather an effeminate and ignoble sort of innovation. It was not until a late period of the reign that Handel, then a young man, began to be appreciated in England. Betterton was still acting during the reign of Queen Anne, although he had passed his prime when Anne came to the throne, and his death was hastened in April, 1710, by his persistency in keeping up his performances when he was suffering from a severe attack of the gout, which had been his constant enemy through life, and then

"THE TRIVIAL ROUND—THE COMMON TASK"

proved fatal to him. Betterton was unquestionably one of the great actors of the English stage. He had to strive against many serious physical defects. He had small eyes and a broad face, a very stout figure, thick legs and large feet, and his voice was naturally low and unmusical. Yet he was able to manage and modulate his voice so that he could make every note and tone of it tell upon the largest audience, and could command the rapt attention of every listener. Addison, Dryden, and other men whose recommendation must carry immortal praise with it, have borne testimony to the commanding power of his dramatic genius. His grave, in Westminster Abbey, was the well-deserved national recognition of the great work he had done for the English stage. Richard Steele declared of him that he "ought to be recorded" among the English "with the same respect as Roscius among the Romans."

Another actor of a very different order, Thomas Doggett, an Irishman by birth, was one of the most distinguished performers of Queen Anne's time. He outlived the reign by many years, but he had given up acting, at any regular theatre, before Queen Anne's death. From all we read of him he would seem to have been inspired by the very genius of comedy. Perhaps he is best remembered in later times by the fact that he left in his will the provision for the annual sculling prize, "Doggett's Coat and Badge," to be contended for by Thames watermen on the anniversary of the accession of George the First.

Colley Cibber was one of the dramatic celebrities of the age. He made himself so much of a celebrity that the satirists and wits of the time found endless theme for droll comment in his personal peculiarities. He was a dramatic author, poet, or, at least, a composer of lines and rhymes, and he was also an actor. He began his career upon the boards at a salary of ten shillings a week, which was increased to fifteen, and at that rate of pay he continued to perform for some time; but he afterwards became successful as a dramatic manager, and held a partnership in some of the best London theatres. As an actor, comedy was his peculiar line, and he seems to have had the good fortune to hit on certain parts which exactly suited his physical peculiarities. He was not one of the performers who insist on playing great parts for which neither age nor appearance gives them natural adaptation. His voice was weak and thin, neither his face nor his figure had anything picturesque or commanding. One or two of his comic parts won for him the praise of Congreve, which was commendation enough to entitle him to be recorded in the history of the stage. Some of his plays, " The Careless Husband," for instance, are still remembered, and the version of Molière's " Tartufe," which he called the " Non Juror," was distinctly a paying success. " The Provoked Husband " he wrote in combination with Vanbrugh. Many years after Queen Anne's death he was actually made poet laureate, and he is the author of some birthday odes which are, perhaps, not much inferior to other works having a similar purpose by authors with much better claims than his to the poet laureate's place. He adapted to the stage of his time some of Shakespeare's plays, and his version of " Richard the Third " might have been called in one sense a theatric success. One is inclined to think that no sharper satire on the poetic taste of the English public in his time could be recorded than the fact that his " Richard the Third " was accepted as a distinct improvement on Shakespeare's dramatic effort.

We have to bear in mind that although the age of

"THE TRIVIAL ROUND—THE COMMON TASK"

Anne produced some genuine poets of a high order, it was certainly not an age which appreciated the genius of Shakespeare. The fact has already been mentioned that Dryden's " All for Love, or the World well Lost " was during Queen Anne's reign regarded as an improvement upon " Antony and Cleopatra." There came, indeed, a long interval in the history of English dramatic art, when the fame of Shakespeare suffered an eclipse, and when it seemed almost doubtful whether it was likely to shine again through the clouds of mannerism and unreality which hung over the intellectual atmosphere. England had apparently to wait for the time when the great German authors, Lessing and Goethe, were to teach the world that the England of Queen Elizabeth had brought forth a dramatic poet worthy to rank with the greatest of classic Greece. Barton Booth—the Booth of Addison's *Cato*—and one or two other actors of the same age are still remembered. Acting by women was comparatively new to the English stage, but Mrs. Barry, Mrs. Bracegirdle, and Mrs. Oldfield were actresses who would have made a mark in the history of any stage.

The ballet was coming into favor about this time, and had a place in the theatrical performances at most of the London houses. But it had as yet reached nothing like the position of importance which was given to it in more recent times. No splendor of decoration set off its unpretending display, nor was it possible then for a ballet-dancer to win by any skill or charm the fame and the fashion of a Taglioni, a Cerito, or a Fanny Elssler. The time had not yet arrived when a successful ballet-dancer could have been thought by fashionable people to make a *mésalliance* when she condescended to marry a rising tragedian like Garrick.

CHAPTER XII

THE LONDON OF QUEEN ANNE

THE London of Queen Anne's day was a metropolis very different in its size, as well as in many other of its characteristic qualities, from the London we know at present. Many of the outlying districts which are now merely a part of the capital, and are lost to ordinary observation in the vast agglomeration of continuous streets, were then divided from the recognized London by wide expanses of meadows and gardens, traversed by connecting high-roads. Piccadilly then, as now, stretched westward as far as what we now call Hyde Park Corner. Bond Street was not yet a completed thoroughfare, and had on its west, north of Piccadilly, the parks and the open country. At the eastern end the occupied houses stretched to Whitechapel Church and but a short way beyond. Covent Garden, Soho Square, and Leicester Square were enclosed within the limits of West End fashionable life. The inhabitants of these regions were held bound by law to keep the roads in front of their houses and shops clean and well swept, and to heap up refuse for the scavengers' carts to carry away, under penalties prescribed for any neglect of these civic duties. It is needless to say that the orders of the law were evaded as much as possible, and that the state of the streets was often a serious trouble to the passengers, who had to pick their steps through masses of neglected refuse. Even at a date later than that of Queen Anne's reign we find it recorded as a matter not calling for any serious observation that the body of a murdered child was found, after a quest of some days, among the dunghills lying at the bottom of Drury Lane.

There was practically no numbering of the houses, and it was as difficult for a stranger to find out some particular building which he desired to reach as some of us have found it in the streets of Constantinople at a time very near the present day. The shops were nearly all proclaimed and identified by the display of great projecting signs, and, indeed, the street signs of that age form a very characteristic and picturesque illustration of the life of the times, as we can see for ourselves in many of Hogarth's pictures. Stage-coaches, hackney-coaches, carts, wagons, and sedan-chairs made up, with the carriages of the wealthy, the means of communication between one part of London and another. The lighting of the streets, if we may thus describe an attempt at illumination which did little more than render darkness visible, was accomplished by miserable oil-lamps and by the frequent use of lanterns, which wayfarers found it necessary to carry with them at night, well knowing that in many of the streets even the oil-lamps could not be expected to shine. The ordinary hackney-coach was a jolting and most uncomfortable vehicle, seldom furnished with lamps. There were all manner of legal ordinances for the licensing and management of the hackney-coaches, and the rates of fare were also prescribed by legislative enactment. But the police conditions did not then exist in the metropolis which might have made obedience to these laws a settled habit, and have provided satisfactorily for the comfort and convenience of street traffic. The private coaches kept by the wealthy were usually very magnificent equipages, and six horses to a carriage were thought necessary for any one who desired to impress the public with a sense of his distinction. Four horses were very common, but the chariot, the calash, and the chaise of more ordinary mortals were considered to be well turned out with even two horses.

The sedan-chair was becoming a regular institution. It took its name from the town of Sedan, in France, a name which has much more lately been associated with an event of immense importance in European history. The sedan-chair had been introduced into England more than a century before Queen Anne's time. Some of the sedan-chairs were finely appointed and even splendidly ornamented according to the taste and the means of their owners. The public sedan-chairs were placed under legal license, and the amount of the fare was settled at one shilling a mile. Any one who has studied the literature of Queen Anne's time will remember that the descriptive prefix "sedan" soon fell altogether out of use, and that the conveyances which we associate so much with the ordinary life of those days were in most cases spoken of simply as chairs.

The streets were even at that time very commonly overcrowded with traffic, although the population of London, of that limited London we are now describing, was so small in proportion to that which now occupies the same space. When once a town completely outgrows the limits and conditions of village life and obtains anything like the size which we are now inclined to regard as that of a city, the traffic of its principal streets is by no means to be measured in its proportions by the actual number of its population. Even in the London of our own days one may turn at any moment, here and there, from a great thoroughfare almost unendurably crowded with wheeled traffic, into long lines of quiet streets where the sound of the wayfarer's step echoes to all but complete loneliness. In Queen Anne's days this striking contrast was much more frequent than in ours. The main bulk of the traffic was confined to the principal thoroughfares which led from one conspicuous centre of life to another, and the mass of the smaller streets were, after night had once set in, almost as silent and lonely as an ordinary highway far out in the country. As we have said, there was nothing like what we in modern times would call a police force to watch over the safety of peaceful pedestrians. The men appointed by the authorities to guard the streets were simply the old-time watchmen, the "Watch," as they were called—a set of men appointed for the purpose with very little regard to their capacity, physical, mental, or moral, for the performance of such important duties.

The literature of the time is full of the terrible doings of the Mohocks. The famous name of these disturbers of the public peace is supposed to be taken from the Mohawk Indians, a tribe which had its home in what is now the State of New York. The Mohocks were, in fact, a race of street ruffians whose doings corresponded in many ways with those of the modern Hooligans, only that the Mohocks were recruited for the most part from a class much higher than that which pesters the streets in London's present days. The Mohocks were the "bloods" and "rakes" of that generation, and were dissipated and reckless scamps, belonging to what are conventionally termed the better classes of society. Their main ambition and chief pastime in life appear to have been to set the ordinary civic laws at defiance and win a fame for themselves by deeds of wanton and utterly unprofitable violence in the streets at night. A man acquired renown among his own set by leading a band of this kind and making night hideous to the peaceful passengers in the streets.

A gang of the Mohocks would probably begin their nightly game of recreation by attacking the watchmen, pricking them with rapier points, fighting them with fists and cudgels, overturning their watch-boxes, and driving them in utter confusion from the positions assigned to them in the discharge of their duties. After a roystering dinner-party it was the delight of these young and middle-aged scamps to begin their midnight revelries by this attack on the watch, and when they had thus cleared a way for their sports to exercise their strength and their pugnacious ingenuity in the terrifying and torturing of peaceful wayfarers. They would stop an unarmed man and force him into a fight from which he was sure to escape, if he could escape at all, with mashed features and lacerated limbs. They did not confine their heroic deeds of conquest to male passengers by any means, but appear to have found a peculiar delight in molesting, terrifying, and maltreating women. One of their choice pastimes was to capture a woman, thrust her into a barrel, and then playfully roll the barrel with its human captive down Ludgate Hill or Holborn Hill. They appear to have found it an occasional variety, in the course of their amusements, to set a woman on her head and thus exhibit her, an indecent sight, for the amusement of themselves and their fellows. Sometimes, if we may believe the stories which were current and commonly received in those days, the women thus tormented did not escape with their shame only, but had to undergo wounds and mutilations before their tormentors set them free to return to their homes.

THE LONDON OF QUEEN ANNE

The poems of Gay, the letters of Swift, and many other memorials of the time bear testimony, at all events, to the common belief in the nature and the frequency of these outrageous barbarities.

From these contemporaneous testimonies the reader might be led to believe that the streets of London were much more dangerous at the time to quiet and respectable wayfarers than would have been a settlement of the genuine Mohawk Indians to the peaceful and civilized traveller. We must, however, make the greatest allowance for the inevitable exaggeration of the stories which record the night history of London life in the reign of Queen Anne. Most of the writers of the time who picture to us the doings of the Mohocks are only told on hearsay, and we find but few descriptions given at first sight, and from direct personal observation. Indeed, if the accounts we read left us anything like an accurate picture of street life at that period, it is plain that the ordinary inhabitants of London would have found existence unendurable and would have been compelled, if the law and the authorities could not protect them, to form committees of public safety out of their own numbers, and to enforce order after the fashion adopted in Western settlements of the American States at a time much nearer to our own.

It may be taken for granted that individual acts or bouts of barbarity were at least multiplied, if not actually magnified, by common report, and that excesses which must even then have been exceptional were given out as the ordinary events of every night in the streets of the metropolis. But when all allowance has been made for almost unavoidable exaggeration, it is beyond doubt that the night life of London was very often made witness to scenes of wanton and brutal lawlessness which would have been a disgrace even to the rudest times of growing civilization. The nuisance was at length becoming so much a public scandal that Queen Anne thought it necessary to issue a royal proclamation against it. The proclamation set forth that the Queen, "being watchful for the Publick Good of Her Loving Subjects," had taken "notice of the great and unusual Riots and Barbarities which have lately been committed in the Night time, in the open Streets, in several parts of the Cities of London and Westminster, and parts adjacent, by numbers of Evil dispos'd Persons, who have combined together to disturb the Public Peace, and in an inhuman manner, without any Provocation, have Assaulted and Wounded many of her Majesty's good subjects."

The Queen promised a reward to any one who should bring to prosecution any offender who could be proved to be guilty of such practices. Perhaps the very nature of this proclamation might suggest that the disturbance of the public peace could not have been quite so common as many contemporary descriptions would make out; for assuredly, if the law was openly defied by bands of armed ruffians every night, there could hardly have been any need of offering a reward for the detection of such offenders. It was evidently only a case for strengthening the force, whether civil or military, at the disposal of the authorities, for the protection of the streets and thus putting down the outbreak of riot by the arm of the law. But however that may be, the mere issue of the proclamation is conclusive as to the fact that an unusual degree of lawlessness did disfigure the London streets, and that Queen Anne, who was a lover of peace and good order, felt it necessary to take some decided measure for the maintenance of public safety in London after dark.

THE LONDON OF QUEEN ANNE

The trouble, of course, mainly arose from the fact that there was no regularly organized police force to guard the metropolis or any of the large towns, and that the very appearance and get-up of the night watchmen only tempted young "rakes" and "bloods" into riotous behavior, which naturally became more riotous, more freakish, and more barbarous because of the impunity accorded to it. Down to a much more modern date in novels and stories which deal with London night life—down, in fact, to the establishment of the organized police force which owes its existence to Sir Robert Peel—we read of assaults upon watchmen and upon peaceful citizens as part of the regular amusement of half-drunken revelry in the midnight streets of the metropolis.

There were some street scenes which, although equally characteristic of the times, were more wholesome and graceful to look at than the amusements of the Mohocks. The milkmaid festivals of early May must have afforded pleasing and picturesque sights for citizens of London who were not too practical or too grim to enjoy such exhibitions. A contemporary writer tells us that "On the 1st of May, and the five or six Days following, all the pretty young Country girls that serve the Town with Milk, dress themselves up very neatly, and borrow abundance of Silver Plate whereof they make a Pyramid, which they adorn with Ribands and Flowers and carry upon their Heads instead of their common Milk Pails." The writer further tells us that "in this Equipage, accompanied by some of their fellow Milk Maids, and a Bagpipe or a Fiddle, they go from Door to Door, dancing before the Houses of their Customers in the midst of Boys and Girls that follow them in Troops, and every Body gives them something." The May-pole, around which lads and lasses used to dance, and around the very name of which so many pretty poetic memories still linger, was not, at this time, any longer seen in the streets of London, although it was yet a cherished institution in most parts of the country. But the Londoners had some reminder of the May-day celebration in the parade of the pretty milkmaids, and that was, at least, better than nothing.

Hyde Park showed some pleasing sights every day. The dinner-hour of that age was very early, and although the fashionable time for riding, driving, or walking in the park was after dinner, it was still long before sunset in most months of the year. The Queen issued more than one set of regulations for the better preservation of the walks and drives and grasses in the park and for securing to visitors an undisturbed enjoyment of the whole pleasaunce. One of these regulations, which survives in part down to our own time, declared that "no stage coach, hackney coach, chaise with one horse, cart, waggon or funeral should pass through the park, and no one should cut or lop any of the trees." It was ordered that wherever a road or path was taken up for the purpose of repairs a lantern should be specially set on the interrupted spot in order to save the wanderer from possible danger. When evening was coming on all such lamps as the park could boast were ordered to be lighted, unless at the height of summer-time or when there happened to be a full moon. Indeed, it is mentioned as a matter of some proper pride for all Londoners, that the whole way through Hyde Park to the Queen's palace at Kensington was provided with lanterns for illuminating the path in the dark nights. The regular illumining of the cities and towns of England, even by such modes of lighting which were then in existence, had not yet become so

THE LONDON OF QUEEN ANNE

recognized an institution but that the condition of Hyde Park might be pointed to as a just source of special pride for all Londoners who lived within easy reach of her Majesty's palace.

What we have already said about the change in the conditions of travel generally will apply with equal force to the conditions of street traffic in the reign of Queen Anne. The great changes did not begin for England until the reign of Queen Victoria. The street traffic in the days of Queen Anne might have been described in very much the same terms as those which were employed in the days of Juvenal or even in much more distant times. All that carriages and horses and the bearers of loads could do was done just after the same fashion, and with the same accessories and consequences, as from the earliest period of European civilization. At a later day the modern conditions of traffic, supplied and stimulated by the application of practical science, began to set in. Tram-cars, drawn first by horses and then impelled by steam and by electricity, motor-cars set in motion by the same impulses, and the ever-present bicycle of our own daily life were as completely unknown and unthought of in the reign of Queen Anne as they were in the days of the Cæsars or of the Antonines. The meditative pedestrian is a personage who seems doomed to vanish before the energetic movements of modern civilization. The pedestrian who would think his thoughts out, and follow meditatively the musings of his fancy, could hardly pursue his favorite pastime even along the country roads of our modern times. A creature endowed or afflicted with such tastes could not indulge them consecutively or even safely where the modern bicycle or the modern motor-car impels its reckless way. The meditative pedestrian of the future will have to follow the example of Gray and indulge his reflections within the limits of the country churchyard. Coleridge, in the *Ancient Mariner*, speaks of

> "One who on a lonely road
> Walks on in fear and dread,
> And having once turned round, goes on
> And turns no more his head."

The reason which Coleridge gives for this sudden impulse of dogged determination is that the wayfarer knows a "frightful fiend doth close behind him tread." The meditative pedestrian of our days has, indeed, no such grisly terror to affect his movements, but he may, at any moment, find that the flying bicycle or the motor-car is following far too closely in his wake, and may have to give up his meditations and seek for safety on the foot-path, if there be one, or close to the bordering hedge. These interruptions and dangers to pedestrian contemplation were wholly unknown in the days of good Queen Anne, and came as little into practical consideration as the sudden appearance of the frightful fiend pictured in the verse of Coleridge.

There were some incidents of London life in Queen Anne's reign which are not known to the life of our modern cities. The duel was then a common adventure even in the streets of London. We read, for instance, of a duel which was fought out within a short distance of the Theatre Royal, Drury Lane, in which one of the combatants was severely wounded. We are told of a duel in Lincoln's Inn Fields, where one of the duellists was killed on the spot. There were certain convenient places set apart by common consent for the carrying out of these deadly disputes. Lincoln's Inn Fields was a favorite scene for such encounters, and so also were the fields behind Montague House. We are told, as an ordinary incident of London life, how a duel was fought behind Montague House in which one of the duellists was done to death, and much about the same time of an arranged duel in St. James's Park, which ended in nothing worse than a severe wound to one of the combatants. There were laws against duelling then as later, and it even happened that the laws were sometimes enforced and the duellists made prisoners. Still the public opinion of the time not merely recognized the duel and favored its accomplishment, as public opinion does still in many European countries, but regarded it as a mode of settling a dispute which ought not to be rudely interrupted by too watchful authorities, which, if necessary, ought to be carried to a conclusion on the spot where the dispute began, with the approval of all well-bred and gentlemanly observers. Thus it happened in Queen Anne's days that the duellists often declined to postpone the settlement of the quarrel until one of the recognized scenes of battle could be sought out, drew their swords just where they were at the moment, and accomplished the work there without any special wonder on the part of the beholders. Some of these duels have an established place in our history, and have been reproduced in many a romance. Unless where an actual death was the result, these extemporaneous combats seemed to have created no greater scandal in those days than would an encounter of fisticuffs between two street arabs outside one of the London theatres in our own more peaceful times.

When we compare the conditions—so far as peaceful pedestrians were concerned—of the street life of London in those days and the street life of London in our own, we shall probably come to the conclusion that even the most devoted admirer of the good old times, if any such admirer still exist, might own that the electric trams and the motor-cars were not quite such disagreeable and dangerous interruptions as the Mohocks or even the duellists. Perhaps the one great difference between the London of those days and the London of ours—and the same remark would apply to all the great English cities and towns of both periods alike—is that the disturbances of the streets in our time are confined almost altogether to the lower quarters, where rowdyism has its congenial home, while in the former time they went on night after night in the regions frequented by the higher and wealthier classes, and, despite all the complaints and the denunciations of enlightened and educated men, were allowed to have their way without any attempt whatever at organized repression on the part of the established authorities.

The river was then as now, and, in proportion to the daily wants of the population, much more then than now, a highway of London life. It could hardly have been called a silent highway even then, and although there were no noises sent out by the machinery of steam-boats, it was probably a noisier thoroughfare than it is at present. The passenger traffic along the Thames was conducted by boats and barges, and we are told that the shouting and screaming of men who managed the boats and barges created an incessant daily disturbance of the river's natural quietude which was a horror to the ears of peaceful Londoners who had to avail themselves of the Thames as a regular highway. At that time the ordinary Londoner found the boat on the river the readiest and quickest way of reaching his destination at any convenient spot between Blackfriars at the one end and Putney at the other. The river boat, indeed, fulfilled to a great extent the duty which is now accomplished by the hansom cab. There were three kinds of boats: the boats which were sculled, the boats which were rowed, and the barges. The wayfarer who at any of the riverside stations called for "sculls" found his appeal answered by a boat with one man in it who sculled it up or down the stream. If the passenger called for "oars," his cry was met by a boat with two rowers in it. The barges were generally owned by private individuals or by private companies, and were often fitted up with some attempt at luxury and ornament. They had usually a sort of canopy erected over the stern which gave protection against sun or rain, were provided with comfortable, cushioned seats, and were sometimes got up with magnificent appointments.

The men who sculled or rowed the ordinary passenger-boats appear to have been a very noisy and demonstrative class of persons, who had strong lungs and a great power of repartee and invective. When one of these little vessels happened to pass another, and such meetings were naturally of almost unceasing occurrence, it was the dear delight of the boatmen in either boat to greet the other with uproarious interchange of what would in later days have been described as "chaff." The jokes were generally of a distinctly personal character, and were flavored with oaths and execrations not recognized as belonging to polite conversation. These uproarious interchanges of sarcasm and denunciation were an amazement and a scandal to all well-bred and decorous citizens who had to make part of the river traffic, and are described with astonishing frankness by writers of the time, even by those who felt the strongest objection to the style of language employed. The language known as Billingsgate was the vernacular of the Thames boatmen.

THE REIGN OF QUEEN ANNE

Blackfriars and Chelsea were the principal stations of these boats, and they went down the river as far as Greenwich or even Gravesend and up the stream until the shouts of the boatmen waked the echoes of some of the loveliest and most famous spots of the upper Thames. The once well-known and fashionable *Folly* was a barge of enormous length, furnished with an immense saloon and moored opposite Whitehall. This barge was a kind of floating Vauxhall or Ranelagh, and was intended for the use of fashionable people, who gave brilliant parties there, where music and dancing, dress and drink, delighted the joyous company. In Queen Anne's time, however, the *Folly* on the Thames was undergoing the fate which in later days befell Vauxhall and Ranelagh Gardens. It had ceased to be the resort of fashion, and the ladies who frequented it were usually of the class which would have been described by the somewhat ill-applied epithet of "gay" in later years. It was a mark of fashion at one time to form one of the company who enjoyed themselves in the *Folly*, but in Queen Anne's reign it was fast becoming an evidence of social outlawry for women to take part in the *Folly's* audacious festivities.

All the passenger-boats on the Thames were placed strictly under the regulations of the authorities, so far, at least, as the fares for proportionate distances were concerned, but the authorities would not hold themselves bound to take any particular pains for enforcing decorum in the language and conduct of the watermen. The river-banks, on the north side especially, must have presented to the passenger, as he went up and down within the reach of the streets and the houses, curious and even startling contrasts. At one moment he caught sight of some stately pile of buildings, a palace, or a church, or some famous national institution, and in the next moment he passed some decaying, dingy wharf, some cluster of tumble-down and poverty-stricken dwellings, some evidences of a life of squalor and filth which would have banished all association with the beautiful from the noblest stream. Parts of the river-banks, as the traveller fared eastward, were the refuge and the Alsatia of a population of outcasts, who could find no abiding shelter even in the poorest quarters of the metropolis, where order and decency were still maintained, or, at least, held in respect.

Happily, in the regions higher up the river, the regions which we should now describe as above bridge, the banks on either side were safe from such desecration, and the beauty of hill and meadow, of luxuriant foliage, and of "Thames' translucent wave," as Pope has pictured it, were seen by citizens and strangers during the reign of Queen Anne very much as we see them now during the reign of King Edward the Seventh. "Man marks the earth with ruin," Byron declares—"his control stops with the shore." But Byron was thinking of the sea when he wrote those lines — the shore does not stop man's power to ruin when it is only the shore of a narrow and beautiful stream. There is comfort, therefore, in the recollection that, for the poets, and the artists, and the lovers of the picturesque in Queen Anne's day, man's power to blot out the beauties of the Thames stopped with the narrow limits of either end of a city which was still of but moderate size when compared with its more recent power of expansion. For in Queen Anne's time the idea does not seem to have found much recognition that it could be any part of the business of the constituted authorities to trouble themselves for the preservation of artistic beauty in the regions which came under their rule.

London as a great metropolis is not even now very rich in noble public buildings, but it was much poorer still in the reign of Queen Anne. St. Paul's was then but a new erection, and had only lately been opened for public service. The Monument, of course, lifted to the skies that inscription which provoked the indignant denunciation of Pope—the inscription which declared that the great fire of 1666 was "begun and carried on by the treachery and malice of the Popish faction." Westminster Abbey and Westminster Hall lent historical and architectural magnificence to the quarter which they adorned, but the vast pile of buildings which we know as Westminster Palace belongs to a much later period of English history, and, like St. Paul's Cathedral, owes its erection to the ravages of a great fire. If the structure which we know as Buckingham Palace can be considered an adornment to London, it did not adorn the London of Queen Anne, for it had not yet come into being after the demolition of Buckingham House. St. James's Palace was then, as now, the centre of royal ceremonial and pageantry. Sir Hans Sloane was only accumulating that vast collection which he left as a bequest to the country—the collection now enshrined in the British Museum. London even then had many hospitals. Bethlehem, or Bedlam, was finished about a quarter of a century before Anne's accession, and the figures which now stand in the hall of the hospital, and are presentments in stone of Raving and Melancholy, were wrought by the hand of Colley Cibber's father. St. Bartholomew's Hospital and St. Thomas's Hospital were well-known institutions, but Guy's Hospital had not yet been established.

There were several prisons and houses of correction, and the treatment of prisoners, whether awaiting their trial or working out their sentences or merely in confinement because they could not or would not pay their debts, was of a nature which to a modern reader would seem almost incredible if the minute descriptions of contemporary observers did not make it impossible for us to have any doubts on the subject. The flogging even of women was a regular part of the discipline practised in the criminal prisons, and in the debtors' prisons an unfortunate inmate might have been left to perish of starvation if he had no friends to provide him with adequate food, or if the mere charity of the outer public did not come to his relief. The strange fact about the management of the prisons, as about the condition of the streets at night, was that its evils were thoroughly understood, and were continually denounced by intelligent observers who could not, with all their efforts, succeed in accomplishing any reform. The age had not yet grown up to a genuine understanding of the true purposes of prison discipline; the conscience of the public had not yet been quickened to the idea that any bad treatment could be too bad for a prisoner, or that good treatment of such a person could result in any good either to him or to the community from which he was an outcast.

A study of the great mass of literature which bears upon the subject will show any one that there were numbers of men and women in those days who were fully enlightened as to the relations between the principles of Christianity and the method of dealing even with the worst offenders, while a study of the actual facts must satisfy every one that the prison reformers of that day were as hopelessly in advance of their age as the opponents of negro slavery would have been about the same period of history. At that time and for long after it was one of the amusements indulged in by fashionable men and women to obtain a sight of the interior of a London prison and of the horrors practised there under the name of discipline. The visitors who indulged in this pastime had for the most part no more feeling of sympathy with the sufferings of the victims than if these victims had been captured wild beasts—only, it has to be said, that at no period of our history could they have seen captured wild beasts treated with anything like the same degree of brutality which was exercised every day upon the unhappy human beings whom the laws had condemned to incarceration.

Yet at this time there was something like a newspaper press existing in England. Some of the newspapers of the reign did actually comment with just severity on the ordinary treatment of prisoners, and the fact only shows how far the newspaper of those days was from being able to exercise any commanding influence over public opinion. The newspaper of Queen Anne's reign can hardly be said to have come within the range or the reach of the general public. To the great bulk of the London population a newspaper was but a luxury or an oddity with which " the man in the street," as we should now describe him, had really nothing whatever to do.

There were about a dozen newspapers published in England, nearly all of them in London, when Anne came to the throne, but most of these made their appearance only three times in the week or less often, and it was immediately after the opening of her reign that the first English daily newspaper came into existence. This remarkable publication, the herald of the great daily press which was before long to come, was called the *Daily Courant*. Its superficial extent was fourteen inches in length and eight inches in breadth. Mr. Ashton, in his volumes on the social life of Queen Anne's reign, to which reference has been made more than once already, gives the readers a fac-simile of this enterprising first number. The *Daily Courant,* thus issued for the first time, bears date Wednesday, March 11, 1702. It consists of one leaf of paper, and is printed on one side only of the leaf. It contains one advertisement, which is the advertisement of the publication itself, and a few scraps of news from the continent. Home affairs are not favored with any notice from this first English daily newspaper. The advertisement at the foot of the page, which proclaims the journal's mission, prides itself upon the fact that the editor, or author, as he is called, will not " take upon him to give any Comments or Conjectures of his own, but will relate only Matter of Fact; supposing other People to have Sense enough to make Reflections for themselves." Finally it announces that the paper " is confined to half the compass to save the Public at least half the Impertinences, of ordinary News Papers."

The resolve of this editor to abstain from giving any comments or conjectures of his own, but to relate only matter of fact, would naturally seem in our days an extraordinary and unintelligible limitation of a newspaper's business. But it may be observed that, even down to our own time, there have been public men who fondly maintained that the true mission of a newspaper was merely to record actual facts and to leave its readers to form their own conclusions and evolve their own opinions out of their heads without submitting to any instruction or dictation on the part of the newspaper editor. The once-famous and very powerful Manchester school of politicians held it at one time as a favorite doctrine that a newspaper was an organ merely for the publication of facts, and ought not otherwise to make any attempt at forming or even guiding the opinions of its readers. The Manchester school did not, indeed, continue to maintain this opinion in the conduct of its newspapers, and some of the most influential journals ever published in England were founded by this school and did their best, with great success, to create a public opinion in the country. Some of the foremost leaders of the school did to the very last uphold as a private doctrine that the true business of a journal was to convey actual information to its readers, and then leave the readers to form their conclusions and maintain their principles according to their own judgment.

It is not necessary now to give a list of the names or to describe the peculiarities of the newspapers which existed, and some of which flourished, during the reign of Queen Anne. Some of them enjoyed but a short existence. One of them, at least, is living to the present day, but it is the *London Gazette,* which was founded before Queen Anne came to the throne, and was then, as it is now, merely the official organ of the government, containing only announcements which belong to the business and the sphere of administration, and owe their special interest and importance to the fact that they are published under ministerial authority. There were some journals, hardly to be described as newspapers in the modern sense, "essay papers," as they were generally called, which helped emphatically to make the reign of Queen Anne famous in literature, and will always be remembered in the history of English letters. These, however, have a position and a renown of their own, are unequalled in their way as illustrations of English journalism, and these, with the men who made them, will require fuller notice in later pages of these volumes.

The English daily or weekly paper as we know it, with its mass of varied information gathered up from the events passing in every part of the world, can hardly be said to have been even foreshadowed by the newspaper press which existed when Anne was queen. The sudden start of progress made by practical science at a much later time created for journalism much the same sort of revolution which it created for travel. The lines of telegraph over the land and under the water have been the touch of science which made the whole world kin in the matter of news, and called into being that journalism which now belongs to every civilized country. The latest newspaper published in the opening years of Queen Victoria's reign bears a greater resemblance to the first attempt at a newspaper ever issued since civilization began to have a press than it does to any of the daily or weekly journals which came into existence with the steamship and the railway and the transmission of news by the agency of the electric wire. Imagination itself in the days of Queen Anne could not have pictured the growth of that newspaper press which was to become one of the common and every-day agencies of civilization in the days of Queen Victoria. What further work of civilization is to be done for travel, for the intercourse of men, for the transmission of news, and for the rapid interchange of ideas among the nations of the world, it would be impossible for us as yet to conjecture, but the new era had not dawned upon humanity at the time when the *Daily Courant* was accounted a venturous speculation just after the last sovereign of the house of Stuart had come to the English throne.

CHAPTER XIII

JONATHAN SWIFT

In the year of Blenheim two books were added to literature which will be remembered in English history forever. One was called *The Battle of the Books* and the other *A Tale of a Tub*. These works were published anonymously, but the authorship was already known to some—was rightly guessed even at the time by many, and was soon made known to all the reading world. The author was Jonathan Swift, whose fame is one of the great glories of Queen Anne's reign. Swift was an Irishman by birth—he was born in Dublin on November 30, 1667. His parents on both sides were English; his father came of a Yorkshire family, and his mother was from Leicestershire. The father died in his prime seven months after the birth of his son, and the young Jonathan Swift was sent in his childhood to a school of some celebrity in Kilkenny. When a youth he was sent to Trinity College, Dublin, where he studied for some years without distinguishing himself particularly in any field of education. He came over to England in 1688, and for a time acted as secretary to Sir William Temple, a distant connection of his mother, at Moor Park, in Surrey, which has become famous in literature rather because of Swift's association with it then and afterwards than because of Sir William Temple's really distinguished services as a diplomatist and success as a writer of essays.

JONATHAN SWIFT

Jonathan Swift was in no sense an Irishman, except by the mere chance of his birth. His own comment on his connection with Ireland was that a man's being born in a stable does not make him a horse. But he lived for a great part of his life in Ireland, and after his first residence in Moor Park he took orders in Dublin and obtained a living in Ulster. He is identified in history with many an effort made to obtain better legislative treatment for the country of his birth than she had been obtaining through successive English governments, and there can be no doubt that while he was at heart a thorough Englishman, he felt the most generous sympathy with the Irish people, and gave some of his finest intellectual efforts to the service of a country which could make him no practical return for his labors on her behalf.

The publication of the works which have been mentioned marked Swift out at once as a great satirical and political writer, and he soon became recognized as a perfect master of English prose. Indeed, it may be questioned whether the whole range of English literature can boast of any other writer of prose who could be ranked as the equal of Jonathan Swift. Mr. Gladstone was only endorsing the opinion of all the best critics of modern times when he again and again declared that Swift was the greatest prose writer known to English literature. We are not attempting here anything like a biography of Swift or a description of his literary and political masterpieces, some of the greatest of which did not make their appearance in print until after the reign of Queen Anne had come to its close. Swift's life, character, and works have been the subject of writings which would almost make a library in themselves. He was in a certain sense a puzzle to his contemporaries, and is apparently a puzzle to biographers, essayists, and critics in general down to the present day. He had the faculty of arousing the most devoted friendship, the most passionate affection, and the fiercest hatred. This was in keeping with the nature and the temper of the man himself, for his whole heart was exuberant in love and in hate alike to persons and to parties. Even among those who are absolutely in unison as to the genius of Swift—and it is hardly possible to believe that any qualified observer could have doubts as to his genius—the most widely different opinions have been formed and maintained through the succeeding generations as to his personal character. The obvious truth is that Swift was one of those great men whose nature and temperament mark them out as the subjects of undying controversy. The more we study the history of great men the more we find that there are some of them who have, above all things, the qualities which make them absorbingly interesting, while there are others whose greatness is universally acknowledged, but whose lives do not give occasion for impassioned dispute.

The word interesting seems but a feeble and inadequate term to describe the qualities of men thus born to be the subject of incessant contention, to create schools of admirers, and schools of opponents in each generation, and yet there is, perhaps, no other word which can so distinctly convey the peculiar idea. There is no controversy about King Alfred; there are no hostile factions contending this way and that way about the character of the man Shakespeare; there is no need of volume after volume to assail or to defend John Milton; and even those who most entirely disagree with the political principles of Edmund Burke at this or that period of his career are generally in complete agreement as to the personal character of Burke himself. On the other hand, we are always listening to fresh discussions on the life and the motives of Julius Cæsar; on the influences which inspired the genius of Dante; on the career of Rousseau; on the real nature of Napoleon Bonaparte. No man has given occasion to warmer controversy of this kind than Jonathan Swift. Men who thoroughly appreciated his genius, like Macaulay and Thackeray, are believed by many of us to have misread and unconsciously misinterpreted the whole nature of the man. To this day we discuss with as much eagerness and with as much conflict of judgment the story of Swift's loves, as if it were some question of party politics destined and open to eager debate. To judge from the recorded opinions of Swift's contemporaries, it would seem to be quite possible for men of clear intelligence and impartial purpose to have been brought into more or less intercourse with him and to form utterly different judgments as to his real character and his ruling motives.

Swift's whole life was one of conflicting impulses. The career into which he was forced by circumstances would appear to have been the very last suited to his temper and his intellect. He would have been a great man of letters if he had been nothing else; he would have been a great politician if he had been nothing else; but nature had not intended him for the work of a clergyman. He seems to have tried hard to do his duty in that field of work for which he was so ill fitted, but he could not compel his passionate temperament to suit itself to the conditions of such a calling, and he sought relief by giving free vent to the stronger and fiercer parts of his nature by plunging into political controversy. His was, above all things, an impatient spirit, and in many parts of his life he reminds us of the old stories told about men visited by demoniac possession. His aspirations appear to have been always for the elevation of humanity, but his impatient spirit was constantly coming into play when the imperfections of the humanity he saw around him were forced upon his attention, and thus he often cursed where his earlier inclination would have been to pray. If we read considerately and charitably some of the writings which especially procured for him the accusation of having a mind burning with hatred for the whole human race, we shall, perhaps, be brought to the conclusion that they were but the indignant outpourings of a disappointed heart, made rancorous by its disappointment. Swift had an unduly sensitive nature, and the difference between his ideal of humanity and the real humanity which he saw everywhere around him was too much for his endurance, and his mind could find, apparently, no other relief than the very extravagance of denunciation.

Let us take one illustration of this morbid impatience. Swift was by natural inclination and by habitude given over to the ways of rigorous personal cleanliness. The social life of Queen Anne's day would be regarded by those who live in our more fastidious age, in our age of universal washing and bathing and changing of linen, as a life absolutely wanting in the elementary conditions of cleanliness and hygiene. It may be safely affirmed, from the unconscious revelations made by contemporary writers as to the domestic habits of Queen Anne's reign that a royal prince or princess of that time would have been set down as a personage of very dirty habits by a well-brought-up working-man in the reign of Queen Victoria. But Swift would have been regarded as a man of scrupulous and fastidious cleanliness if he were living at the present hour. He carried his love of it so far that whenever he washed his hands, which he did very often in the course of a day, he usually took care to wash his feet as well. He became furious now and then because of the personal habits of those he saw around him, and he relieved his mind by satirical verses revelling in descriptions which many a reader in our days would find it impossible to get through because of the utter loathing which they bring with them. Swift has been denounced again and again for those really abominable verses by critics who never seem to have remembered that the verses only testified to the man's inborn and ingrained horror of dirt.

The most devoted admirer of Swift must wish that he had never written satires of this peculiar order, but the harshest critic of Swift might, at least, do him the justice to admit his perverted and fanatical zeal in the cause of cleanliness. We have taken this one illustration because it throws some light on the character of Swift, and on the manner in which he has been unfairly judged by many of those who fully recognize his genius. When he was a reformer he became a reformer who knew nothing of compromise and who scorned moderation of language. It may probably be taken for granted that the whole of Swift's life was to some degree affected by that disordered mental tendency which showed itself at last in downright madness.

Some of his biographers tell a strange story of an adventure which befell him in his infancy. When he was a year old " his nurse, who was a woman of Whitehaven, being under an absolute necessity of seeing one of her relations who was then extremely sick, and from whom she expected a legacy, and being extremely fond of the infant, she stole him on shipboard unknown to his mother and uncle and carried him with her to Whitehaven, where he continued for almost three years. For when the matter was discovered his mother sent orders by all means not to hazard a second voyage till he could be better able to bear it." This is a strange story, but there seems to be no question as to its accuracy, and it might, if we could know but all, contain some possible explanation as to the peculiarities of temperament which marked so emphatically the life of Swift. For three years after his first year of infancy he was wholly out of the care of his widowed mother, and was brought up under conditions of which his family and friends could know little or nothing. Who can tell what accident might not have happened through carelessness or ignorance or other such cause which might have had a lasting effect on the health and the temper of the child thus curiously withdrawn from his home? This earliest adventure of Swift's might remind us of one of the many stories told about children stolen by gypsies and bearing with them through all their after lives some effect or influence of the temporary removal from parents and home. It must be said in the case of Swift, as in that of some of the stolen children in romance, that there was no lack of love or kindness to him on the part of the woman who had carried him off. We read that his nurse was very careful about giving him such education as she could, and that before he returned to his mother's house he had actually learned to spell.

The whole story has a sort of artistic fitness as an opening to the life of a man whose career was one of strange contrasts and unexplained moods. Perhaps some ingenious and bold romancist might find in it a suggestion for an entirely new theory embodying and explaining the paradoxical character of Swift's life. The bold romancist might start the idea that the young Swift died almost immediately after his removal to Whitehaven, and that the nurse, driven almost to despair by the thought of having to tell Mrs. Swift that her child was dead, became possessed with the idea of substituting a changeling for the dead child and bought an infant of some gypsy mother which she kept and brought up for the three following years, and then carried back to Dublin and palmed off on Mrs. Swift as her boy, and thus gave to English politics and literature the man whose extraordinary career history has found it so difficult to explain.

Swift's love affairs, each one so intense in its character, have perplexed commentators and given rise to all manner of theoretical explanations. That he loved Stella seems beyond all manner of question. Why, then, did he not marry her, when he came to know of his love for her and her love for him? Or if he did marry her, why did he hesitate in proclaiming his marriage at once? An explanation has been invented by some which resembles the dark and melancholy story made by Walter Scott a part of his immortal novel, the *Antiquary*. Is it possible that Swift may have had the idea brought wrongfully into his mind that there was some mysterious degree of consanguinity between Stella and him which would have precluded him from loving her in the lover's fashion, and that he may have discovered the mistake, and only found himself free to marry her at a late period of their association? Biography has generally declined to adopt Swift's own frank explanation as to his unwillingness to enter on the married state, and has sought otherwise some plausible theory to account for his conduct. Did he really love Vanessa? And what was the nature of his feelings towards Varina? It is certain that Swift had in his heart a deep capacity for love, and even for passionate love, and that he had a marvellous power to arouse the warmest and tenderest affection in women. No love stories ever told in romance are full of deeper emotions than the authentic records, most of them left by his own hand, of the love which Swift felt towards some women and the love which they and others felt for him. Was it that Swift was always looking out for the one woman who could be his perfect and complete affinity, and that his failure to find any such may have been the explanation of the passages in his life which have most taxed the divining powers of his biographers? We may take it for granted that the explanation, if there be any, will never now be forthcoming, but the story of Swift's quest for a perfect love has given to the world some of the most deeply interesting, perplexing, impassioned, and melancholy chapters in the life of any great man known to modern or to ancient history.

A Tale of a Tub made its appearance, as has been said, in 1704, the year of Blenheim. We now know, on Swift's own authority, that the work had occupied him off and on for a long time. The greater part of the book was finished about eight years before it was published. "The author was then young, his invention at the height, and his reading fresh in his head." The author, in his preface, tells us that "seamen have a custom, when they meet a whale, to fling him out an empty tub by way of amusement, to divert him from laying violent hands upon the ship." Then he goes on to say: "The whale was interpreted to be Hobbe's Leviathan; which tosses and plays with all schemes of religion and government; whereof a great many are hollow, and dry, and empty, and noisy, and wooden, and given to rotation. This is the Leviathan, from whence the terrible wits of our age are said to borrow their weapons. The ship in danger is easily understood to be its old anti-type the Commonwealth. But how to analyze the tub, was a matter of difficulty; when, after long inquiry and debate, the literal meaning was preserved; and it was decreed, that, in order to prevent these Leviathans from tossing and sporting with the Commonwealth, which of itself is too apt to fluctuate, they should be diverted from that game by a Tale of a Tub. And my genius being conceived to lie not unhappily that way, I had the honour done me to be engaged in the performance."

The *Tale of a Tub* is introduced by more than one preface, and is varied by several carefully set-out digressions. The prefaces and digressions are, indeed, part of the whole essay, and have their direct bearing and influence upon its satirical meaning. Every page of the work is a satire upon somebody or something, on some school of thought, some group of critics, some literary novelty proclaimed as a masterpiece, some political or religious phantasy, some goblin called into shadowy existence to distract the reasoning powers of men. To make its meaning perfectly clear at all points to modern readers would require a volume of annotations and explanations. The whole form of this satire was then quite new to the reading public, and it is not too much to say of *A Tale of a Tub* that it took the political and literary world by storm. Those who knew Swift intimately had no difficulty in making up their minds as to its authorship, and the word was quickly passed from mouth to mouth, so that there can hardly have been a moment of actual secrecy concerning the origin of the satire.

"No man," says the author in his concluding pages,

"hath more nicely observed our climate than the bookseller who bought the copy of this work. He knows to a tittle what subjects will best go off in a dry year and which it is proper to expose foremost when the weather glass is fallen to much rain." Then he goes on to tell his readers of the various devices which the bookseller and he agreed upon adopting in order to make the work hit the passing taste at the time of its publication, and how it should be privately ascribed to this writer or to that, "naming whichever of the wits shall happen to be that week in vogue." The title-page of the work announces it as *A Tale of a Tub,* "written for the universal improvement of mankind," to which are added "An Account of a Battle between the Ancient and Modern Books in St. James Library and a Discourse concerning the Mechanical Operation of the Spirit." The narrative opens with the familiar "Once upon a time," and tells us that "There was a man who had three sons by one wife, and all at a birth; neither could the midwife tell certainly which was the eldest." Then we learn that the father came to die while the sons were very young, and on his death-bed called his sons around him and delivered to them a parting discourse, which may be quoted here at full length, because, if we may put it so, it sets forth the terms of the riddle which the reader has afterwards to make out to the best of his capacity.

"Sons, Because I have purchased no estate, nor was born to any, I have long considered of some good legacies to bequeath you; and at last, with much care as well as expense, have provided each of you (here they are) a new coat. Now, you are to understand, that these coats have two virtues contained in them. One is, that, with good wearing, they will last you fresh and sound as long as you live. The other is, that they will grow in the same proportion with your bodies, lengthening and widening of themselves, so as to be always fit. Here, let me see them on you before I die. So, very well; pray, children, wear them clean, and brush them often. You will find in my will (here it is) full instructions in every particular concerning the wearing and management of your coats; wherein you must be very exact, to avoid the penalties I have appointed for every transgression or neglect, upon which your future fortunes will entirely depend. I have also commanded in my will, that you should live together in one house like brethren and friends; for then you will be sure to thrive, and not otherwise."

Then the story tells us that the good father died, and the three sons went out together to seek their fortunes. Now it should be said that the sons were called, respectively, Peter, Martin, and Jack, and perhaps the intelligent reader will already begin to form some idea as to the conditions of the riddle. Peter, who is sometimes called Lord Peter, and later on assumes the imperial title, typifies the Pope. Martin represents the Church of England, and Jack stands for the Protestant Dissenters. An explanatory note in one of the early editions of the narrative helps us to an easy understanding of the story by telling us that " in the character of Peter, we see the Pope seated on his pontifical throne, and adorned with his triple crown. In the picture of Martin, we view Luther and the first Reformers. And in the description of Jack, we behold John Calvin and his disciples." To clear the ground still further, the note tells us that " the author's arrows are chiefly directed against Peter and Jack "; and that " to Martin he shows all the indulgence that the laws of allegory will permit." Further it is explained to us—" by the coats are meant the doctrine and faith of

Christianity, by the wisdom of the Divine Founder, fitted to all times, places, and circumstances."

It might be thought at first that the writer of the notes showed a curious simplicity in thus explaining, at the very outset, the meaning of his author's satirical parable. It might appear to some at the first glance that there could be but little interest in following out any further a puzzle which had been thus prematurely unravelled. But the truth is that the satirical wit and humor of Swift's story continue to fascinate the reader, and to hold him with undiminished power of fascination long after he has completely mastered the meaning of the riddle. Indeed, only a very dull reader could have the slightest difficulty in guessing at the identity of Peter, Martin, and Jack, and most readers may safely be reckoned upon to follow the fortunes of these personages with undiminished interest long after they have obtained the most complete insight into the purpose of the author's parable. What may be called the double identity of each of the three characters is so well maintained that the reader may for a considerable part of the narrative take it, if he will, that he is only reading of three young men who came up to London and were exposed to the temptations of a London life without remembering, for the moment, that he has three allegorical figures before him. It is only when he goes over the early part of the story for the second time that he fully realizes how well every thought and action of the three fits in with the allegorical meaning of the characters.

The brothers make the acquaintance of three great ladies, the Duchesse d'Argent, Mademoiselle de Grands Titres, and Comtesse d'Orgueil, who, as the careful annotator informs us, represent " covetousness, ambition, and pride, which were the three great vices that the ancient Fathers inveighed against, as the first corruptions of Christianity." All that part of the story which immediately follows this new acquaintanceship might pass as a mere satire on the follies and corruptions of town life and their demoralizing effect on young men from the country. It would be a very interesting story even from that point of view. The three brothers are supposed to be bound strictly by the conditions of life laid down for them in their father's will, and we are told of the wonderful devices by which Peter succeeded in persuading Martin and Jack that any course of conduct they desired to follow can be made to agree exactly with the terms of the document. One of these devices, if only it had been chronicled in more modern days, might seem as if it were intended to be a droll satire on a certain alleged discovery with regard to the writings of William Shakespeare, which created a great deal of controversy in the United States and afterwards in England. The three ladies already named to whom the brothers are paying their addresses " were ever at the very top of the fashion, and abhorred all that were below it but the breadth of a hair." But it will be remembered that the conditions of the father's will were very precise as to the wearing of the coats he had given them, without the change of a single thread in them, unless such change found sanction in the terms of the document itself.

Now it so happened that before the brothers had been a month in town the wearing of large shoulder-knots came into fashion, and no one could be received at the house of a great lady unless he came ornamented with these evidences of social distinction. " Our three brethren soon discovered their want by sad experience, meeting in their walks with forty mortifications and indignities. If they went to the play-house the door-keeper showed them into the twelve-penny gallery." "If they stepped to the 'Rose' to take a bottle, the drawer would cry, 'Friend, we sell no ale.' If they went to visit a lady, a footman met them at the door, with 'Pray send up your message.' In this unhappy case they went immediately to consult their father's will; read it over and over, but not a word of the shoulder-knot." The question then arose what were they to do? The terms of the will were absolutely to be obeyed, and yet they could not get into fashionable society without the wearing of shoulder-knots. Now, then, comes the device which might be taken as a prophetic forecast of the ingenious discovery which an American author, made thereby famous for a time, professed to have found in the text of Shakespeare. Thus Swift tells the story:

"After much thought, one of the brothers, who happened to be more book-learned than the other two, said, he had found an expedient. 'It is true,' said he, 'there is nothing here in this will, *totidem verbis,* making mention of shoulder-knots; but I dare conjecture, we may find them *inclusive,* or *totidem syllabis.*' This distinction was immediately approved by all; and so they fell again to examine. But their evil star had so directed the matter, that the first syllable was not to be found in the whole writing. Upon which disappointment, he, who found the former evasion, took heart, and said—'Brothers, there is yet hope; for though we cannot find them, *totidem verbis* nor *totidem syllabis,* I dare engage we shall make them out *tertio modo* or *totidem literis.*' This discovery was also highly commended; upon which they fell once more to the scrutiny, and picked out S, H, O, U, L, D, E, R, when the same planet, enemy to their repose, had wonderfully contrived that a K was not to be found. Here was a weighty difficulty! But the distinguishing brother, for whom we shall hereafter find a name, now his hand was in, proved, by a very good argument, that K was a modern illegitimate letter, unknown to the learned ages, nor any where to be found in ancient manuscripts. ''Tis true' (said he) 'the word Calandæ hath in Q.V.C. been sometimes written with a K; but erroneously; for in the best copies it has been ever spelt with a C. And, by consequence, it was a gross mistake in our language to spell knot with a K; but that from henceforward he would take care it should be written with a C.' Upon this all farther difficulty vanished; shoulder-knots were made clearly out to be *jure paterno,* and our three gentlemen swaggered with as large and as flaunting ones as the best."

"But as human happiness is of a very short duration, so in those days were human fashions, upon which it entirely depends. Shoulder-knots had their time; and we must now imagine them in their decline: for a certain lord came just from Paris, with fifty yards of gold lace upon his coat, exactly trimmed after the court fashion of that month. In two days all mankind appeared closed up in bars of gold lace. Whoever durst peep abroad without his complement of gold lace," was " ill received among the women. What should our three knights do in this momentous affair? They had sufficiently strained a point already, in the affair of shoulder-knots. Upon recourse to the will, nothing appeared there but *altum silentium.* That of the shoulder-knots was a loose, flying, circumstantial point; but this of gold lace seemed too considerable an alteration without better warrant, . . . and therefore required a positive precept. But about this time it fell out, that the learned brother aforesaid had read *Aris-*

totelis dialectica; and especially that wonderful piece *de Interpretatione* which has the faculty of teaching its readers to find out a meaning in everything but itself; like commentators on the *Revelations,* who proceed prophets without understanding a syllable of the text. 'Brothers,' said he, 'you are to be informed, that of wills *duo sunt genera* nuncupatory and scriptory, that in the scriptory will here before us, there is no precept or mention about gold lace, conceditur: but, *si idem affirmetur de nuncupatoria, negatur.* For, brothers, if you remember, we heard a fellow say, when we were boys, that he heard my father's man say, that he heard my father say, that he would advise his sons to get gold lace on their coats, as soon as ever they could procure money to buy it.' 'That is very true,' cries the other. 'I remember it perfectly well,' said the third. And so, without more ado, they got the largest gold lace in the parish, and walked about as fine as lords."

It is not necessary to our present purpose to follow this satire to its conclusion. Enough has been said to show its central idea and to illustrate the manner in which that idea is adorned with literary shape. The modern reader who sits down to study this masterpiece of sarcastic humor must make up his mind not to be too fastidious as to its phrases, or to be too easily offended by any of its strictures. The essay, in fact, has startling irreverence on every page of it, and it is not too much to say that there is hardly any class of Christians which might not take offence at its caricatures of religious doctrine and feeling. The one excuse to be made for its worst irreverence is that Swift had for his main purpose to draw a striking contrast between the professions and the practices of too many proclaimed believers in the several denominations of

Christianity. Swift was terribly in earnest about everything which he undertook, and he was filled with a detestation for any manner of religious hypocrisy. This feeling carried him so far as to make him seem often to regard the man who did not quite and always act up to his religious professions as if he were really no better than a deliberate, and what might be called a professional, hypocrite. There was certainly no charity in his way of estimating his fellow-mortals when he came thus to describe them for satirical purposes. Judged by the test which he appears to have adopted in the *Tale of a Tub,* there would be little difference between the man whose mode of life fails to be in full harmony with his avowals of creed and principle and the man whose whole existence is a living lie.

So much of excuse, if it be an excuse, has to be made for the wild irreverence of many passages in this remarkable production. The Roman Catholics, as might be expected, come off the worst in these satirical descriptions, and it is easy to understand that many Roman Catholics would find it impossible to appreciate the artistic cleverness of a satire so repulsive to all their reverential feelings. But, indeed, there is much in the whole essay for which the believers in any form of Christianity would find it hard to make allowance or excuse, and one can understand that many a pure and pious Christian might regard the worst errors of belief and the worst worldly contrast between profession and action as less offensive and dangerous in themselves than Swift's manner of exposing and satirizing them. Then, again, it is hardly necessary to say that the literary style of Swift's age allowed and was accustomed to a coarseness of expression which would be impossible in more modern times, and it is not always easy for a later generation to distinguish between coarseness of expression and impurity of purpose.

Cicero has observed in one of his letters that certain phrases which had been considered quite seemly and tolerable for writing and talk among even the best educated in his younger days had since that time come to be regarded as positively indecent, though precisely the same ideas were meant to be conveyed in the later days as in the earlier, and he is curious to know how far that process of supposed refinement is to go, and whether mere fastidiousness in the choice of words is to be the one supreme merit in the expression of ideas. Each succeeding age sets up, of course, its own standard of propriety in speaking and writing, and the purest and healthiest writers in Swift's time sometimes adopted a freedom of language which would be impossible in more recent days. Yet we have had some schools of literature in France, and even in England, during our own age which never offended against the canons of propriety in mere words, but nevertheless contrived to emit sentiments and teachings which would have seemed corrupt and loathsome to Pope, or Addison, or even to Swift himself. We must judge the *Tale of a Tub* as we should judge one of the plays of Aristophanes or one of the satires of Juvenal.

The publication of the *Tale of a Tub* was one of the events of the time. To all readers of English literature it became at once apparent that a great master of satire had suddenly come up to claim his place. When the authorship was made known it brought upon Swift, naturally and necessarily, much anger and denunciation from those who regarded the satire as irreligious and blasphemous, but it settled Swift's rank in literature, and made it clear to the world that the author of *A Tale of a Tub* was a man destined to play a great part in politics as well as in letters. During his frequent visits to London Swift became an accepted member of the brilliant company of authors and wits who used to meet together and exchange ideas and repartees at Button's coffee-house. Swift's greatest achievements in literature were yet to come, but he was already recognized as one of the foremost writers of the age, and time since then has only added to his fame.

The Battle of the Books belonged to a narrower field of controversy, a field of controversy which has but little interest even for the literary world of more modern days. The essay is described on its title-page as "A full and true account of the battle fought last Friday between the Ancient and the Modern Books in St. James' Library." It was composed and written during one of Swift's residences with Sir William Temple at Moor Park. Sir William Temple had written an essay on the relative merits of ancient and modern culture, and a passionate dispute arose upon the subject in which Dr. Bentley and many other distinguished scholars and authors took part. Swift's contribution sparkled with brilliant wit, and was made amusing by droll and fantastic ideas. Swift sets out his humorous purpose in the opening pages of the essay.

"This quarrel first began, as I have heard it affirmed by an old dweller in the neighbourhood, about a small spot of ground, *lying* and *being* upon one of the two tops of the hill Parnassus; the highest and largest of which had, it seems, been, time out of mind, in quiet possession of certain tenants called the *Ancients;* and the other was held by the *Moderns*. But these disliking their present station, sent certain ambassadors to the *Ancients,* complaining of a great nuisance; how the height of that part of Parnassus quite spoiled the prospect of theirs, especially towards the *east;* and therefore, to avoid a war, offered them the choice of this alternative: Either that the *Ancients* would please to remove themselves and their effects down to the lower summity, which the *Moderns* would graciously surrender to them, and advance in their place; or else that the said *Ancients* will give leave to the *Moderns* to come with shovels and mattocks, and level the said hill as low as they shall think it convenient. To which the *Ancients* made answer, How little they expected such a message as this, from a colony whom they had admitted, out of their own free grace, to so near a neighbourhood: That as to their own seat, they were *Aborigines* of it, and therefore to talk with them of a removal or surrender, was a language they did not understand: That if the height of the hill on their side shortened the prospects of the *Moderns,* it was a disadvantage they could not help; but desired them to consider, whether that injury (if it be any) were not largely recompensed by the shade and shelter it afforded them: That as to the levelling or digging down, it was either folly or ignorance to propose it, if they did not know, how that side of the hill was an entire rock, which would break their tools and hearts without any damage to itself: That they would therefore advise the *Moderns,* rather to raise their own side of the hill, than dream of pulling down that of the *Ancients;* to the former of which they would not only give license, but also largely contribute. All this was rejected by the *Moderns,* with much indignation: who still insisted upon one of the two expedients. And so this difference broke out into a long and obstinate war; maintained on the one part by resolution, and by the courage of certain leaders and allies; but on the other, by the greatness of their number, upon all defeats affording continual recruits. In this quarrel, whole rivulets of ink have been exhausted, and the virulence of both parties enormously augmented."

One sentence, or, perhaps, it should be said one phrase, in *The Battle of the Books* has already passed into almost universal quotation and repetition. The author introduces an ingenious account of the discussion between the bee and the spider as to their relative claims on the regard of the world. Æsop, who happens to be a listener to the debate, decides in favor of the bees, on the ground that, instead of dirt and poison, they have rather chosen to fill their hives with honey and wax—" thus furnishing mankind with the two noblest of things, which are sweetness and light." Matthew Arnold adopted the phrase " sweetness and light," and made it popular for his generation and for many generations to come. Men are constantly quoting it who have no idea what they are quoting from, just as men are constantly repeating certain phrases from Horace, from Dryden, and from Pope, without remembering or knowing where the phrases are originally to be found. Sweetness and light may not seem to be appropriate as a motto for Swift. Light he had, indeed, to an almost marvellous degree. He saw everything clearly, no matter what mists of superstition, of perverseness, of hypocrisy, or of conventionality might hang around it. As John Bright once said of John Stuart Mill, " he lived in light." But sweetness? One might at first be disposed to think that bitterness was the essential and pervading property of Swift, but, perhaps, if we study his letters to Stella and to others of his friends we shall become willing to admit that in his strange, combative, aggressive nature there was a rich store of sweetness as well.

Mr. Herbert Paul, in his thoughtful and brilliant volume of essays, *Men and Letters,* has described Swift as the "prince of journalists." The title is just, and is historically appropriate. Swift might fairly be called the creator of the modern leading article. Mr. Paul points out that "he was also the father of what is now called society verse." The world will readily adopt Mr. Paul's concise summary of Swift's claims to our admiration. "His value to posterity," says the concluding sentence of the essay on the "prince of journalists," "lies in his matchless humour, his statesmanlike wisdom, his hatred of pretence and sham, his intellectual integrity, and above all the sustained perfection of his English style." We are yet only at the opening of Swift's career as a politician and a man of letters. Much will have to be said with regard to Swift as a party man; with regard to his change from one party to another; with regard to the motives which may be supposed to have influenced him in the course he followed upon this or that great question of public debate; with regard to the manner in which this or that man was treated by him at various periods of his life. About his position as a writer of English prose there can be no controversy. He took his place at once in the foremost rank, and the age of Queen Anne will have one of its highest claims to historical importance in the fact that it was the age which saw the opening of Swift's literary career.

CHAPTER XIV

RAMILLIES AND ALMANZA

THE war, meanwhile, was going on, and, for a time, with successive victories for the allies, one more splendid or, at all events, more important in its results than the other. The year 1706 was one in which Marlborough was especially fortunate, and, as his destiny would so often have it, by virtue entirely of his own plans and his own instinctive knowledge of the right moment and the right place for striking a decisive blow, and in spite of increasing difficulties put in his way by some of his allies. Every reader must have observed the extraordinary flexibility of Marlborough's mind. Again and again he had formed plans which, owing to the obstruction caused by his own side of the field, he found himself compelled, for the hour, at least, to modify or even to abandon. But his genius, for all its bold conceptions and its vivid imagination, was, above all things, practical, and the moment he found that one particular conception of his could not just then be carried into effect, he was able to put it away for the time and to devise, without delay, the best use to be made of the means actually within his reach. He was not given to petulance, or to sulking, or to the waste of a single hour in futile lament because he could not carry to instant success, or even attempt, the very project which appeared to him the most appropriate and the most commanding.

It was one of the special qualities of his genius that he could make instant calculation as to his actual possibilities, and, to use a vulgar expression, "cut his coat according to his cloth."

After the victory of Blenheim his immediate idea was that he should move at once into Italy, but he was not in the position of a general commanding one great national army, bound to take its orders from him and to march when and where he could operate most successfully to bring the war nearer to a triumphant close. His force was made up, to a great extent, of small armies belonging to his different allies, and he had to consult his military colleagues, who were themselves necessarily dependent upon the decision and the support of their several governments. The forces of the United Provinces represented a state which was beset by the dread that the frontiers of their country might at any moment be left undefended, and, therefore, at the mercy of the French. That the army of Louis the Fourteenth might overrun the Netherlands, and seize and hold commanding positions there, was the idea which, above all others, occupied the attention of the Dutch government and made them reluctant to agree to any scheme which might take Marlborough and his troops too far afield. For this reason he had to accept very unwillingly, indeed, the policy which prevented him from carrying into execution his own favorite plans, and to put up with the necessity of accomplishing as much as he could on the somewhat narrow field the condition of affairs allowed to him. He had at his command an army of about sixty thousand, mainly made up of English and Dutch troops. The French army opposed to him was about equal to his in numbers, and was under the command of Marshal Villeroy.

Marshal Villeroy seems to have got at a thorough

understanding of the difficulties and delays which were obstructing the execution of Marlborough's projects, and he had apparently become convinced that a bold and dashing policy would be his surest way to success. His hope probably was that, if he were to make a sudden forward move upon the army of the allies, the forces of the Netherlands would be likely to leave Marlborough to fight out the battle for himself, and by this means he might be enabled to secure a victory. The attempt was made in the province of Brabant. The village of Ramillies was the central point of the scene where the two opposing armies came into direct antagonism. Marlborough thoroughly understood the meaning of the French stratagem. He adopted one of his favorite plans, and concealed his real purpose by a movement which seemed designed to concentrate his whole attack on the left of the French line. The immediate result of this movement — the very result which Marlborough hoped to gain—was that a sudden concentration of the French troops was made on the spot where Marlborough seemed determined to begin his assault. Then the French commander found out that he had, all unconsciously, played into the hands of his enemy. He found, too, that the English commander was not left to fight with only his British troops to follow him. The forces of the Netherlands made a gallant charge on the French line where it was least strong in numbers, and for a while they carried all before them, for the Dutch then, as at all other times, were splendid fighters when it came to be their policy to fight. The second line of defence on the French side was made up of some of the best soldiers in France, and the Dutch soon had the worst of it, and were actually beginning to fall back.

Then came Marlborough's golden hour of opportunity. He summoned up all the cavalry under his command, and himself led a splendid charge on the confident and exulting French. It was now altogether a cavalry battle. Marlborough was twice in imminent danger at a critical moment of the fight. He was recognized by some of the French dragoons, who all but succeeded in making him prisoner, and he had to fight his way through, as some commanding officer of the olden days might have done. In the struggle his horse fell under him. " Withdraw, my Lord—I'll help you to a horse," are the words addressed to Shakespeare's Richard the Third, when sudden relief comes to him at a critical moment of battle. But Marlborough could not withdraw, and one of the officers who helped him to a horse had his own head shot off by a cannon-ball just at the moment when he came to his commander's relief. Marlborough was now safe, and he led the charge as if nothing particular had happened. The French force was utterly defeated, the French line was practically cut in two, and the village of Ramillies was taken. The French, however, rallied, and still held a neighboring village on their left. Marlborough composedly called a halt, and got his men again in order. He commanded another advance, but the battle was already practically over. The French saw that the struggle was hopeless, their lines became broken, something like a panic set in among many of them, and a general dispersal of their troops was the result.

The rest of the work was nothing but a long pursuit of the enemy by the cavalry whom Marlborough had brought to the final charge. The battle itself, with all its incidents, had not occupied more than three hours. Nearly the whole of the French artillery became the capture of the English and the Dutch. The loss of the

RAMILLIES AND ALMANZA

French in killed, wounded, and prisoners amounted to some fifteen thousand, while the loss of the allies was little more than three thousand men. No victory could well have been more complete, so far as the forces actually engaged were concerned.

One of the most popular songs in the Irish national literature of modern times, a song still familiar to Irish gatherings all over the world, tells with pride that—

> "When on Ramillies' bloody field
> The baffled French were forc'd to yield,
> The victor Saxon backward reeled
> Before the charge of Clare's dragoons."

This ballad records the fact that one incident in the fortunes of the battle of Ramillies was the gallant effort made by an Irish regiment, serving on the side of the French, to retrieve the fortunes of the day. The same story might be told of many a battle-field during the reign of William and of Anne, and later still when Irish exiles, under the command of gallant captains, driven from their own country by the hostility of English laws and English systems, devoted their lives to the vain effort to uphold the cause of France against that of conquering England. The story has its lesson, which the greatest English legislators of more recent years have not failed to understand and to act upon. The relations between Great Britain and Ireland will become all the better and all the more productive of brotherhood and of peace the more the lesson is taken to heart, understood, and acted upon.

The comments of Bishop Burnet are always interesting and important, if only because they come from one who had personal observation of the immediate effect produced by the events of the time, and who was in frequent intercourse with some of those who mainly helped to make its history. Burnet, indeed, is naturally fond of telling what this or that great personage said to him about the day's doings, and what he has to say about the battle of Ramillies becomes an important part of its history. " The duke of Marlborough said to me "—these are Burnet's words—" the French army looked the best of any he had ever seen; but that their officers did not do their part, nor show the courage that had appeared among them on other occasions. And when I asked him the difference between the actions at Hockstadt and at Ramillies; he said, the first battle lasted between seven and eight hours, and we lost above twelve thousand men in it; whereas the second lasted not above two hours, and we lost not above two thousand five hundred men. Orders were presently sent to the great cities, to draw the garrisons out of them, that so the French might have again the face of an army; for their killed, their deserters, and their prisoners, on this great day, were above twenty thousand men. The duke of Marlborough lost no time, but followed them close; Louvain, Mechlin, and Brussels submitted, besides many lesser places; Antwerp made a show of standing out, but soon followed the example of the rest; Ghent and Bruges did the same; in all these King Charles was proclaimed. Upon this unexpected rapidity of success, the duke of Marlborough went to the Hague, to concert measures with the States, where he stayed but a few days; for they agreed to everything he proposed, and sent him back with full powers. The first thing he undertook was the siege of Ostend, a place famous for its long siege in the last age. The natives of the place were disposed to return to the Austrian family, and the French that were in it had so lost all heart and spirit, that they made not the resistance that was looked for. In ten days after they sat down before it, and within four days after the batteries were finished, they capitulated."

The King of France saw as clearly as any one could the immense importance of Marlborough's successes, and he sent one of his greatest soldiers, Marshal Vendôme, to encounter the English commander. Vendôme was not able to do anything to retrieve, at that moment, the fortunes of the war; for the splendid victory of Ramillies had left in French armies but little heart for a trial of strength with the English commander. Place after place surrendered to Marlborough. Of the surrender of Dendermonde, Marlborough himself says in his despatch: "That place could never have been taken but by the hand of God, which gave us seven weeks without rain." Before the surrender King Louis had defiantly said that, owing to its watery surroundings, only an army of ducks could succeed in taking Dendermonde. The sudden and timely cessation of rain enabled Marlborough's troops, although not web-footed, to accomplish their object. Then there happened what had often happened before in the campaign and was to happen again. Marlborough would have pushed his conquests still farther in the same direction but that his Dutch allies were not ready, or were not willing, to keep up the supplies which were necessary for the accomplishment of his purpose. The campaign had been a splendid success so far as it had gone, and it filled the minds of Englishmen at home with the full hope that the whole struggle was about to draw to an immediate end. These hopes, however, were not realized. Europe had yet to wait some time, and England had to undergo many disappointments before the final triumph was to bring about the restoration of peace.

It was the desire of the Emperor and of the Archduke Charles that Marlborough should be made governor of all the region which he had thus invaded and occupied. Marlborough himself was ready to accept this important post, and the government of Queen Anne would have been quite willing to sanction the appointment. But there was a strong feeling of jealousy among the Dutch allies at the suggestion that such a position should be assigned to an English commander, and Marlborough, with that caution and prudence which never left him even in the midst of his greatest successes, thought that it would be unwise to give occasion to any feeling of dissatisfaction, reasonable or unreasonable, among those on whom he had to rely for support. Owing to his influence, therefore, the proposition was not pressed any further.

Prince Eugene was skilful enough and fortunate enough to follow up Marlborough's success by another victory which might in its way be called decisive. Eugene had gone into northern Italy with men and supplies, which, owing to the efforts of Marlborough, had been made fairly adequate for the work they were desired to accomplish. Eugene's appearance just now on the Italian battle-field was, to say the least of it, timely. The imperialists had just sustained a severe defeat at the hands of Marshal Vendôme. The French were laying siege to Turin, which was held by the Duke of Savoy. The Duke of Savoy saw clearly enough that unless some sudden relief took place the city could not hold out, and as he believed that the presence of himself and his court might only add to the difficulties of the besieged, he withdrew from his capital, leaving the work of defence in the hands of the best general he could find, but having little faith in the possibility of successful resistance. Eugene, when

RAMILLIES AND ALMANZA

campaign of 1707 under conditions which were very trying, even apart from the retirement or removal of Peterborough. There had been a sudden and unexpected rally of the Castilians against the advance of the allies, whom the national pride of all this region of Spain had now come to regard as invaders and enemies. The occupation of the capital and other cities by the allies was followed almost immediately by this sudden movement of national reaction, and it would have taken a much better general than Lord Galway to hold his own under such difficulties.

The Duke of Berwick, the son of James the Second and Arabella Churchill, was in command of the French forces, and we can easily understand how his close kinship with the house of Stuart inspired him with an undying determination to do his very best for the cause of the French King, whose court had been a sheltering-place for the exiled Stuarts, and whose public recognition of their cause and its living representative had done so much to bring about the war. In any case, Berwick was a man of far greater military capacity than Galway, and the fact soon made itself evident in the field. The two armies met on the battle-field of Almanza, a name destined to be famous in the annals of the war. Almanza is a town in Murcia, on the border of Valencia, standing on a broad plain. The situation was in itself favorable to the Duke of Berwick, because his cavalry was his strong force, and in this arm of the service he was superior, so far as numbers were concerned, to his antagonist. Lord Galway began the attack. For a while the struggle went on with doubtful success, but Galway's forces were composed, in part, of Portuguese and Spanish cavalry, and the Portuguese were unable to resist the impetuous charge of the French. Some of the Spanish troops made but a poor fight of it, and perhaps, indeed, had little heart for the business which they were expected to do. The English infantry, who held the centre, were outnumbered and utterly overborne by the French, and most of them had no option but to surrender. The defeat became a complete disaster, Galway lost most of his men, and had to abandon all the artillery he had brought with him.

Lord Galway, in a letter to Marlborough, written soon after the battle, described his defeat in the frankest terms. "I am under deep concern," he wrote, "to be obliged to tell your lordship we were entirely defeated. Both our wings were broke and let in the enemy's horse, which surrounded our foot, so that none could get off." Galway himself had received a severe wound on the forehead during the battle. His despatch to Marlborough declares that he "cannot but look upon the affairs of Spain as lost by this bad disaster," and adds, "all the generals here are of opinion that we cannot continue in this kingdom." Bishop Burnet, whose opinions on such subjects are worth quoting, because, such as they were, he is sure to have obtained them from men who bore a leading part in the event, ascribes the defeat mainly to the fatal advice, representations, and directions of the Archduke Charles, who had been proclaimed King of Spain. Charles persisted in dividing the force, "when the whole together was not equal to the enemy's," and marched into Catalonia to encounter an army of the French, which he declared to be moving in that direction, and thus left only about sixteen thousand men under Lord Galway.

"A council of war had resolved to venture on a battle, which the state of their affairs seemed to make necessary: they could not subsist where they were, nor be subsisted if they retired back into Valencia; so on the 14th of April, the two armies engaged in the plain of Almanza. The English and Dutch beat the enemy, and broke through twice; but the Portuguese gave way; upon that the enemy, who were almost double in number, both horse and foot, flanked them, and a total rout followed in which about ten thousand were killed or taken prisoners. The earl of Galway was twice wounded; once so near the eye, that for some time it put him out of a capacity for giving orders; but at last he, with some other officers, made the best retreat they could. Our fleet came happily on that coast on the day that the battle was fought; so he was supplied from thence, and he put garrisons into Denia and Alicant, and retired to the Ebro, with about three thousand horse, and almost as many foot. The duke of Orleans pursued the victory; Valencia submitted, and so did Saragoza; so that the principality of Catalonia was all that remained in king Charles' obedience."

The defeat proved a most serious check to the policy of the allies. It had a disheartening effect on the counsels of the Queen's administration. Queen Anne herself, it need hardly be said, had never been at heart in favor of the war. The whole policy of the alliance was essentially the policy of William the Third and of the Whigs who supported his views. When Anne succeeded to the throne the war was popular everywhere throughout England, and it would have been impossible for her to resist the public spirit, or to prevent the opening of hostilities. She had nothing for it but to carry out the policy of William, although at heart she was a Tory, and liked nothing less than to make war against that foreign sovereign in whose protection and support the Stuarts saw their only hope of success. The ministers were Tories, and even Marlborough and Godolphin inclined to the Tory view of the whole question. But the public feeling in favor of the war was too strong for the Tories, and Marlborough was about the last man in the world likely to forego his chances of personal success and greatness for the sake of any romantic fidelity to a political cause.

The Tory ministers, therefore, had to maintain a policy which distinctly belonged to the Whigs, and they found themselves in the predicament which English ministers have had to encounter in many instances since that time, of having to carry out their predecessors' policy or give up their places. The spirit of the war soon began to take possession of them, and their natural ambition forced them into the desire to make a better business of the Whig policy than the Whigs could have done for themselves. All this went well enough so long as victory after victory delighted the English public and made the government almost universally popular. We have seen in more modern instances how the temper and spirit of war can sweep away an administration from what might have seemed to be its natural moorings, and how the passion for mere success can subdue and silence for the time all considerations of traditional policy and all thought of constitutional consistency. But when a sudden and serious defeat seemed to portend a complete change in the whole course of the campaign; when the fruits of the most recent victories appeared to be wholly blighted by one great failure, then indeed a change came over the mood and temper of the administration. The armies of the allies had apparently gone so near to success that at one moment it seemed as if nothing remained but to make it an accomplished fact, and to dictate terms of surrender to the defeated enemy. If Marlborough had been at the head of the allied forces in Spain, or if there could have been found another Marlborough to take the command in Spain, the disaster of Almanza could without doubt have been easily retrieved. But there was no other Marlborough, and at various points of the campaign there were already indications that the first rush of victory had spent its force.

"The battle of Almanza," says Macaulay, "decided the fate of Spain. The loss was such as Marlborough or Eugene could scarcely have retrieved, and was certainly not to be retrieved by Stanhope and Staremberg." But the war was still to drag on for a long time, and other alternations of good or evil fortune had to bring their moods of hope or despondency before the day could arrive when peace was to be accomplished at almost any price.

CHAPTER XV

THE FIRST PARLIAMENT OF THE UNION

The new Parliament of the United Kingdom was held at Westminster on the 25th of October, 1707. The Queen opened Parliament in the House of Lords, and the members of the new House of Commons were summoned to attend her. There was but little of public demonstration. The event passed off quietly, to all appearance a mere state ceremonial and nothing more. The thoughts of the people were occupied for the most part with the events which were passing on the battle-fields of the Low Countries, Germany, and Spain. But it soon began to appear as if the work of accomplishing a thorough union between two countries and two parliamentary systems was not a work quite easy of accomplishment. The essential laws and practices of Scotland had been secured to the Scottish people by the express terms of the act of union. The religious institutions of Scotland had been guaranteed by declaration in the compact made between the two countries. The laws and institutions of the two ancient kingdoms thus made into one differed most widely in many of their actual principles as well as in all their forms and practices, and it was found no easy task to carry out any new work of legislation with due regard to the existing conditions which had been recognized and guaranteed by the act of union. The very phrases and terms belonging to each system were constantly coming into sudden antagonism, and there was something occasionally ludicrous as well as serious in the attempts which had to be made to bring them into a state of seeming reconciliation. The difficulties were most immediate, most practical, and most obvious where questions of trade and commerce came into consideration. Scotland had been in all matters of trading and navigation a foreign state, and often a competing and rival state where England was concerned, and the political and constitutional necessities which had naturally overborne all other considerations of the moment in bringing about the union could not be expected to overbear all at once the mass of conflicting interests which still existed and had to be cautiously dealt with.

Then, again, there could be no doubt that a large proportion of the Scottish gentry and the Scottish people were yet far from being reconciled with the new constitution, the new succession, and the new foreign policy established in England. In the north of Scotland especially large numbers of people of all classes, high and low, still held in their hearts a strong sentiment of allegiance to the cause of the dethroned and exiled Stuarts. France was relied upon by such persons as the natural ally of the Stuart cause, and for many years to come Scotland had to be regarded as the campaigning ground of any new attempt to be made for the restoration of the Stuart dynasty. The literature of Scotland, prose as well as poetry, bore testimony through several successive generations to the feelings of sympathy which existed here and there in the minds of the Scottish people for the dethroned dynasty. Nothing could bear more convincing testimony to the necessity and the practical advantages of the act of union than the fact that all these difficulties were got over in the end, and that the union gradually became a reality in feeling as well as in terms. Any attempt to establish the supremacy of England and of the English crown over the people of Scotland by a mere decree would have proved an utter failure, and would have converted the northern part of the kingdom into a rebellious state perpetually endeavoring to overthrow the predominance of the southern kingdom. Thus the very difficulties which at first seemed to make the work of thorough union almost impossible were, in fact, the best securities for its continuance and its success. In days much nearer to our own Thomas Carlyle declared that the thoroughness of the union between England and Scotland had been mainly secured by the fact that the Scotch had been the victors at the battle of Bannockburn. Carlyle's meaning was, of course, that in this event, which closed an important chapter in the history of the two countries, the Scottish people had given enduring evidence that they could not be regarded as a conquered race subjected to the imperious will and ways of the conqueror.

The British statesmen who helped to make the act of union must have had this great fact always in their minds, and must have known that Scotland would have to be treated as an independent state willing to agree to the terms of a suitable alliance, and not as an inferior power which must, for the sake of its own existence, consent to accept any terms which the state of superior strength and importance might out of its favor and its good-will be ready to offer for acceptance. In our own times we have seen how the words "predominant partner" became a phrase of rather ominous significance when spoken by a highly placed British statesman. The Scottish people at the time when the act of union came to be passed would have been little inclined to put up with the suggestion that England was the predominant partner whose right it

FIRST PARLIAMENT OF THE UNION

was to dictate, according to its own judgment, the conditions of the partnership. On such a principle we may safely affirm no union could ever have been made between the two kingdoms. The statesmanship of Queen Anne's days was wise enough to see that if Scotland were to be a partner at all, she must be treated as an equal partner, whose inclinations and interests had to be consulted and cared for at every stage of the new arrangement. Therefore, the Scottish people were allowed from the beginning to see that their own national institutions were not to be interfered with in any way by the constitutional agreement which was intended to convert the two countries into one United Kingdom.

The time cannot be far distant when it will be clearly and universally understood that there is no way of blending different nationalities into one imperial system but that which recognizes the complete independence, so far as local laws and usages are concerned, of each of the populations which are to make up the new empire. We use the word "empire" in this case not as describing merely some system which has a monarch at its head, but as a term applying to any combination of states into one system, whether monarchical or republican. The common-sense of the matter is very clear. Each country or each state naturally understands best what is suited to its history, its traditions, its religious sentiments, its inherited usages, and its ordinary ways of life. The work of the central representative authority is to provide for the welfare of the interests which are common to all, for the defence of the united countries against possible dangers from enmity abroad, and for the maintenance of the elementary conditions which best provide for the development and improvement of the commonwealth.

The world has seen in the history of the house of

Hanover how the principle of the predominant partner led to utter failure when applied to the American colonies of those days, and how at a later period still the other and better principle created the loyal, contented, and prospering Dominion of Canada. Scotland has now, as she had before the act of union, a whole code of civil and criminal law widely, and in all its details, differing from that which prevails in England. The mere fact that the continuance of that system, so long as she saw fit to continue it, was guaranteed by the conditions of the act of union, has been the main cause of the success and prosperity which attended that signal stroke of statesmanship. The statesmen who brought about the act of union may claim the praise of having been in advance of their time when they thus recognized existing realities and renounced all idea of striving after a compact based upon an untenable and impossible uniformity of system among peoples of differing race, traditions, usages, and temperament. Probably, at the time, the statesmen of Queen Anne's reign did not enter into any such philosophical considerations, but they saw that the union with Scotland was essential to the safety of the two countries, and that it could not possibly be brought about except with the full and free consent of the Scottish people. Even for this, however, they must have their due meed of praise, for there were great European statesmen living at that time who had formed no higher conception of political principle than the domination of the stronger and the submission of the weaker partner in the proposed alliance.

It was not at first a very easy matter to blend into one working parliamentary system the procedure and the purposes of the two representative bodies. The Estates of Scotland had had a kind of work to do which did not call for the same arrangements as those found necessary for the maintenance and the objects of the English Parliament. The principal purpose of the Scottish Estates was to secure the northern part of the island against the domination of the English crown and the English houses of legislature. The work that had to be done was, for the most part, strictly local work on the general objects of which the Scottish Estates were already well agreed, and the Estates were therefore in the condition of an assembly which had to arrange for the discharge of business about which no inherent antagonisms existed. Their work was like that of a representative association which had merely to devise the best and most convenient methods of putting into operative form the general wishes of the community. They were not impeded by the constant necessity of protecting their resolutions against the interference of some authority which was always ready to take advantage of any mistakes or omissions arising in their legislative arrangements.

The English Parliament had to guard itself carefully, at every step, against the ever-encroaching privileges of the crown. The resolutions of the English Parliament had to be drawn up with all the critical precision which belonged to an act of Parliament under a system which would have made the slightest error in expression have the destroying effect of a flaw in the act, and thus render its whole purpose inoperative and futile. The proceedings of the English Parliament have, to this day, to be protected by a number of forms which must be taken into account, must be strictly observed, must be literally obeyed, if the whole work of legislation is not to become worse than useless. The business, therefore, of the Scottish members in the Union Parliament was, above all things, to see that the local interests of Scotland should not be injuriously affected by the conditions new to them, under which the Parliament of England had to carry on its labors.

This fact alone rendered necessary a good deal of give-and-take on both sides. Both began with the general and cordial recognition of the fact that the union of the two parliaments was absolutely necessary for the maintenance and welfare of both countries alike. Therefore the English members were for the most part quite willing that the purely local interests of Scotland, so long as they did not absolutely interfere with English interests, should be left to the dealing and the management of the Scottish representatives. The Scottish members were, on the other hand, willing to submit to the casual inconveniences put in their way by the English forms of parliamentary procedure so long as they were allowed the practical management of their own affairs. It is plain that if there had not been some common understanding of this kind the work of satisfactory legislation would have become impossible, for the mere majority could always have overborne the will of the minority, and thus have given the predominant partner a complete mastery over the wishes and the interests of the partner who could not claim or assert predominance. Down to our own days this principle of reasonable compromise has been practically recognized and acknowledged in the English House of Commons. The understanding was and is that the affairs of Scotland should be left as much as possible to the management of the Scottish representatives. Every English member had and has a perfect right, so far as parliamentary procedure is concerned, to interfere with and oppose any motion which has to do with purely Scottish business, even though it had the support of the whole body of members who represent Scottish constituencies. But, of course, if such a right were constantly or even frequently acted on it is quite clear that the position of the Scottish members would become unendurable. The men who best understand, who alone could thoroughly understand, the real interests of their country would be liable at any moment to be overborne by some sudden opposition coming from a larger number of English members, and the presence of the Scottish representatives in the assembly would be absolutely futile for the very purposes which they were sent into Parliament to accomplish.

It is not usual, therefore, for English members to interfere with the progress of any measure dealing purely with Scottish local interests except in the rare and extreme case where such measures might come into antagonism with some great legislative principle affecting the general interest of the whole country, some principle which English members were bound by their national duty to maintain. In recent days it has been the usual practice of the Scottish members to hold private councils of their own when preparing some measure applying strictly to the interests of their own country, and to come to a general agreement as to its object and its form. In these cases the common understanding is that the English members should interfere as little as possible with the legislative progress of the measure. Nothing could be more harmonious and more satisfactory than the manner in which this common and reasonable understanding has been found to work for the benefit of both countries and of the whole parliamentary system. The fundamental difference between the principles and practices of English and Scottish law which for a long time were found very perplexing in the business of legislation render some such understanding all the more needful.

The law of Scotland, like that of many or most European countries, is founded mainly on the basis of the old Roman law, while that of England is a somewhat rough and wild-grown accretion of time and chance, change of varying dynasties and systems, of foreign innovations, and sudden temporary devices. The delightful fictions of English legal procedure were wholly unknown to the Roman law and to the Scottish law which was derived from it. The Scottish law set itself to carry out the objects it sought to attain in the clearest and most direct manner. It did not occur to Scottish legislation, for instance, to fancy that there could be any advantage in the creation of imaginary characters like the once familiar John Doe and Richard Roe, in order that a simple lawsuit involving the interests of real and living personages should be properly conducted to its conclusion. English youths and maidens of the present day have probably forgotten all about those fantastic creatures John Doe and Richard Roe, whose names were at one time familiar to every one who attended English courts of law or read the published reports of English cases. Even the more mature readers who belong to the present generation will probably not remember that at one time such picturesque creations of the legal fancy as Paul Pry and Peter Thrustout were named in English legal proceedings as personages seeking the protection of English law in order to assert their claims against real and living citizens or corporations. On the other hand, many of the phrases and terms habitually used in the law courts of Scotland were absolutely unintelligible to an English listener, although in these instances it was merely a question of different names applied to identical proceedings.

If any serious effort had been made to bring about an actual assimilation between the legal systems of the two countries, the difficulties would have proved insurmountable and the union could never have been accomplished. The Scottish people were absolutely devoted to the principles of their own law, while the English people would probably have thought that the end of the world was coming if they had been expected to submit to any radical alterations in their familiar and time-honored ways of conducting their legal business. Happily, it was thoroughly understood on both sides that each country was to have its own principles and its own forms of legal procedure, and the law systems of the two countries remain to this day absolutely independent, and even in many fundamental attributes quite different. The arrangements for the completion of the union were satisfactorily carried on, each of the countries fully understanding that there were certain points on which a compromise was out of the question.

There were, however, some serious obstacles to be got over where the trading interests and usages of the two kingdoms were concerned. England and Scotland had long been rivals in trading activity, and it proved, for some time, very hard to arrive at a common understanding which should give to the one country no unfair advantage over the other. Scotland, so far as wealth and population came into account, was the weaker partner of the two, and therefore the Scottish people were naturally jealous of any part of the new system which might seem to give undue advantages to the stronger partner. Scotland had always up to this time carried on arrangements of her own for the promotion and maintenance of her trade with foreign countries, and many objections were raised to some of the arrangements under the new system which confined her dealings within the same limits as those set up by England for the regulation of her commerce with foreign states. John Hill Burton, in his history, gives many interesting and some decidedly amusing illustrations of the antagonism which arose out of the effort to mould these rival claims into one compact and uniform system. He tells us how "After the union had been carried and was absolute law, there was still mischief in store for that 1st of May, 1707, when merchandise was to pass free between the two countries — the great point that had throughout been demanded by Scotland and resisted by the trading interests of England." Scotland had had a system of very low customs duties, and under the union she had to adopt the high customs duties which prevailed in England, and had even received under the act of union a large compensation in money for the new burdens now to be imposed upon her trade. The 1st of May, 1707, was the period prescribed for the acceptance by Scotland of the higher scale of duties, and therefore the interval was turned to account by Scottish traders for the purpose of making as much profit as possible meantime. Burton, himself a Scotchman, frankly acknowledges that the trading community of England had "to protest against extremely dishonest uses made of the vast privileges so acquired by Scotland." But he points out that there was no remedy, because "the revolution in the trading organization of the empire gave opportunity for private persons to speculate on the event as a source of profit, and they could not be prohibited from drawing the profits realized by their skill." The mercantile problem, as he points out, was to import as much foreign merchandise as possible into Scotland during the interval. The object was to turn that interval to the greatest amount of profit which could be extorted from it, and Burton declares that, in all probability, " a far greater amount of English than of Scots money was thus embarked, as the market was open to all speculators of both countries, and England had at

FIRST PARLIAMENT OF THE UNION

least twenty times the capital of Scotland." A large amount of the duties of Scotland were actually farmed. "The farming was to come to an end on the 1st of May, and the natural question with the farmers was how to gather in the largest amount of customs duties before that time." "So it came to pass that on the 1st of May a large stock of goods had accumulated for the English market, imported partly at the low Scots duties and partly at less even than these."

The accumulation of merchandise was easily made, but the difficulty began when the fatal 1st of May came round. Then arose the question how the goods were to be got into England without having to submit to the charge of the newly constituted rate of duties. Of course, if the merchandise, thus put together for a special speculative purpose, were to pay the new and heavy rates of charge, then the object of the whole game of speculation would be completely frustrated. It was thought by those who had started the game that it would be better, on the whole, to fight out the question in one concentrated and decisive battle than to undertake a large number of individual struggles by sending in the different consignments of merchandise in separate lots and at various points of the customs frontier. The impression was that the customs officers would find it much more easy to enforce the high rates on small accumulations of goods at various places than to conduct what might almost be called a great international struggle under new conditions on one battlefield. Some time was lost by the speculative owners of the goods in making up their minds how and where to accept battle, and Defoe tells us in his *History of the Union* that the middle of June had arrived before "the fleet sailed for London, consisting of about forty sail, mostly loaded with wine and brandy." The English custom-house officers, as Burton tells us, " could see nothing in this but an attempt on a large scale to smuggle foreign goods through Scotland into England." The English custom-house officers, one may readily admit, could hardly be expected to take any other view of the venture. They acted on this very reasonable principle, and simply laid an embargo on the whole fleet and all the goods it contained. Even here the importers were able to secure a sort of advantage. " The officers," says Burton, " would not permit the ships to be unladen on bond or other security for the duties, if any, that might be found exigible." That was, in fact, an accommodation usually allowed to importers of goods on any occasions when the exact amount of duty was open to question, in order that the amount might be satisfactorily settled by the proper authorities after a quiet discussion of the conflicting claims.

In ordinary cases the dispute was merely one which might arise naturally between the customs officials and the owners of merchandise, acting in perfect good faith and only anxious to secure themselves against accidental or mistaken overcharge. But the vast mass of merchandise now claiming entrance into England was regarded by the custom-house officers as merely contraband. The goods, as we have seen, consisted chiefly of wines and brandies, and it was perfectly clear that wine and brandy are not articles of Scotland's home manufacture. The goods thus sought to be imported evidently came from France, and France was then the national enemy of England, actually engaged in war against English armies on foreign fields of battle. This fact naturally made the attempt of the importers seem more audacious than ever to the customs officials, and these officials, if left to themselves, would probably have made short work of the whole dispute by exacting the full amount of the duties on the new goods, or absolutely prohibiting their importation, if they did not insist on dealing with them as the property of a lawless band of smugglers. But the higher authorities, the government in London, soon saw that the dispute was something too serious to be settled in a moment according to the legal principles of the custom-house. The government, as Burton justly observes, "had the responsibility of keeping the peace between Scotland and England, and saving the treaty, that had cost so much patience and anxiety, from being scattered to the winds."

The legal rights of the question were perfectly clear. The new rate of customs duties to be imposed on goods entering England from Scotland had been settled by the act of union. But the carrying of the act had met with many difficulties, especially coming from the rivalry of trade between these two parts of the kingdom, and nothing could have been more inauspicious than to arouse a general feeling in Scotland that the first effect of the union was to exhibit the stronger partner filling his pockets at the expense of the weaker. Such an exhibition would have been particularly undesirable when the nature of the goods sought to be imported gave fresh evidence of the sort of trade sympathy between Scotland and France. The crown lawyers were consulted on the subject and set themselves to work to devise some happy means by which anything like an open antagonism between the two parts of the kingdom could be avoided. The immediate result was, in the words of Burton, that "in some of the deep recesses of the law of England a method was found for warehousing and preserving the goods, reserving the rights of all parties concerned for deliberate adjustment." Then came a sort of conflict of opinion between the officials of the custom-house and the ministers of the crown. The custom-house officers argued that if the audacious attempt of the importers were allowed to meet with any semblance of success, a precedent would be established which might lead to a complete practical exemption of Scottish trading companies from the rates of excise imposed by law upon their English rivals. But the advisers of the Queen took a different view of the crisis. They were of opinion that, if anything like a reasonable, or to them endurable, settlement of this existing dispute could be brought about, the discouragement and difficulty put in the way of the Scottish importers would prevent them from venturing on such reckless experiments in the future. Defoe tells us how the troublesome question was finally brought to an arrangement.

"That the merchants might be made easy, it was proposed to them that they should land their goods upon condition that they gave security to stand to the judgment of the British Parliament. This was thought but reasonable, and some complied with it and had their ships unloaden; others refused such securities, and their goods lay longer and suffered more. At length a medium was found out which was to let all the merchants have possession of their goods, serving the possessors of the goods with a writ of *devenirunt* out of the Exchequer. This is a kind of writ which puts the matter in a form of prosecution only, that in case of farther occasion the Queen might recover her dues; and so the merchants had their goods, and the decision of it was left to time and to the British Parliament. Thus it continued in a course of law, but not under prosecution, till the meeting of the British Parliament, when, by a vote of the House of Commons, the whole affair was discharged, and all prosecutions ordered to be stopped."

FIRST PARLIAMENT OF THE UNION

Thus the government got out of the trouble, not perhaps in the most dignified manner, but by the adoption of the most prudent policy which could have been devised under the trying conditions. There was no further temptation to import vast quantities of goods from France with the hope of passing them through English custom-houses at the low duties which existed before the union, and the government acted wisely, on the whole, in not regarding the one great enterprise of trading speculation as worth a serious disturbance of the friendly relations between England and Scotland. With this settlement ended the whole dispute, so far as custom duties were concerned, between the two kingdoms now united and made one.

In order to regulate and assimilate the methods for collecting customs and excise duties in England and Scotland, a commission of excise and of customs was immediately established. The commission was made up of men representing the two nationalities. Burton gives us an amusing account of one effect produced by the combination of English members with Scottish in the commission. "The new process made the Scots acquainted with a curious testimony to English persistency in ancient customs. It had been found of old, when writing was a rare accomplishment, that when a sum of money represented a claim on the Exchequer, the way of recording it so that neither party had a possible chance of gaining anything by maintaining the record to be inaccurate, was to take a baton or bar of wood, smoothen one side of it, cut into the wood the sum in question — generally in Roman figures — and then split the wood through the figures, each party keeping one slip or tally. When the two were brought in union and fitted by the split there could be no question as to the exact figures engraved on them. An importation of vast bales of the materials for this kind of record caused much amusement among the Scots, and was perhaps a diversion from more dangerous excitements."

We may follow the story of the Exchequer tallies. The system was not abolished until an advanced period in the reign of George the Third, and in the reign of William the Fourth it was decreed that the accumulated tallies should be destroyed. The tallies, however, had their revenge, for they succeeded in destroying the Houses of Parliament. The antiquated calculating machines were burned in a stove in the House of Lords, but the stove, becoming overheated, set fire to the room in which it stood, the fire spread with amazing rapidity, and on the evening of October 16, 1834, the two Houses of Parliament were completely destroyed. It was well for England and for the world that Westminster Hall and Westminster Abbey were saved from the flames.

The only change made in the Scottish laws of procedure was where the change merely affected some action or practice to which a law common to both countries might apply, without controverting any of the legal principles or practices peculiar to Scotland and hallowed by the traditions of the Scottish people. One civil council was established for the whole kingdom. The powers of justices of the peace were made the same for England and Scotland. The law relating to high treason was made the same for both countries. But in all cases, and these were many and were often of great national importance, where the feelings of the Scottish people in general made them strongly inclined to hold to their own principles and practices of jurisprudence, the national sentiment was justly and wisely allowed to have its own way, and no at-

FIRST PARLIAMENT OF THE UNION

a change accomplished for the convenience and the furtherance of local legislation in both countries, and will indicate no severance of national interests or feelings, but only a general honest thought for the common good of the empire.

CHAPTER XVI

SACHEVERELL

The comet of a season is a familiar figure in history and in romance. The phrase has become famous since Byron applied it to Churchill, but the phrase was not particularly apt when set out as the summary description of a man of genius, whose works are likely still to outlast many seasons and many generations. The common understanding of the words is that they typify the career of some human meteor flashing upon mortal vision for a short time and then disappearing altogether from sight. The comet of a season often brings with it commotion and disturbance in human affairs, but it generally passes away as suddenly as it came, leaving the world uncertain how far it helped to create and how far it served merely to forbode the temporary storm. A straw can show which way the wind blows, but there are human straws every now and then which seem to have some strange power to call up the gale of which their movement indicates the direction. Such a comet was the once-famous Dr. Sacheverell; such a human straw he may at least be called if the phrase which Byron applied to Churchill seems too glowing and too poetical to be taken as typical of his career.

Henry Sacheverell was born in 1674, and was the son of a High Church rector. He got his first share of education at Marlborough grammar-school, and by the help of some of his father's friends he was sent thence to Magdalen College, Oxford. There he had the great good fortune to make the acquaintance, and, indeed, to obtain the friendship of Joseph Addison, and he must have been a youth of much promise and of winning manners, for when Sacheverell was twenty years of age Addison dedicated one of his books to him, and called him in the dedication "My dearest Henry." He entered the Church, and obtained a vicarage in Staffordshire. He soon began to distinguish himself by delivering sermons and printing them afterwards for the instruction of the public, or, at least, of such of the public as had got into the way of reading published sermons. These discourses were couched in well-chosen and graceful English, were apt in their use of quotations, and showed a certain faculty of studied if not spontaneous eloquence. Sacheverell, however, seems to have soon made up his mind that he had some other business in life besides the mere delivery of sermons on the ordinary subjects of a High Church clergyman's discourse. He determined, apparently, to identify himself with the declaration of political as well as religious doctrines which, for some time before, had been allowed by virtue of a sort of recognized truce to remain without emphatic expression.

Bishop Burnet says of him that "Dr. Sacheverell was a bold insolent man, with a very small measure of religion, virtue, learning, or good sense, but he resolved to force himself into popularity and preferment, by the most petulant railings at Dissenters and Low Churchmen in several sermons and libels written without either chasteness of style or liveliness of expression; all was one unpractised strain of indecent and scurrilous language."

If Burnet is just in this description of Sacheverell's style, his style must certainly have greatly changed from that of the sermons by means of which he first sought to bring himself into public notice; but it is easy to understand that such a man, if determined to make his way, and finding the language of moderation did not help him to accomplish his purpose quickly, would be very apt to suit his general bearing and language to the work of popularity-hunting which he had chosen for himself. For a time even the vehement style did not produce all the effect which Sacheverell appears to have desired. Bishop Burnet says that when he had pursued this method—the method already described in Burnet's words—" for several years without effect, he was at last brought up by a popular election to a church in Southwark, where he began to make great reflections on the Ministry, representing that the Church was in danger, being neglected by those who governed, while they favoured her most inveterate enemies."

Now there was undoubtedly a strong and growing feeling at that time among a large body of the public that the doctrines of the Whig party were obtaining too wide an influence over the governing classes, and that the cherished sentiments of Queen Anne herself were compelled to give way to the levelling counsels of those whom she had allowed to act as her advisers. Men who were well known to be Tories when they took office in the administration had been seen to act in thorough co-operation with their Whig colleagues, and an impression was growing up among large sections of the public that the Whigs were generally pretty safe to have their way in everything. The nation, in fact, had not yet quite settled down to the principles established by the popular revolution and by the reign of William the Third. The doctrine of divine right had been deposed, indeed, but it had not been completely disestablished. A large section of society everywhere, which had been privileged, influential, and powerful under the old system, saw its privileges, its influence, and its power passing away, and was not willing to abandon without a struggle its claims to its ancient position. We are not speaking now merely of those who still had some faith left in the forlorn cause of the Stuarts, and were willing to make sacrifices and to run risks in an effort for their restoration. There were large numbers who had no real hope of any such counter-revolution, and who had not the least idea of incurring sacrifice or risk for its sake, but who yet detested in their hearts the new system, and were ready to welcome with acclamation any voice which gave emphatic utterance to their cherished feelings.

Then, again, the war had been dragging on for a long time without any of the dazzling successes which carried away the minds of many who at its opening were not very enthusiastic about it. Among certain sections of society it had, of course, always been unpopular, because it brought the country into antagonism with France on the battle-field, and France was the only state from which the adherents of the Stuart cause had any hope. But apart from these there was a large proportion of the population who had had little or no feeling in favor of the war when it was first proclaimed, but who had been roused into national sympathy and enthusiasm by the victories of Marlborough and Peterborough. As the war dragged on and on, and there seemed no near prospect of its termination, and of late there had been no brilliant triumphs to dazzle the public, a feeling of dissatisfaction and of disappointment had been growing up in many minds, and the war was beginning to be regarded by large sections of the community as a costly, futile, wearisome, and apparently endless game, a national burden to be borne without hope of recompense. Now the war was a Whig war from the outset, and many among the political opponents of the Whigs were in a frame of mind to seek some consolation for the national sacrifices in the thought that they were brought about by the perverse policy of their political antagonists. Under all these conditions there was a large amount of sullen discontent, brooding here, there, and everywhere, which needed only some sudden impulse or temptation to stir it up into outspoken and uproarious manifestation.

Whether Sacheverell had been carefully watching and estimating all the various conditions which might give him a favorable opportunity to become a prophet and leader of public opinion, or whether mere chance put the opportunity in his way and he found it, is a question scarcely worth while taking any time to discuss. The opportunity came, and it was recognized and turned promptly to account. There were two great commemoration days still cherished by preachers in England, and still celebrated by special services. One of these was the 30th of January, the anniversary of the execution of Charles the First. The other was the 5th of November, the anniversary of the Gunpowder Plot, an event which has a sort of popular commemoration, although after a somewhat burlesque fashion, even in our day. Sacheverell had the good fortune to be chosen to preach the 5th of November sermon in the year 1700 from the pulpit of St. Paul's Cathedral.

The preacher began with an elaborate, and what

would be thought a somewhat superfluous, denunciation of the Gunpowder Plot and of all who were concerned in it. It has been suggested by some historians that Sacheverell was anxious to make it clear from the very first that his detestation of Whiggery had not led or driven him into any weak or sentimental toleration for Popery. However that may be, he certainly began his discourse with a condemnation of the Church of Rome which might have satisfied the sternest fanatics described in *Old Mortality*. The climax of his denunciation of the plot itself was reached when he described it as "a conspiracy, so full of the most unheard-of malice, most insatiable cruelty, most diabolical revenge, as only could be hatched in the cabinet council of hell, and brought forth in a conclave of Romish Jesuits." On the other hand, the preacher was careful not to indulge in any emphatic diatribes against the general body of Dissenters. The full force of his denunciations was levelled against the men who, while professing to be themselves members of the Church of England, were yet willing for their ignoble purposes to "play fast and loose with faith" to suit the enemies of the Church, and to support measures of toleration for "occasional conformity."

Sacheverell had taken his text from the Epistles of St. Paul, where the Apostle speaks of the perils through which he had gone. "In journeyings often, in perils of waters, in perils of robbers, in perils by mine own countrymen, in perils by the heathen, in perils in the city, in perils in the wilderness, in perils in the sea, in perils among false brethren." The perils by mine own countrymen and those among false brethren were the dangers to the Church of England on which Sacheverell poured forth the full flood of his eloquence. Was it, he asked, indignantly, the spirit and doctrine of the Church "to assert separation from her communion to be no schism; or if it was, that schism is no damnable sin; that occasional conformity is no hypocrisy, but rather for the benefit of the Church; that any one may be an occasional conformist with schismatics, and yet not guilty of schism; that a Christian may serve God in any way or congregation of worship as well by extemporary prayers as by a prescribed form and liturgy; that conformity to the Church and ecclesiastical authority are no parts of morality and a good life; that the orders and ceremonies of the Church are only carnal arbitrary obediences, to be dispensed with as men please both by clergy and laity; that the censures and excommunications of the Church are mere *bruta fulmina;* canonical obedience and absolution, spiritual tyranny and usurpation—and, in a word, that the whole body of the worship and discipline of the Church of England is nothing else but priestcraft and Popery in masquerade?"

Then the preacher went on to give this part of his discourse a more direct application to the existing condition of things and to the manner in which the influence of her Majesty's ministers was used for the purpose of practically denying the doctrines of the Church. He besought his audience, and he besought them in the name of God, to consider "what must be the consequence of this scandalous fluctuation and trimming betwixt the Church and Dissenters, both in conscience and prudence." Could the surrender, he asked, of one point or article in the faith of the Church be allowed without violating and affecting the whole frame and body of it? "Will not such a base and time-serving compliance give the enemies of our Church an occasion of blaspheming her as weak and inconsistent?"

Then he went on to insist that nothing could be gained in form of genuine support from the Dissenters by the renunciation of this or that article of faith to suit their convenience.

Here Sacheverell made use of that argument which has been familiar to the civilized world against every measure of reform, religious or political, proposed in favor of an oppressed minority since legislative enactments began to be matters of public discussion. We have had the same sort of argument put forward again and again in our own days, and applied to all manner of proposals for civil and religious liberty. The Dissenters, he declared, were not to be gained over by even the most generous measures of relief compatible with the safety of existing institutions. "A man," he proclaimed, "must be very weak, or something worse, that thinks or pretends that Dissenters are to be gained or won over by any other grants and indulgences than giving up our whole constitution; and he that recedes the least tittle from it to satisfy or ingratiate with these clamorous, insatiate, and Church-devouring malignants, knows not what spirit they are of." He reminded his hearers that Queen Elizabeth, in her wisdom, saw through all that sort of thing, knew that it meant the overthrow of the monarchy as well as of the Church, "and, like a Queen of true resolution and pious zeal" for Church and monarchy alike, pronounced that such demands came from the restless spirits of factious people, "and that no quiet was to be expected from them till they were utterly suppressed, which, like a prudent princess, she did by wholesome severities, that the crown for many years sat easy and flourishing upon her head." He gave emphasis to this part of his discourse by insisting that if Elizabeth's successor, King James, had followed her wise politics, his son would never have fallen a martyr to their fury.

Sacheverell pointed his moral by some tolerably direct allusions to what was going on at that moment in England, and by one phrase, at least, which had a direct and intelligible, and, indeed, a perfectly unmistakable, application to a living statesman. Denouncing the men in power, whoever they might be, who were utterly without zeal for religion in any form of faith, he referred again to the passage which he had made his text, and called upon his hearers to remember " in what moving and lively colour does the holy Psalmist point out the crafty insidiousness of such wily volpones!" This latter phrase could not but have gone home to the minds and the feelings of the large majority among the congregation which Sacheverell was then addressing. The word had been taken from Ben Jonson's famous comedy, "Volpone," in which it was meant to represent a crafty and fox-like nature. It had been applied to Godolphin as a nickname, intended to be at once sarcastic and characteristic, and at the time when Sacheverell was delivering his discourse it had already passed into the slang of the day. Comic verse had got hold of it and made its application intelligible even to him whom we should now describe as the " man in the street," and we can easily imagine that a thrill of amusement and satisfaction must have passed through that listening crowd when Sacheverell thus gave it utterance.

It may easily be imagined that the storm which was created by these utterances and allusions was exactly the effect which Sacheverell's ambition for notoriety would have led him to welcome with delight. Sacheverell took every opportunity of impressing on the public mind his desire to be a martyr, his determination to be a martyr, even before it was by any means certain that his efforts were destined to be rewarded by the martyr's crown. He advertised himself immediately by the publication of his two sermons, both harping on the same string, in cheap and popular pamphlet form, and he introduced each of them by a dedication impressing the meaning and pointing the moral of his utterances; he did not even allow it to be supposed that he had adopted his plan of publication merely to remove the whole argument out of the sphere of the Church and the pulpit, and to accept battle as a political gladiator on the ordinary field of fight. On the contrary, he boldly asserted, in the introductions to his printed pamphlet, the right of the pulpit to perform a leading part in political controversy.

In the dedication to the " Perils of False Brethren " Sacheverell declared that " We are told by these men who would fain shut both our ears and our mouths, in order the more effectually to undermine and destroy us, that the pulpit is not a place for politics; and that it is the business of a clergyman to preach peace and not sound the trumpet in Sion—so expressly contrary to the command of God to ' cry aloud and spare not ' !" This sermon was dedicated to the Lord Mayor, and the dedication announced that " By your Lordship's command this discourse ventures to appear in public, in contempt of all those scandalous misrepresentations the malicious adversaries of our Church have traduced it with, and that impartial sentence it had the honour to receive from some of those acute and wise judges who condemned it without sight or hearing; and it is set before the world, and especially the affluent citizens of London, that they may not be flattered into ruin, but seeing the fatal consequences of these damnable false doctrines which some seditious impostors have laboured to poison them with, may forsake and detest them." These erring personages who thus endeavored to deceive the public were recommended by Sacheverell to abandon their ignoble ways, and to adopt "the same open undaunted resolution" which the Lord Mayor himself had displayed.

The Lord Mayor himself was, apparently, not much gratified by the distinction thus conferred upon him, and it was publicly asserted that the printing of the sermon had not taken place, as Sacheverell asserted, by command of the Lord Mayor, and that other members of the corporation were entirely opposed to the doctrines proclaimed by the preacher. Now it was certain that the Lord Mayor had given every countenance to the preacher, and had expressed in very direct fashion his approval of the sermon by publicly carrying off Sacheverell to dine with him at the Mansion House when the service of the day had come to an end. It is quite possible that the Lord Mayor had not put any command upon the preacher to publish the sermon, and, indeed, the Lord Mayor, in his official capacity, had no sort of authority to issue any such command. The Lord Mayor happened to be then a member of the House of Commons, and probably felt that he might find himself in a very awkward predicament if Parliament should order the impeachment of Sacheverell, and it should appear that Sir Samuel Gerard, M.P., had, as Lord Mayor of London, pledged his authority, whatever it was, to an approval of the preacher's doctrines. The Lord Mayor had many influential friends in the House of Commons, and the question as to his responsibility for the publication of the sermon was not allowed to come to any direct issue. It may fairly be assumed that he thoroughly approved of the preacher's doctrines, and sanctioned their issue in pamphlet form, but that he had not at the time quite understood the seriousness of the responsibility which he was taking on himself, and was only too glad to escape out of the difficulty with as little of personal controversy as possible.

The first sermon, preached at the Derby assizes on August 15th of the same year, on "The Communication of Sin," was dedicated "To the Right Worshipful George Sacheverell," a near relation of the preacher, "High Sheriff of the County of Derby, and to the Honourable Gentlemen of the Grand Jury." The dedication pointed more especially in this case than even in the other to the direct identification of the culprits against whom the preacher had thundered from his pulpit. Without the dedication the sermon might have been regarded merely as a general declamation against evil-doers in whatever class of society. The dedication, however, relieved the preacher from any imputation of having merely wasted his breath in a vague and general denunciation of evil-doing. Sacheverell took care to inform his relative and the gentlemen of the grand jury that the offenders whom he mainly denounced were the Whigs and the Low Churchmen who lent their help and their patronage to the Dissenters. Such persons, he declared, "in commending, approving, or defending any crime . . . become the guardians of iniquity, and commence the devil's champions to fight his battles and maintain his cause, and represent him in the most detestable quality of his nature—a delight in the dishonour of God and the misery and ruin of mankind." There could be no mistake, therefore, as to the direct purpose of this sermon, which otherwise might have passed off as a conventional and commonplace discourse against what Shakespeare's " Richard the Third " describes as " the formal vice iniquity."

The question then arose for the government whether any steps ought to be taken by them, and, if any, what steps, to answer the challenge—for it could not be called by any other name—which had been flung at them by Dr. Sacheverell. The wisest course, as we can all clearly see now, would have been to pay no attention whatever to the preacher, his sermons, or his pamphlets, to let them have their blaze of fame and then sink into obscurity. Even if this course was not taken, there might have been proceedings instituted against Sacheverell in the ordinary courts of law, without recognizing him as an antagonist important enough to call for the action of government and Parliament. It was believed at the time, and probably with good reason, that the wisest of Queen Anne's advisers, Somers, was opposed to the taking of any direct action by the crown and Parliament. This advice did not prevail, and it was understood that Godolphin had set himself against it. Some of Queen Anne's ministers were, no doubt, anxious to seize the opportunity of disclaiming any sympathy with the views expressed by Sacheverell. These men probably thought that public opinion was beginning to regard them as too well inclined to pander to the passions of the Tory mob, and were eager to put it on evidence that they were thoroughly sound constitutional statesmen of the new order. There can be no doubt, moreover, that a large proportion of the public was growing weary of the long war, with its recent lack of brilliant victories, and some of the Queen's advisers may have felt that a crisis was approaching which could not but end disastrously for them, and that they could not be any the worse if they were now to make a stand

SACHEVERELL

on something like a respectable constitutional principle.

One cannot help believing that Queen Anne herself must have felt in her heart a certain sympathy with the doctrines proclaimed by the preacher. Queen Anne was always a sincere believer in the principle of divine right, and although she was doing her best to perform with integrity her part as a constitutional sovereign under the new order of things, she had no more natural inclination for the principles of the revolution than she had for the Hanoverian succession. But whatever her secret feelings may have been, she was able to control them, and when the ministry determined on the impeachment of Sacheverell she put no difficulties in the way. It was arranged, therefore, that the House of Commons should move in the matter and obtain a decision for the impeachment of Sacheverell before the House of Lords. The whole question was raised in the House of Commons on December 13, 1709. A resolution was proposed and carried that Sacheverell should be impeached before the House of Lords on a charge of high crimes and misdemeanors, and a committee was nominated to prepare the articles of impeachment in due form. The promoters of the resolution had laid before the House two printed papers which were deemed evidence enough to justify the impeachment. The first of these was the famous sermon preached at St. Paul's, while the other was merely the dedication of the sermon preached at the Derby assizes on August 15, 1709. John Hill Burton explains that "the object of bringing up the dedication appears to have been, like the previous convictions cited against an ordinary criminal, to show that the great sermon was no single unpremeditated outburst, but that its author, in a distant province, when he addressed his own relations and personal friends, scattered around him the same perilous matter."

The preamble to the articles of impeachment made the charge against Sacheverell distinctly one of treason to the constitutional principles of the revolution and the Act of Settlement. The debate was long, and would probably have been considered very wearisome by any mere political or historical student who happened to listen to it. It was one of those debates which occur not infrequently even in our own times on occasions of great public crises when the desire of every man who takes part in the discussion is rather to make his own position clear to the outer world than to deal in arguments which may affect the immediate and practical issue. Every speaker seems to have acted on the assumption that the debate gave him a Heaven-sent opportunity of showing how loyal he was to the Act of Settlement and the Hanoverian succession, or, on the other hand, how incorruptibly devoted he was to the principles of a supreme state Church and a divinely inspired sovereign.

The debates dragged on for weeks and even for months. Thackeray, in one of his humorous ballads, has declared that even the trains on a certain English line of railway come in at last. The discussion on the proposed impeachment of Sacheverell came to an end at last, and then solemn preparations were made for the arraignment of the accused man before the House of Lords. Sacheverell might well have thought himself a proud man as he followed with mind or eye the progress of these preparations. Westminster Hall was to be the scene of the great ceremonial, that same hall whose vast and majestic enclosure had witnessed the trial of William Wallace and the trial of Charles

SACHEVERELL

the First, and was in a later generation to look upon the impeachment of Warren Hastings. A court for the business of the trial was constructed in the hall, and a cabinet was partitioned off for the reception of the Queen herself, which she could enter without being seen by the crowd. It was made known that Queen Anne took a deep interest in the proceedings, and desired to be present at the trial as often as her other engagements would allow.

The business of each day was opened by a solemn procession of the peers from their own House, and the procession moved in regulated order, led by the parliamentary officials, and after these the peers according to their rank and order, the nobles of greatest rank closing up the procession of peers. When any question arose which involved some disputed point of law or of procedure, the peers did not discuss the subject in Westminster Hall itself, but withdrew to their own House and returned to the public court when they had made up their minds as to their decision. The greatest public interest was aroused by the knowledge of the fact that the Queen intended to be present as often as possible during the progress of the trial, and it was the opinion of many that her presence was another tribute to the popularity of the preacher, and was evidence of a personal sympathy with the doctrines for the utterance of which he was put upon his trial. Bishop Burnet tells us that each day as Sacheverell stood at the bar "many of the Queen's chaplains stood about him, encouraging and magnifying him; and it was given out that the Queen herself favored him; though, upon my first coming to town, which was after the impeachment was brought up to the Lords, she said to me that it was a bad sermon, and that he deserved well to be punished for it."

Whatever doubt there may be as to the sentiments of the sovereign, there could be no doubt whatever as to the sentiments of the London mob. There were processions every day of a less august and ceremonious order than those which the peers made from their own chamber to Westminster Hall and back again, and these were the processions of the crowds who accompanied Sacheverell to and from Westminster Hall. Sacheverell lived in the Temple, and he took care to pass through the Strand on his way to and from Westminster Hall. He went in a sort of state coach, through the windows of which he could easily be seen as he passed along. Such a carriage would naturally have attracted public attention if it only contained a Lord Mayor or a foreign ambassador. But it was accompanied on the first day of its movement by a crowd of especial friends, who conducted themselves as if they were the body-guard of the preacher going to his trial. Of course the whole population of that quarter of London knew perfectly well that Sacheverell was about to take his trial, and the very first day that his state carriage made its appearance in the streets with its escort of friends there could be no doubt in the mind of any passer-by that the accused preacher was the occupant of this ostentatious vehicle. Therefore an enormous crowd, growing greater and greater with every moment, soon gathered around and followed Sacheverell's coach, impeded its progress by their mere multitude, and proclaimed to all the inhabitants of the quarter, by enthusiastic shouting and cheering, that the hero of the hour was on his way. Cheers for the High Church and Sacheverell, from thousands and thousands of throats, awakened the echoes even in far-distant streets and brought new crowds to try to force their way into the great thoroughfares through which his triumphal procession had to pass.

One can easily imagine how these tumultuous demonstrations in favor of Sacheverell began to deepen and darken in their character and to become more ferocious and dangerous with each succeeding day. The acclamations for the popular hero were soon mingled with wild and vehement denunciations of all those who were supposed to be his enemies and his persecutors. Public men, even prelates who were believed by the mob to be in favor of Sacheverell's impeachment, were hooted, execrated, and threatened with bodily injury as they endeavored to make their way into Westminster Hall, and many a harmless passenger was knocked down and beaten merely because he refused to pull off his hat or was slow about pulling it off as Sacheverell's state carriage passed along, or because he did not seem to join with sufficient energy and good-will in the acclamations for the High Church and the idol of the hour. The uproused and infuriate spirit of the mob could not, however, content itself for very long with cheers for Sacheverell and curses or blows for any unlucky by-stander who did not seem to engage quite readily in the demonstrations of hero-worship. The passion of the crowd soon began to need some more definite objects on which to expend its fury. There was no need to look far or long for such objects. Were there not to be seen in all quarters of the town the chapels and meeting-houses of the various dissenting denominations, and were not these most legitimate objects on which to make effective demonstration of High Church principles?

Bishop Burnet tells us that "there happened to be a meeting-house near me, out of which they drew everything that was in it, and burned it before the door of the house." Indeed, the Bishop was threatened with a similar illustration of mob fury, for he tells us that " they threatened to do the like execution on my house; but the noise of the riot coming to Court, orders were sent to the Guards to go about and disperse the multitudes, and secure the public peace. As the Guards advanced the people ran away, some few were only taken; these were afterwards prosecuted, but the party showed a violent concern for them; two of them were condemned as guilty of High Treason, small fines were set on the rest, but no execution followed; and after some months, they were pardoned." As Burnet goes on to say, " this remissness in punishing so great a disorder was looked on as the preparing and encouraging men to new tumults." Burnet declares that the mob, in many of their outrages, were directed " by some of better fashion . . . who followed the mob in hackney-coaches, and were seen sending messages to them." He mentions one little incident of which he was a witness. "Before my own door, one, with a spade, cleft the skull of another, who would not shout as they did."

The tumult rose to extraordinary dimensions, and at last took the form of an organized attack on all the chapels and meeting-houses of the dissenting denominations which happened to be within reach. Day after day these scenes were witnessed. It became a regular part of what may be called the pageantry of the occasion that, after the mob had escorted Sacheverell safely to Westminster Hall, they immediately turned back and sought out some dissenting chapel, in order to wreak their vengeance on it. In New Court, near Drury Lane, there stood the meeting-house of a conspicuous nonconformist minister. The mob sacked the building completely; carried away all its furniture, and made a huge fire of it in Lincoln's Inn Fields. This is only one incident out of many which might be described as the doings of that particular day. Just the same story would have to be told of several other meeting-houses in various quarters of the town.

Of course, it was not long before the news of these outrageous disturbances reached the ears of the Queen, and she seems to have behaved with much sense and spirit. She sent for Lord Sunderland, one of her secretaries of state, and commanded him to send her Guards, horse and foot, at once to disperse the mob. It was nightfall when the conference took place between the Queen and her Secretary of State, and Sunderland, who did not seem very eager to act in the business, made some excuse on the ground that it would be dangerous to leave her Majesty's palace unguarded at such a moment. The Queen quietly answered that God would be her guard, and told the Secretary of State to do his duty. Whatever the Queen's secret feelings may have been with regard to the doctrines preached by Sacheverell, it is only justice to her to say that she could be every inch a queen when it was needful to maintain the authority of the laws and to put down the temporary rule of a raging mob. Sunderland, however, seems to have found some difficulty in putting the Queen's orders into execution. Some officers in command had, apparently, got the idea into their minds that there was no very serious desire on the part of the authorities to come down too severely on the supporters of Sacheverell, and even stipulated that the orders should be given by the Secretary of State in writing, and that the officers should not be held responsible for the consequences of energetic action. Lord Sunderland would appear to have had a very reasonable apprehension that the fury of the mob, if not soon repressed, might become inspired by something more than a purely religious zeal, and might not content itself with attacks on dissenting chapels and meeting-houses. The Secretary of State, we read, told one of the officers in command that he had better send a body of troops to take care of the Bank.

Of course, when the military power was really put into operation the disturbances soon came to an end. The Guards easily dispersed the crowds who were making bonfires in Drury Lane and Lincoln's Inn Fields with the wreckage of the dissenting chapels. Then they moved on to the City and found another mob disporting itself at Blackfriars over another work of destruction. The Guards charged this crowd, wounding some of them with their sabres and capturing others, and, as usually happens in such cases, the majority of the rioters, finding that the authorities were really in earnest at last, scattered themselves in flight and left the neighborhood in comparative quiet. We may anticipate the course of events so far as to say that no great pains were taken to discover the real ringleaders of these riotous outbreaks, and that the offenders against public law, even when captured and convicted, were not visited with any very severe penalties. The authorities probably found themselves well contented when the actual rioting was brought to a close, and were not particularly anxious to trouble themselves overmuch with elaborate perquisitions or prosecutions.

Meanwhile the impeachment before the House of Lords went along its formal way. The Queen's ministers were made the managers of the impeachment, at least they had the nominal charge of the proceedings. Sacheverell was defended by several of the leading counsel of the day, and he was also allowed to deliver a speech in his own defence. There was no need for the production and examination of witnesses, for the sermons and dedications contained all the evidence that was necessary for the purposes of the trial. The arguments on both sides were, therefore, arguments as to the full and real meaning of this or that impugned and defended passage in the printed pamphlets. Sacheverell delivered a written speech in his own defence, which, according to Bishop Burnet, " he read with much bold heat; in which, with many solemn asseverations, he justified his intentions towards the Queen and her government; he spoke with respect, both of the revolution and the Protestant succession; he insisted most on condemning all resistance, under any pretence whatsoever, without mentioning the exception of extreme necessity, as his counsel had done; he said it was the doctrine of the Church in which he was bred up; and added many pathetical expressions, to move the audience to compassion." Burnet adds that " it was very plain the speech was made for him by others; for the style was correct, and far different from his own."

When the actual trial was ended the House of Lords set to debate the question of the impeachment. The Bench of Bishops was divided on the question, some of the prelates speaking, as Burnet puts it, " in excuse of Sacheverell," while Burnet himself and several others took the opposite side. When the division was taken on the distinct question of impeachment — in other words, whether Sacheverell was guilty or not guilty of the charges brought against him—sixty-nine peers voted for the condemnation and fifty-two against it. Then came the question as to the amount of punishment to be imposed upon the convicted offender. It was proposed to suspend him from preaching for one year, but another proposition was made that the suspension should be extended to six years. Finally it was carried by vote that the period of suspension should be only three years. A motion was then made that Sacheverell should be declared incapable of any preferment during those three years, and a division was taken which ended in the proposed disqualification being rejected by the very narrow majority of sixty votes against fifty-nine. Then it was ordered that the sermon should be burned in the presence of the Lord Mayor and the sheriffs of London. This order was carried out, but not in the actual presence of the Lord Mayor. That distinguished functionary, whose connection with the original publication was, as we have already seen, a matter not fully cleared up, seems to have made up his mind that, *pro hac vice,* he was essentially a member of the House of Commons and not a City magnate, and he therefore excused himself from attendance at the public cremation.

Then once again Sacheverell became the hero of the hour. The mildness of the judgment pronounced against him gave his enthusiastic supporters not unreasonable ground for regarding the result as a victory and not a defeat, and bonfires blazed and windows were illuminated and shouting crowds proclaimed the triumph of the preacher, not only in the metropolis, but in various cities and towns, and, indeed, all over the whole country. Addresses of congratulation poured in upon Sacheverell from all quarters, and wherever he travelled for some time to come his journey was like a triumphal procession. The sermons, their publication, and their impeachment were destined yet to have important political consequences, but Sacheverell himself may be allowed to pass out of this history. Not many years after he was selected by the House of

SACHEVERELL

Commons to preach a sermon on a great public occasion, and received the especial thanks of the House for his services. He was appointed to a rich rectory in Holborn, and although the passionate enthusiasm about him had somewhat faded in the mean time, he must have had good reason for being well content with the practical results of his career. But so far as this narrative is concerned that comet of a season had ceased to blaze.

CHAPTER XVII

"HARLEY, THE NATION'S GREAT SUPPORT"

MEANWHILE events were occurring which seemed at one time destined to exercise a serious influence on the career of Robert Harley. One of these was the event which is recorded as the treason of Gregg. The story would be a curious one in itself even if it had not led to a momentous crisis in the fortunes of a successful minister. A distinguished French exile, Tallard, had been carrying on a secret correspondence from London with the French Minister of War. His letters were forwarded through the foreign department of the Secretary of State in London, and it was understood that every care was taken to see that the correspondence contained no matter which it would have been unsuitable for the English government to send out. For some reason or other it appears that one of the letters, bearing date the 28th of November, 1707, became an object of suspicion on its way through Holland, and was opened there. It was found to carry in it the clearest evidence that a clerk named Gregg, engaged in the foreign department of the Secretary of State, had been inserting letters of his own in some of the correspondence before sealing it up. A letter from Gregg thus despatched contained a distinct offer to place his services at the disposal of the French government and the Stuart exiles in France for the supply of secret information as to the purposes and

"HARLEY, THE NATION'S GREAT SUPPORT"

plans of the English government. In order to prove that he really could make himself the master of important secret information, Gregg enclosed a copy of a letter written in the Queen's own hand and addressed to the German Emperor. The Queen's letter urged upon the Emperor the importance of sending Prince Eugene at once into Spain, and Gregg's copy of it, if it had not been intercepted on its way, would have reached the French court at Versailles several days before the letter itself could arrive in Vienna. Thus the French government, the government of the country with which England was at war, would have obtained a knowledge of the military movements contemplated by England before that policy could have been made known and commended to the Emperor, her ally.

Gregg had peculiar advantages for the carrying out of his plans, inasmuch as the letters sent home to France by French prisoners of war in the charge of the English government passed regularly through his hands. It was, of course, only thought courteous and fair that French prisoners should be allowed to write to their friends at home, but at the same time it was absolutely necessary that all such letters should come under the eyes of some accredited English official in order that they might not convey any information which could be of service to the French military authorities. Gregg had been holding a position of absolute confidence in the Secretary of State's office, and if his plans had not been discovered in time he might have enabled the French government to anticipate and to counteract many an important movement which the ministers of Queen Anne were preparing. In the very letter which contained the copy of the Queen's missive, Gregg gave many particulars about the manner in which that document had been obtained from the Queen and the alterations which had been made in the original draft before it was finally copied out in Anne's own handwriting. He seems to have made up his mind that if he were to commit an act of treason he might as well make it as complete in its treason as he possibly could. Gregg was instantly charged with high treason and put upon his trial. He saw at once that the game was up, and he promptly pleaded guilty. There could be no possible defence as the case actually stood, and although he could not hope to escape extreme punishment by the mere admission of his crime, he may perhaps have had interest enough in the Stuart cause to make him anxious that no prolonged judicial investigation should lead to any further discovery as to his plots and his accomplices.

The House of Lords intervened at this stage of the proceedings, and sent an address to the Queen urging that for the future safety of the kingdom everything should be done "to find out the rise and progress of this dangerous correspondence." The Lords requested that all the papers in the possession of the government which could help them in their investigation should be laid before them, and their request was at once complied with. The Lords then appointed a committee of their own House to carry on the inquiry. Some of the information which they received threw a startling light on the manner in which business was conducted in one of the most important departments of the Queen's administration. It came out that the man Gregg, who had been employed in such delicate and confidential work, was a person not merely without credit or character, but had actually been a professional criminal in his time, and had been put on his trial as a coiner of false money and convicted of the crime. His people were of the poorest and humblest class, but he was a native of Scotland, and like most natives of Scotland, even at that time, he had obtained a good education to begin with. He had sought again and again for employment in the office of the Secretary of State, and at last had succeeded in obtaining it. He was to some extent taken up by Harley, and it was even stated that he had sometimes made himself very useful to Harley by pointing out defects in the style of some of the despatches which he had been ordered to copy, and by correcting Harley's bad French.

When the story of Gregg's early life became known through the inquiry of the Lords' committee, it need hardly be said that a good many people in England made invidious comment on his Scottish birth, and declared that if he had not been a Scotchman he would never have been so readily admitted to ministerial patronage. At that time, as at other times, there was a certain jealousy of Scottish influence among many classes in England, and it was a common doctrine that the canny Scot could always find patronage which was denied to the honest but unfavored Englishman. The general impression was not likely to lose much of its force when it came out, in the course of the investigations, that Gregg had been employed by the Secretary of State as a confidential agent when the arrangements for the union with Scotland were in progress, to descend upon Scotland and find out how the public opinion of that country was divided with regard to the proposed union of the two kingdoms. Evidently a man employed in such a capacity must have been intrusted by the Secretary of State with the pursuit of many private inquiries which the government would not have cared to submit fully to parliamentary and public notice. That such a man should have been intrusted with the reading and forwarding of all letters sent by French prisoners of war and other French exiles back to their own country, and with the power of transmitting or detaining the documents, seemed to bring Harley into something like a direct responsibility for the actions of his subordinate. The time was full of trouble. France was actually at war with England, and while it would hardly have been fair or even decent conduct to prevent distinguished prisoners of war from keeping up any communication with their families, yet it seemed quite evident that the man who had charge of forwarding or withholding such letters might, if he were so inclined, have allowed much news to be carried to France which ought to have been kept back in the interest of France's greatest enemy, England.

When it became clear from actual facts, and even from Gregg's own confession, that he had made use of the opportunities given by the confidence reposed in him to send to the French court a copy of a royal letter addressed to the German Emperor, then it was impossible that people should not ask themselves whether the Secretary of State was himself a willing party to such a betrayal of state confidence. The progress of the war with France had not for some time been quite satisfactory to the people of England. It was still believed, and indeed was still known, that there were in Scotland, and especially in the northern parts of the country, many men of leading position who were devoted to the Stuart cause. At one time a great alarm was aroused in England by the news that a French fleet was actually about to invade the English shores, with the object of compelling the English government to bring back Marlborough and a portion of his troops for the defence of the island, and with the

"HARLEY, THE NATION'S GREAT SUPPORT"

hope, it was believed by many, of creating a rising in Scotland on behalf of the exiled Stuarts. The project came to nothing, for the English government had learned enough about it to enable them to send a fleet to sea which marred all the chances of the French expedition; but the minds of men in England were much disturbed by this new scheme on the part of King Louis, and were ready to believe that treachery or treason of some kind must have helped to create it.

Not very much came of the examination of Gregg beyond what the intercepted letter and his own confession had already made known to the public. The peers who were nominated to conduct the commission of inquiry must have been disappointed if they expected to get any evidence of a great and organized treasonable plot. The truth would seem to be that Gregg had but lately begun his treacherous work, that he was acting entirely on his own account, and was not a member of any secret organization. He told the committee that the state papers used to lie so carelessly on the desks and tables of the Secretary's office that anybody going in or out of the room might have read them if he pleased, and that it was open to all the doorkeepers to make such a study if they felt so inclined. He stated that Harley's custom was to come to the office late on certain nights and write his letters there, and that when he had written them he took his departure at once, and left the letters or other state papers to be copied after he had gone. It was in this way, Gregg declared, that he himself had come to see the Queen's letter to the Emperor. He volunteered the information that he might, if he had thought fit, have communicated to the French government some important movements designed by England several months before, but he told the committee that, as a matter of fact, he had not then taken to his evil practices, and therefore did not make any treasonable use of his opportunity.

Now it was generally known of Harley that he was one of the most careless of men; that he was given to taking most things for granted, and when an order of any kind had been issued by his department he had got into the way of thinking that the order would be properly carried out in due course, and that there was no need for him to trouble himself any further about its execution. He had often the air and manner of a noon-day dreamer; of a man whose mind and thoughts are engaged on something quite different from the matter actually in hand; and this was sometimes his way even when he was engaged on the most important affairs of state. All this, it should be said, was now pointed out and dwelt upon, not so much by Harley's enemies as by Harley's friends, for it was thus that the friends went about to explain the utter lack of system and of proper watchfulness in the department over which he had control. His friends, in fact, pleaded for him by saying: "You know what sort of a man Harley is; you know that he often becomes for the time a mere John o' Dreams, and the greatest irregularities might go on in his office and under his very eyes without his knowing anything about them or having any suspicion that such things might occur."

This was the defence made by Harley's friends, for the reason that Harley's enemies were beginning to find a very different explanation of his conduct, and were actually going the length of saying that his heart was all the time with the cause of the Stuarts, and that he was only too willing to connive at lending a helping hand to them and to the state which had given them shelter and recognition. The investigations of the committee were spread over several weeks, and the report was then presented to the House of Lords, who sent it on to the Queen, in which was strongly urged upon her the necessity of making Gregg a public example by exemplary punishment. It should be stated that Gregg, in his confessions, expressly declared that Harley had nothing whatever to do with his treasonable practices and had no knowledge of their existence. The Queen was naturally a very good-natured woman, but she did not find it possible to resist the recommendation of the Lords for the punishment of the man convicted by the evidence, and upon his own confession. Gregg was sentenced to death, and executed. "He died," Burton says, "much better than he had lived." It is stated that Harley behaved with generous charity to the widow of the unfortunate man whom Harley's own negligence had probably tempted into crime, and that he made her an allowance of fifty pounds a year out of his own private means.

The Queen now found herself placed in a position of great difficulty. Harley felt that after what had happened he could not possibly continue just then to hold office, and he made known to the Queen that he must ask her permission to resign. Marlborough and Godolphin had already urged upon the Queen that she could not retain Harley any longer in her service, and they had called her attention to many perilous irregularities, quite apart from the treasonable practices of Gregg, which had been allowed to go on in his department. Anne still desired to hold by Harley, and for a while she positively refused to give him up. Harley actually attended a meeting of the cabinet council at which the Queen was present. Marlborough was not present, and the Duke of Somerset bluntly declared that it would be impossible in his absence to discuss any question of foreign policy with the slightest practical advantage. Other members seemed to agree in his opinion, and such a general feeling of dissatisfaction and unwillingness prevailed that the meeting of the council soon came to an end, without any result other than that which must have been wrought on the Queen's own mind. Marlborough and Godolphin had already informed the Queen that they could no longer remain in her service if Harley were permitted to retain his office. Perhaps she might have held out to the last but for Harley's own resolve that it would be impossible for him just then to think of holding his place. That fact seems to have decided her course, and when Marlborough and Godolphin came to confer with her again and repeated their announcement that they could not possibly continue in her service if Harley were retained in office, Anne informed them that her mind had already been made up and that Harley could not continue to hold his place as one of her advisers.

Other influences also were beginning to prevail over the mind of the Queen. There were peculiar qualities in the temperament and character of Anne. It sometimes seems as if she had a double sort of nature—as if she were made up of two minds and two hearts in the one human form. Her womanly sympathies, her personal sympathies, were undoubtedly with the Tories, and not only with the Tories but with the Jacobites. That was, in fact, Anne the woman. But then Anne the sovereign was quite a different sort of person, and had an understanding which conformed entirely with the position of a constitutional ruler. Anne the sovereign had intelligence enough to understand that the days of divine right had quite gone by for England, and the days of constitutional monarchy had come into

"HARLEY, THE NATION'S GREAT SUPPORT"

being. Anne the woman was a devout believer in the divine right of kings, but Anne the Queen was able to recognize and accept established facts, and to see that an English monarch could thenceforward only rule by popular support and by acting upon the advice of a minister who might be supposed to study and represent the public opinion of the country. The explanations generally given of Anne's sudden changes in policy and in advisers set her down merely as a woman who had to be governed by the rule of some favorite, and was incapable of initiating any course of conduct for herself. It is quite certain that Anne loved to yield herself to the domination of some will more strong and masterly than her own, and that it was a relief to her to give herself up, for the time, at least, to such a personal guidance. But this theory alone is not enough to supply a full explanation of Anne's occasional changes in policy and conduct. The more fair, and, on the whole, the more reasonable, explanation is that which we have suggested, that Queen Anne the woman and Queen Anne the sovereign had different inclinings, and that the sovereign sometimes had the better in the contest.

It would have been impossible that a woman brought up as Anne had been brought up could by any effort of growing observation and intelligence shake herself completely free from all the traditions of her ancestry and the teachings and habitudes of her early days. But, on the other hand, she was, with all her weaknesses and her many errors of judgment, quite too intelligent and reasonable a woman not to recognize, in her brighter and better moods, the fact that a new system of monarchical government had set in for the country which she was called upon to rule. Even in her weakest moods she had a far better understanding as to the duties of a constitutional sovereign than was shown by any monarch of the house of Hanover down to the days when William the Fourth saw himself compelled to surrender his own most cherished convictions to the advice of his ministers. It is beyond question, however, that in her repugnance to the course she took with regard to Harley's resignation she was much influenced by the advice and guidance of the new favorite whom she had allowed to obtain dominion over her. When the crisis came, and she saw that it was necessary for her as a constitutional sovereign, she yielded to the pressure of the emergency; but she never changed in her inclinations towards Harley, and Harley probably felt he had good reason to believe that the sun of court favor for him was only undergoing a temporary eclipse, and that it would, before very long, shine out more brightly than ever.

We find it somewhat hard to understand at this distance of time how Harley ever came to be accounted a really great statesman. That he had intellectual qualities may be taken for granted when we remember the praise he received from men of genius and understanding, who would never have showered their compliments on him merely for the reason that he had come to be a power in the state. We cannot find any evidence that he represented great political ideas or that he had any conception of England's true national policy. He was a remarkable and astute manager of parties and of parliamentary affairs, but in the higher and nobler sense of the word he does not seem to have been a statesman at all. He could make his Tory principles so far subservient to his political ends and personal ambitions as to be willing to work in that sort of coalition which, according to one of the cleverest of later parliamentary leaders, England always de-

"HARLEY, THE NATION'S GREAT SUPPORT"

tests. He could for immediate purposes cry content to that which grieved his heart, if we may apply to him the expression which Shakespeare puts into the mouth of a very different historical personage. He could help to carry on a war with which he had no manner of sympathy because his adoption of a policy which in his heart he detested enabled him to hold office and to direct affairs of state. Perhaps, if he inwardly reasoned about the matter at all, he may have come to the comfortable conclusion that, as the war certainly had to go on, and as he was quite powerless to stop it, it might as well go on under his management as under that of anybody else. Even when he seemed to go the whole way in recognizing the new state of things which had arisen and in accepting the constitutional principle of government, we know that he was all the time still hoping and waiting for some turn of affairs which might enable him to help in bringing about a Stuart restoration.

Harley was seen, no doubt, at his best among those who knew him in private life and had little or nothing to do with affairs of state. He was a lover of books—perhaps it might be said rather a lover of books than of reading—he had an appreciation of art, and enjoyed the conversation of scholars and poets. In the company of such men the finer and better qualities of his nature came out, and his literary companions were not compelled to think of the shifts and dodges, the private and ignoble influences, the swallowing not merely of formulas, as Carlyle might have put it, but of actual principles in order to maintain himself at least in power even while he could not maintain himself in office. For the moment his rule had come to an end, but no doubt he was enabled to assure the Queen that she would not have to wait very long for his return to office. So Queen Anne put up with the change of affairs as well as she could, but did not attempt to conceal from Marlborough and Godolphin that she grieved at the condition of things which had compelled her to yield to their representations. For the present the words used by the Duke of Somerset at that meeting of the Privy Council over which the Queen had just presided gave a perfectly accurate description of the crisis. There was no going on without Marlborough and Godolphin. The war had to be fought out, and Marlborough was the only man who could conduct it to anything like success, and Godolphin was the best manager of the national resources who could be found in England at such a time. So Marlborough and Godolphin had their way, and Harley went out of power, but which of the conflicting parties was to have the better fate only the high gods, as Socrates said to his judges, could tell.

Meanwhile it is necessary to say something about the new influence which had come over the moods and actions of the Queen. The rule of the Duchess of Marlborough was over. The favorite who had now come into power was a very different sort of creature. One can well understand the sway which a woman like the Duchess of Marlborough obtained over the mind of the Queen, for a woman who could govern Marlborough himself may be set down as capable of governing almost any one. There was no one with whom Sarah Jennings ever came into companionship who did not feel the influence of her charm, her humors, her versatility, and even her audacious self-assertion. But the impulse to self-assertion may easily be carried too far, more especially when the subject is dealing with a sovereign princess, and this was the one defect which filled the Duchess of Marlborough

"HARLEY, THE NATION'S GREAT SUPPORT"

with faults. Hers was a very passion of self-assertion, and it was coupled with an extremely bad temper. Because she had ruled the Queen so long she had got into the way of believing that there was a sort of divine right sustaining her rule, and that Anne could not, under any provocation, dare to rise in rebellion against her. Because she had found Anne yielding, submissive, and glad to be governed, she had got it into her head that the Queen would put up with being bullied and trampled on, and there her spirit of domination overleaped itself and fell on the other side. Anne was ready to give up a good deal of her own way for the sake of being made comfortable in her own way, but she could not long submit to being made uncomfortable for nothing. The rule of the Duchess would probably have come to a close before very long, in any case; for as soon as Queen Anne found that she was being made constantly uncomfortable, the spirit of revolt was certain to rise within her. In this instance, however, a rival had come on the scene, and the convenient entrance of a rival naturally suggested to Anne the possibility of relief from her state of aggravated subjection.

There was a period of French history when the King of France was said to have passed under the successive reigns of three petticoats. In that sense Queen Anne may be said to have passed under the reigns of two petticoats, the one typified by the Duchess of Marlborough and the other by the new favorite, Mrs. Masham. The worst of it, for the Duchess of Marlborough, was that she herself had been the means of introducing to the Queen's notice the very woman by whose influence she was destined to be supplanted in the Queen's favor and in the right of dictating the policy and the movements of the Queen. Abigail Hill, who afterwards became Mrs. Masham, was a cousin of the Duchess, and a very needy woman, and the Duchess thought she was doing a good service to her own family when she obtained for her poor relation employment in the Queen's household. Abigail Hill was made bedchamber-woman to the Queen, and nothing could have been further from the mind of the Duchess than any suspicion that this exercise of her personal influence was ever likely to bring about a serious disadvantage to herself.

Miss Hill appears to have been a woman of gentle and genial manners, who made herself agreeable to all with whom she came into contact, and showed herself especially devoted to the promotion of Queen Anne's personal ease and comfort. There must have been something refreshing and delightful to the Queen in the close companionship of a woman who could influence her without causing her any discomfort, who had the faculty of guiding, when she seemed only to be guided and to obey. Gradually and insensibly the Queen found the close society of Miss Hill becoming more and more essential to her daily happiness, and it must have been the opening of a new chapter of life to her to have a woman always at her side who could tell her what to do without seeming to dictate to her, who could show her the way to go without pushing her along that path, and could prescribe a course of policy for her without cramming the prescription down her throat.

Thus the companionship between Queen Anne and her new friend grew and grew steadily for a long time without exciting the least suspicion or jealousy in the mind of the domineering Duchess. Sarah Jennings would probably as soon have thought of some respectable regimental officer becoming a military rival of the

"HARLEY, THE NATION'S GREAT SUPPORT"

Duke of Marlborough as of Abigail Hill rising to be a rival of Marlborough's Duchess in the favor of Queen Anne. The story goes that the Duchess only began to realize the actual condition of affairs when she suddenly heard that Abigail Hill had been privately married to a gentleman of the Queen's household named Masham, that Queen Anne herself had been present at the marriage ceremony, and that it had all been done without any appeal for the advice or the approval of the Duchess herself. Mrs. Masham was not merely a cousin of the Duchess of Marlborough, but was also a cousin of Robert Harley—a fact which came to have an important bearing on the political history of the reign.

It may be said, in passing, that Mrs. Masham does not seem to have always retained the gentle and considerate temper which is understood to have been for a long time her chief recommendation to the favor of Queen Anne. One historical writer bluntly describes her as "vulgar and mean in her manners, petulant and passionate." But she probably knew when and with whom to be petulant and passionate, and she certainly did not make exhibition of petulance or passion in her early intercourse with Queen Anne. The Queen, indeed, had acquired so great a dread of such qualities in a favorite that when it was first proposed to her that Mr. Masham should be raised to the peerage she met the suggestion with a flat refusal, declaring that she never intended to make a peeress of Mrs. Masham, on the ground that if she did so she should only lose a useful servant and get a grand lady in her place. Anne was afterwards induced to change her mind in this instance, as in many others, but the mere objection which she raised to the suggestion was enough to show that experience had filled her with a reasonable dread lest in seeking for a confidential adviser and a faithful servant she might only find a self-opinionated and ostentatious ruler. It soon became clear enough to those who were around the court that the rule of the Duchess of Marlborough was drawing to a close, and that she was destined before long to be formally supplanted by her poor relation who happened also to be the cousin of Robert Harley.

The force of events, therefore, private and public, was working silently in the one domain and very noisily in the other—for the personal importance of the statesman who had been put out of office. Then came the Sacheverell episode and the passionate popular declarations in favor of Church and state, and in favor, likewise, of the principle of non-resistance. All these public demonstrations aroused a sympathetic echo in the mind and the heart of Queen Anne. The Queen had accepted the war with France only because it seemed at the time too widely and intensely popular to give her any hope of successfully setting up her own will and her own principles against it. Now she thought she found in the outburst of apparently unmingled public enthusiasm for Sacheverell a direct appeal to her to come forward and put herself at the head of her people by asserting her own predilections and maintaining her own favorite advisers.

Harley was kept well informed as to the moods and hopes of the Queen, and it was easy for him to put on the manner of one who bears with truly philosophical composure a retirement into political exile. Nothing suited Harley's turn of mind better than the opportunity of thus enacting the part of a philosopher and affecting utter indifference to the loss of high office, when all the while he had good reason for the comfortable conviction that it was only a question of time,

"HARLEY, THE NATION'S GREAT SUPPORT"

and not of very long time, when he should be invited once again to mount his ministerial throne and make his enemies his footstool. Lord Palmerston once described a certain political crisis of his time as destined to make him "the inevitable." Robert Harley must have felt before he had long been out of office that a crisis was coming in the movement of events around him which was destined to make him "the inevitable." It was easy and must have been to him very delightful, under such conditions and with such prospects, to posture before his friends as one whose philosophic temperament uplifts and sustains him above the disappointments which might have broken the spirit and bowed the head of a less serenely minded statesman.

About this time, too, Bolingbroke was playing the part of a philosopher in retirement. He had followed the footsteps of Harley in retirement more or less enforced from office. We find him writing to a noble friend a letter in which he discourses on recent events and on his present mood of mind. "My health," he says, "which you are so kindly concerned for, is extremely good. Those opportunities of spoiling it are at a distance; and to own the truth, as I have them seldomer so I want them less. You see, My Lord, one effect of my retreat. The men of profound wisdom form to themselves a scheme of life; and every action is preceded by a thought. We who are of a more ordinary size of understanding act by chance at first and by habit afterwards." Bolingbroke, however, had much of the genius of a philosopher, and the mood of contented retirement came as natural to him in its turn as the active, unresting spirit of a leader of men in the world of politics. He, too, could probably see, at least as easily as Harley could, that the world of politics was not likely to do without him for long.

CHAPTER XVIII

THE TRIUMPH OF THE TORIES

QUEEN ANNE had to bear a heavy trial in the autumn of 1708. Her husband, Prince George of Denmark, had been suffering from a severe asthmatic malady, and during his illness the Queen nursed him with constant and affectionate care. His illness proved mortal. The state lost nothing by the death of Prince George, for he was at best only a harmless, muddle-headed sort of man, who had been put to hold high commands for which his capacity and temperament gave him no qualification, and the most that could be said in his favor was that he had not done so much mischief to the state as might have been done by a more meddlesome person placed in the same position. The Queen loved him, however, and, indeed, her affection for him was one of her few strongly developed qualities. It may be mentioned here that, after a decorous interval, addresses were presented by both Houses of Parliament to the widowed Queen requesting her to turn her thoughts towards a second marriage, and that the Queen, in graceful, touching, but decisive words, declared that it was impossible for her to act on the recommendation.

At this time the most eminent among the leaders of the Whig party, the Whig Junto, as it was called, was undoubtedly Lord Somers. He was a man who had risen from a comparatively humble position, but his

THE TRIUMPH OF THE TORIES

great natural capacity, his integrity, his reputation for benevolence and generosity, and his winning manners had gained for him gradually a commanding place in public life. His profession was that of a barrister, and he had early attained to a high position at the bar. He acted as one of the counsel for the seven bishops in the momentous and memorable trial, and after the revolution he became Solicitor-General, Attorney-General, and Lord Keeper of the Great Seal, and finally Lord Chancellor, with the title of Baron Somers of Evesham. There was no statesman in whom William the Third showed a greater confidence, but the position which he had won in public affairs and the favor which his sovereign was showing to him naturally made him many enemies, and some of the most powerful of these succeeded in creating a party against him and made him an object of frequent attack.

Some charges were brought against him, and the story of one of them, at least, is worth recalling here, although it belongs to the history of the previous reign. The extreme Tories and Jacobites, who found Somers all the more formidable as an opponent because of his moderation and his impartiality, got up an accusation in connection with an event for which he had no moral responsibility whatever, and concerning which, even if he could be shown to have had any responsibility, the burden must have been equally shared by other advisers of the King and even by the sovereign himself. There had been some trouble about threatened piratical attacks on British commerce by the Great Mogul, as the Tartar or Indian sovereign was then called, and King William was advised to charter privateer vessels to defend the merchant shipping of England. One of the men appointed to take the command of a privateer for this service was a Captain

Kidd, who has in later days been made the hero of many a romance, and whose exploits, real or imaginary, have delighted whole generations of boyish readers. Now, the resources of the state were at that time rather heavily overtaxed, and there was no public money available for the expenses of the privateering. The King offered to advance a sum of money out of his own pocket, and Lord Somers, with several others of his Majesty's advisers, agreed to make up the necessary amount. As a matter of fact, it would appear that the King was not able, after all, to contribute his share of the fund, but Lord Somers and some of his colleagues made up the money between them. Now comes the critical point of the story. Captain Kidd, when he got his vessel and his command, threw over the service of King William, became a pirate on his own account, sailed the seas in quest of prizes for himself, and sailed likewise into a celebrity which has not even yet wholly faded from his name.

An outcry was raised against Somers by the extreme Jacobites and Tories not altogether unlike that which assailed the career of Harley when the discovery was made of Gregg's treasonable practices. As in the case of Harley, so in that of Somers, the statesman was made a victim for the offences of one in whom he, like others of his colleagues, had mistakenly put his trust. An attempt was made to impeach Somers on the ground that he had become a patron of piracy. To the eyes of modern readers such a proceeding would seem to be an outrageous absurdity, better suited for the realms of comic opera than for the serious business of Parliament. But the party passions of the time found any stone good enough to throw at a political opponent, and the agitation against Somers seemed to become really formidable. There was nothing for it, under these conditions, but that Somers should resign all his public offices and meet the charges against him, if charges there were to be, as an ordinary subject. King William would have stood by him if he were to follow his own inclination, just as Queen Anne would have stood by Harley, but in the one case as in the other the victimized statesman thought it better to retire than to bring public trouble on his sovereign. Several attempts were made in the House of Commons to get up an impeachment against Somers on the case of Captain Kidd, and on other charges which merely amounted to a condemnation of the advice he had given to his sovereign in several great questions of policy. The impeachments, however, which included other statesmen as well as Somers, came to nothing, and Somers out of office still remained a leader of the Whig party, and was always a power in the state. His name remains through all time a synonym for judicial and political integrity. For a while he lived a quiet life, withdrawn from any active part in public affairs, but more lately he had returned to his high place in politics.

Queen Anne felt well inclined to strengthen her councils by calling to her aid the services of such a man, and perhaps had then especially some faith in the possibility of governing the country by means of a ministry made up from the moderate men of both parties. She probably regarded Somers as the most likely of living Whigs to help her with her task, seeing that just at the moment there did not seem to be any chance for a Tory government, and she appointed Somers President of the Council. The ministry, therefore, was composed altogether of Whigs, and to the ordinary observer it might well have appeared as if the doors of office had been peremptorily closed, for a long time, against all who belonged to the Tory party.

But, as we have already seen, events were moving in different places and in different ways, events wholly independent of each other and not alike in character or in cause, which were destined to encourage and enable the Queen to effect a sort of constitutional *coup d'état* of her own, and recall to power the statesmen whose principles and whose counsels were congenial with hers. The reign of the Duchess of Marlborough was practically over, and that of Mrs. Masham had set in. The populace of London and of other great cities and towns had made a hero and an idol of Sacheverell, and notwithstanding all that Marlborough's genius as a commander could do, the war had lately been dragging on without any splendid victories to boast of and without any apparent prospect of soon coming to an end.

Marlborough himself had helped directly, although with no such purpose in his mind, to bring about the total overthrow of the party with whom he had lately been acting. He could not fail to see that the mind of the Queen was working in the direction of a complete change of ministry, and he probably feared that with the loss of personal favor to his wife and himself might come a change in the war policy which he had been carrying out, through so many difficulties, to the promise of a complete success. He therefore made up his mind to lay before the Queen and her advisers a proposal that his appointment as commander-in-chief should be converted into a life office for him. His enemies naturally suggested that this was but another illustration of Marlborough's ambition and avarice alike, and that he wanted to obtain a position which must give him a practical mastery not only over the Queen and her ministers, but over the whole state and the country. Now, it is beyond dispute that in a

THE TRIUMPH OF THE TORIES

kingdom professing constitutional government it would be out of the question to invest any private citizen, no matter how splendid his services and how high his position, with an appointment which would make him absolute master of the army and navy during the whole term of his life. A soldier of Marlborough's genius and success, if endowed with such powers, would unquestionably become the military dictator of the realm. Constitutional government had not at that time developed itself so fully as to offer any secure guarantee against the ambition of a military dictator, and the recent history of England itself told how a conquering soldier might become the crowned sovereign of the realm.

We have it on the excellent authority of the late Lord John Russell that the dethroned Emperor Napoleon, during his temporary exile in Elba, had had his mind possessed with the idea that the Duke of Wellington, if he should win any more great battles, would be certain to seize the crown of England and set it on his own head. Lord John Russell has told how, in his conversations with Napoleon in Elba, he found that this idea had got full hold of the illustrious exile's mind. Now, in the days of Napoleon such a fancy was, of course, an utter chimera, born of the dethroned Emperor's experience of his own people and ignorance of the conditions which had become settled in England. But in the reign of Queen Anne constitutionalism had not become so thoroughly established a principle of government as to preclude all possibility of a military dictator making himself master of the state. Thus, at least, it appeared to the political enemies of Marlborough, and even among his political friends the general conviction was that such a proposal could not possibly obtain acceptance. The Lord Chancellor of the day, a friend of Marlborough, told the Duke frankly that his proposal was utterly unconstitutional, and that he as Lord Chancellor could not venture to put the great seal to the patent which conferred such an appointment. Yet, on the other hand, it seems only fair to assume that Marlborough was not inspired by mere love of power or love of money, but by a genuine conviction that the appointment would be for the good of the country.

Marlborough's mind was naturally set on the successful completion of the war which he had conducted thus far. He was a man of genius, and he knew well that he and he alone could be relied upon for the full accomplishment of the task which he believed to be essential to the security and the greatness of his country. He had seen, over and over again, some of his best projects brought to failure by the changes of political parties and by private influences at home, by the doubtful, hesitating, and laggard ways of this or that ally, by the intervention of counsels over which he had no control, and by the reactionary movements of public opinion both at home and abroad. He may well have felt an earnest and unselfish conviction that if the war were to be brought to an end with anything like the result for which it had been undertaken by his country, he was the only man who could achieve such a triumph, and that it would be impossible even for him to achieve it if he were liable at any moment to be deprived of his command by a change of mood in the sovereign or in the sovereign's advisers.

Throughout the whole course of the war Marlborough had had to do the work of a diplomatist and a statesman, of an envoy and a political negotiator, as well as of a general in command. He was despatched over and over again to this or that foreign capital or foreign camp; he was summoned back to London again and again from the battle-field itself. We have ceased in this history to make any record of his visits to London, and have taken it for granted that the intelligence of our readers would enable them to understand without specific explanation that whenever Marlborough's counsels were needed at home Marlborough would be there at the right time to set them forth and to sustain them. The proposal he made was undoubtedly one which it would have been impossible for the Queen or her advisers to accept, but it seems only justice to the memory of a great man to assume that, whatever other errors his love of power and money may have led him into, this mistake at least came of general honest thought and common good to all. Marlborough disregarded the advice of the friends who warned him against pressing forward his proposal, and made his proposition to the Queen herself. Queen Anne was probably at this time not much inclined to listen with great favor to any suggestion coming from Marlborough, but we may credit her with a clear enough understanding as to the duties of a constitutional sovereign to make her refusal of such a demand quite certain. The Queen promptly and absolutely refused her consent to the scheme urged by Marlborough, and the dream of a military dictatorship for life came to a sudden end.

By this time it must have become quite clear to Marlborough's friends, as well as to his enemies, that his influence over the Queen was losing its power. The great soldier does not look to much advantage in the persistent and futile efforts which he made to retain the favor of the Queen for his wife. One does not like to think of the almost unrivalled commander soliciting, beseeching, and even begging of his royal mistress that his wife should not be dismissed from the places which she held in the Queen's household. But the Queen was quite resolute this time, and, indeed, the new influence she had accepted as her guiding power was strong enough just then to sustain her in any exercise of authority which came from its dictation. The Duchess of Marlborough was dismissed from all her offices, and the new favorite reigned supreme. Then came on a general election, and almost all the recent events, including, of course, the popular triumphs of Dr. Sacheverell, seemed as if specially destined to rouse up and bring into action the strong Tory feeling which filled the minds of so many people all over the country. A general election then did not reflect even the passing feeling of the hour with anything like the fidelity belonging to our time of household suffrage and cheap newspapers. But it did at least serve to reflect faithfully enough the political attitude of the limited class which alone was endowed with the franchise, and the opinions of those who were not thus favored counted for little in the estimation of sovereigns and statesmen. Moreover, the demonstrations of the unenfranchised populace, the crowds in the streets, proclaimed that the popular feeling was just then on the side of the Tory electoral majority.

Queen Anne thought she now saw her way clearly enough to accomplish an object which had long been dear to her heart, and to surround herself with Tory advisers. She did not at first desire to make a clean sweep of all her Whig ministers. She was willing and even anxious that Somers should retain his place, and she again and again urged Lord Cowper to remain in his position as Lord Chancellor. But both Somers and Cowper felt convinced that they could not, in justice to their colleagues, consent to be made exceptions to the general decree of the royal policy. The Whig leaders were resolute to stand or fall together, and the result was that their ministry came at once to an end, and that a new administration was formed which had Harley and Bolingbroke to guide it. Harley held the higher position of the two, and was, in fact, what we should now call prime-minister. In mental powers he was not to be compared with Bolingbroke, for Bolingbroke was a man of genius, and, intellectually at least, the greatest English statesman of his time.

The name of Bolingbroke stands out as distinctly among the leading men of Queen Anne's reign as does that of Marlborough himself. Judged by an exalted moral standard, there is not much to be said for Harley or Bolingbroke or Marlborough. Each man was, above all other things, a self-seeker; with each man his own personal ambitions and his own desires were the inspiring principles of action. But with Bolingbroke and Marlborough these grave defects were often lost to men's sight by the dazzling genius which fascinated while it conquered. Harley was just as much of a self-seeker as Bolingbroke or Marlborough, but the prosaic and commonplace composition of his intellect was not illumined by any ray of genius. Macaulay sums him up as "a solemn trifler," and the wonder which fills most readers when they study his career is a wonder how he could ever have contrived to pass himself off with his contemporaries as a high-minded and intellectual statesman. We see such men, however, rising to a prominent and even a commanding position in almost every political generation. With unlimited resources of self-satisfaction, a faculty for endowing commonplaces with an aspect of philosophic wisdom, and with an unquestioning conviction of their own right to a place in the front, such men have been prime-ministers before Harley was born and such men have been prime-ministers since Harley was laid in the grave.

Soon after the change of ministry had been accomplished, Harley came in for what proved to be a stroke of good fortune, although fortune delivered the stroke in a manner which at first seemed likely to be fatal. An attempt was made upon his life, and the mere attempt, although it only proved fatal to the man who made it, obtained for Harley an immense amount of sympathy and popularity. The author of the murderous attack was a French refugee named Guiscard, who was said to have been an ecclesiastic in his own country, but was charged there with grave offences, and being apparently unwilling or unable to meet the accusations against him, had contrived to escape from France. He managed to pass himself off upon the Duke of Savoy as a man capable of rendering great service to the cause of the allies. The Duke of Savoy recommended him to the court of Queen Anne, and Guiscard came over to England and settled himself there for some time in the hope of getting advancement. Queen Anne, however, had no faith in Guiscard's sincerity, and was not inclined to enter into any arrangements with him, and she steadily refused to admit him to speech with her.

Guiscard became despondent and even desperate. He tried to enter into negotiations with the court of France, and undertook to render some signal service to the French cause during his stay in London. The terms of some of his letters made it seem as if he meditated a design upon the Queen's life, although it is hardly possible to suppose that a man in his senses could have persuaded himself that such a plot would be likely to find favor with any one of influence at the French court. Some of his letters were opened at the post-office, according to a practice which we have already seen was not very uncommon in those days, and were submitted to a council of ministers. Even the most lenient interpretation which could be put on the meaning of what he had written seemed to lay him open to a serious criminal charge. The cabinet council at once decided that he must be arrested, and a messenger was instantly despatched to seize on him and bring him up for examination. The messenger found him walking in St. James's Park, and, having carefully disarmed him, effected his arrest and brought him to the council-chamber. Bishop Burnet's narrative of the events which followed is clear and concise:

"As" Guiscard "waited without, before he was called in, he took up a penknife, which lay among pens in a standish; when he was questioned upon his letter, he desired to speak in private with the secretary St. John, who refused it; and he being placed out of his reach, whereas Harley sat near him, he struck him in the breast with the penknife again and again, till it broke; and indeed wounded him as much as could be done, with so small a tool. The other councillors drew their swords, and stabbed Guiscard in several places; and their attendants being called in, they dragged him out. Harley's wound was presently searched; it appeared to be a slight one, yet he was long in the surgeon's hands; some imputed this to an ill-habit of body; others thought it was an artifice, to make it seem more dangerous than indeed it was. Guiscard's wounds were deeper, and not easily managed; for at first he was sullen, and seemed resolved to die; yet after a day, he submitted himself to the surgeons; but did not complain of a wound in his back, till it gangrened, and of that he died."

Before the death of Guiscard, Bolingbroke writes to a friend in the Queen's service abroad: "Your Lordship will see in the newspaper from my office a short account of a villainous action which, I think, is not to be paralleled in history. M. de Guiscard has four wounds, but none of them mortal, as we hoped. The chirurgeons believe that he will recover, there being no bad symptoms as yet; and it is a pity he should die any other death than the most ignominious which such an attempt deserves. Mr. Harley is in a very good way at present, and, I hope, in not the least danger of his life." A few days after Bolingbroke writes to the same friend a letter in which he tells him that "Our friend Mr. Harley is quite out of danger, his fever having this day entirely left him." Yet a little later Bolingbroke writes that "M. de Guiscard is dead, and has thereby escaped being made that public example which his villanies deserved."

It was a common belief at the time, as we have seen, among those who were not particularly friendly to Harley, that the Tory leader was making as much as he possibly could of the hurt which he had received, and was putting on the ways of one in a really dangerous condition, long after the physicians had made it perfectly clear to him that the wound was not of a nature likely to do him any serious bodily harm. At the same time it was certain that the attack made upon Harley had had an immense effect in augmenting his popularity. He was regarded as the victim of a French political plot, and this prevailing public impression came in with peculiar advantage to him. The worst which had been said against him and his friends was that, in their secret hearts, they were opposed to the

THE TRIUMPH OF THE TORIES

policy of the war, and had, in fact, a sneaking kindness for the court of France, and now here comes a miscreant who appears to be in mysterious communication with the French court, and he singles out Harley as the object of attempted assassination. What does this prove, people asked, but that the miscreant regarded Harley as the one most dangerous enemy to the designs of France and the main support of the English state? The thrust of De Guiscard's stolen penknife had raised Harley at once to the position of a popular hero. The Queen felt the deepest interest in Harley's condition, and when his danger was quite over thought the time had come to reward him with an especial mark of royal favor. She created him Earl of Oxford and Mortimer, and conferred upon him the office of Lord High Treasurer.

Anne was not so eager to bestow a testimony of her approval on Bolingbroke, partly, it may be assumed, because she had no relish for the tendencies of some of Bolingbroke's writings, which were sceptical, and, indeed, anti-Christian in their tone. Still, having conferred so great a reward upon Harley, she could not well leave his colleague long out in the cold, and within a year after Harley's elevation she conferred on Bolingbroke the title by which he is now always known in history. He was created Viscount Bolingbroke. It may be remarked here that we have, throughout the earlier part of this history, anticipated this long-delayed act of favor on the Queen's part, and described the "nobly pensive St. John" by that title which is forever associated with his career in the minds of all who read history. It was said very often, at the time, that the marked difference which Queen Anne had made in her way of treating the two leading Tory statesmen did not tend to increase the feeling of personal friendship between the recipients of the two titles, but it may be fairly assumed that a sovereign seldom confers royal favors without leading to a general belief that one man thinks he has got too little, while his colleague has got too much.

The events which have just been described had, of course, a direct and an immense influence on the conduct of the war. Many writers and students of this part of English history have ascribed the change of policy which was now brought about to the triumph of Mrs. Masham over the Duchess of Marlborough— to the rivalry, in fact, of the two petticoats and the victory of the one. Now, there can be no possible doubt that Queen Anne's whole nature craved for the guidance of some spirit more resolute than her own, and that when the Duchess of Marlborough made herself intolerable the Queen was only too ready to welcome any other influence which could give her at least a relief and a change from the old dominion. But we cannot help thinking that somewhat too much is made of Anne's subjection to her successive favorites and too little of her own tendencies and inclinations. It must be borne in mind that Queen Anne's sympathies never went with the statesmen and the policy of the Whig party, and it must be remembered, too, that when she accepted the war policy, the men who, like Marlborough, had to carry it into action avowed much the same Tory principles which she cherished in her own mind and heart. As the war went on Marlborough found that he had to rely on the support of the Whigs, that at certain periods such support was absolutely indispensable to him, and his great and supreme object was the successful prosecution of the war. But as the war went on the Queen only liked it less and less, and she soon began to regard Marlborough as

THE TRIUMPH OF THE TORIES

practically identified with the policy of the Whigs. If nothing had occurred to make her believe that that policy was not fully acceptable to the country, she would probably have put up with Marlborough just as she put up with the war itself. But when events came which brought to her mind the hope and belief that the Tory policy was, after all, the policy most welcome to the majority of Englishmen, she probably would have sought for new advisers and new guides if Abigail Hill had never been in existence. Queen Anne had come to believe that the principles most dear to her own heart were also the principles most dear to the country. She was only too glad to seize the opportunity of pleasing herself while yet keeping within the limits imposed upon sovereign rule by the scheme of constitutional government which came in with the revolution.

The student of history may, therefore, be advised not to accept in an unqualified sense the general theory which ascribes the change in the fortunes of parties and in the policy of the war to the triumph of Lady Masham over the wife of Marlborough. There is no more curious, amusing, and sometimes humiliating chapter in English history than that which tells how the rule of favorite number one asserted itself, demonstrated itself, overworked itself, and finally worked itself out, and how the rule of the second favorite came to be established in its place. The story has too much of the comic element in it to lose its hold upon readers of any time since then, or of any time to come, and it has supplied material for many interesting volumes and created a literature of its own. But much as we may find fault with those peculiarities of Queen Anne's character and caprice which led her to make herself the willing slave of this or that feminine influence, there is no just reason to believe that the policy of Queen Anne and the direction of her reign were absolutely dictated or created now by Sarah Jennings and now by Abigail Hill.

Queen Anne was right in her assumption that the country was growing more and more weary of the long war. We know by modern experience how a people, much more widely educated than the people over whom Queen Anne ruled, may be expected to become weary of a long war which seems to promise no immediate end, and has ceased to dazzle by a succession of brilliant successes. The war in which England was engaged during so great a part of Queen Anne's reign was one which could not possibly be said to have any direct interest for the English people. The ordinary Englishman who had nothing to do with camps or with courts might well have been excused if he failed to see how it greatly concerned the position and the prosperity of England whether a prince of this foreign house or that should ascend the throne of Spain. Perhaps even the most accomplished historical student of our own days would not find it easy to persuade himself that the question was one of vital interest for the English people of any generation. There is, however, always something captivating to a spirited people about the opening of a new war. The excitement which it brings along with it carries men's minds away from any prudential comparison of its objects, with its possible risks and its certain costs. Then, when the struggle has fairly begun, the passion of national feeling comes into play and men are, for the time, ready enough to make any sacrifice for the glory of the national flag. But if the war drags on for year after year, and if the longer it drags on the rarer become its moments of dazzling success, it is inevitable that a large proportion of those in whose name the war has been undertaken should begin to count the cost, to lament the sacrifices, to ask themselves when the time of trouble is likely to end, and what particular advantage is to come to them, let it end how it may.

This was the questioning mood into which the lapse of time and the lack of exciting successes had brought a large proportion of the English people, when Queen Anne began to form the conviction that her best advisers were those who could help her to follow the teachings of her own instincts and to bring the whole struggle to the earliest possible end. With the triumph of the Tory party it must have seemed clear to every reasonable observer that the War of the Succession was destined to come to an end before long, although even the keenest and best qualified observer might have failed to form any idea, or even any conjecture, as to the terms and the conditions under which England was to shake herself free of the contest and settle, for the time at least, into a state of peace.

CHAPTER XIX

WHAT THE WAR WAS COMING TO

WE broke off from the story of the war after the fatal battle of Almanza had been fought and lost by the forces engaged on the side of the allies. The result of that defeat left the Archduke Charles, the candidate of the alliance, in possession only of the province of Catalonia, in Spain, and in the merely nominal possession even of that province. The Catalonian population still clung to the cause of the Archduke, but his forces were small in number and very inadequately provided with the means of carrying on a serious struggle. The provinces of Valencia and Aragon had given themselves completely up to the French occupation. Indeed, the inhabitants of the town of Valencia had made no attempt at resisting the approach of the French, and had even thrown open its gates and given a welcome to the invaders. If Spain were to be recovered for the allies, the struggle there must begin all over again, and at the same time the campaigns in the Low Countries and in Italy had to be carried on.

Marlborough had formed a great idea for the invasion of France herself in the southeast, with the object, at least, of compelling King Louis to withdraw some of his attention and some of his forces from Spain. Marlborough's idea was that the point of attack should be Toulon, and that the expedition should be put under the command of his ablest coadjutor, Prince Eugene. There seemed some good reason to believe that such an expedition under such a commander would cause the Protestants in that region of France to renew their movement of insurrection, and thus give a fresh chance to the invaders, who professed to come in the name of religious freedom. The policy of King Louis had converted French Protestants everywhere into a hostile race, and Marlborough might well believe that his plan of campaign must have the help of these allies. Of course an important part of the scheme was that the English fleet should co-operate in the attack.

The expedition was placed by Marlborough's direction under the command of Prince Eugene and the Duke of Savoy. But it was found very difficult to prevail upon the Emperor to take any interest in Marlborough's plan, and all the usual delays and difficulties were put in its way. The trouble in this instance, as in so many others, was that each of the allies had at every critical moment distinct and different purposes in view. The Emperor was always thinking of what seemed to him the immediate interests of himself and his own realm, and was disposed to regard every proposal made by England or by the United Provinces only as it bore on those particular interests, and not as it involved the joint business of the campaign. The Dutch allies, as we have seen over and over again, were always anxious to estimate every proposal according to its bearing on what seemed to them the direct advantages of their own country, while we may take it for granted that the imperialists and the Dutch allies, differing as they did on so many other points, were often agreed in thinking that England had an eye chiefly to her own aggrandizement, and was making use of their co-operation for the mere benefit of her own policy.

In this particular instance it was the doubtful mood of the Emperor which marred the success of Marlborough's plan. Eugene was so badly supplied with the means of making a great attack that, finding it impossible to carry on the siege of Toulon with any effect, he had to make up his mind to the abandonment of the attempt. The imperialist army itself—at least that part of the force which was occupied on the Upper Rhine, under the command of a very incapable leader, the Margrave of Baireuth, was surprised and completely defeated by a French force under Marshal Villars. Villars was thus enabled to make his way into the Palatinate and to lay it waste, as other commanders sent out by King Louis had done before. One result of this defeat inflicted on the imperialist forces deserves to be recorded as a curious and interesting historical incident. On the urgent advice of Marlborough the Emperor deprived the Margrave of Baireuth of the command, and gave it to George, the Elector of Hanover, the man to whom the crown of England was to pass on the death of the reigning sovereign. Not much change, however, in the fortunes of the war was brought about by this change of command, even though it took place on the advice of Marlborough, and gave a chance of military distinction to the future King of England.

England suffered a severe loss about this time, but the loss was not inflicted by any successful effort on the part of the enemy. A stormy sea and a rock near the Scilly Isles closed, on a foggy night, the brilliant career of the brave Admiral Sir Cloudesley Shovel, who had co-operated with Peterborough in the capture of Barcelona. Shovel's vessel went down with its crew of some eight hundred men, and the wrecks of that night cost about two thousand lives to the British naval service. The dead body of the gallant admiral was flung high on the shore by the waves, and was there seen by some fishermen, who stripped the corpse of any article of value which took their fancy and then dug hastily a grave for it in the sands. Among the articles the plundering fishermen had carried off was a valuable emerald ring, which was recognized by some in the nearest town as a personal possession and ornament of Sir Cloudesley Shovel. The fisher-folk who had found the body were probably not worse than many of their friends and neighbors who were accustomed to take advantage of any chance that a storm might bring them when it tossed a stranger's corpse ashore. They had not had any suspicion that they were plundering the body of a great English admiral, and they gave up the ring and revealed the place where they had laid its owner beneath the sand. The corpse of the brave seaman was dug up and carried to London, where it received the well-merited ceremonial of a grand funeral service and a tomb in Westminster Abbey. When the Queen had to appoint a successor to Shovel's position of rear-admiral of England, she chose Sir John Leake. She spoke some words of feeling which were at once a tribute to the dead and to the living when she told Leake that she knew no man so fit to repair the loss of the ablest seaman in her service.

Some biographers record the fact that an unlucky expression used in the prayer prepared by Archbishop Tenison in this same year invoking a blessing on the fleets and armies of England was the occasion for some dismal and rather irreverent pleasantry. The prayer besought Heaven to be "the rock of our might." A facetious person threw off on the spur of the moment the lines which we quote—lines which are said, we hope not truly, to have been actually laid upon Sir Cloudesley Shovel's grave:

> "As Lambeth pray'd, so was the dire event,
> Else we had wanted here a monument,
> That to our fleet kind Heaven would be a rock;
> Nor did kind Heaven the wise petition mock:
> To what the metropolitan did pen,
> The bishop and clerks replied, Amen."

The feeling of discontent with the progress of the war had been of late growing more and more in England, and it began to affect the cohesive efficiency of the alliance. Marlborough became convinced that the time had come when some decisive blow must be struck if the alliance was to be held together and if the public of England were to be encouraged to support the campaign. We have seen that Marlborough had often endeavored to arouse his own government and the other governments of the alliance to the imperative necessity of adopting some onward policy which might lead the way to a successful close of the war. Again and again he had striven to obtain the authority which might enable him to carry his policy into effect, and again and again his inspiration had been rendered futile by objections, by delays, by counter-projects, by purposes which would not agree with each other, and by lack of faith in the possibility of complete success. Perhaps there is no story of great military enterprise in which the genius of one man shows itself so well qualified to accomplish all the desired results, if only it had not been hampered, harassed, and frustrated at every crisis by the interposition of some impediment on the part of those whose prompt co-operation was indispensable to complete victory. The more closely we study the events of this long war the more clearly

WHAT THE WAR WAS COMING TO

do we see that Marlborough was always right in his policy, that he was always successful when allowed to give that policy a fair chance of working out its ends, and that he only failed when for one reason or another some other policy was allowed to prevail over that which was the birth of his genius as a commander.

Marlborough now found that new difficulties were rising in his way. He had had warnings from qualified advisers that the people of the United Provinces were beginning to feel utterly weary of the war, and were even turning their minds towards the formation of plans which might end in their making terms of peace on their own account. To some men of influence in Holland it seemed possible that advantageous terms for themselves might now be obtained from the French government if, at a time when active operations in the field seemed to have come almost to a stand-still, the Dutch were to express a willingness to enter upon terms of peaceful arrangement for their own separate advantage.

A curiously expressive, although somewhat grotesque, phrase was used within the memory of most of us by a clever and audacious American adventurer in finance and politics, to describe a crisis when there seemed nothing left for every one concerned in it but to look out for his own safety. He declared that the time had come for every man to drag his own corpse out. Some of the allies at the time which we have now reached in the story of the war were unconsciously anticipating the judgment of the modern adventurer, and were making up their minds that the hour had come for every one to drag his own corpse out. The trouble was not that the spirit of brave comradeship was utterly wanting to any of the allies. No people had ever given more splendid evidences of heroic determination to carry on what might seem to be an unending struggle than the Dutch had given to the world not so long before. The trouble was that no one common and single purpose inspired the counsels of the alliance, that each of its members was jealous, or, at least, doubtful about the objects and the policy of all the others, and the disheartening moment had arrived when each began to think that if he did not promptly endeavor to save himself the others would anticipate his action and save themselves by deserting him.

Other difficulties, too, began to show themselves in that field of action which was more especially Marlborough's own. The populations of the regions which we should now describe as Belgium were by no means satisfied with the dominion which the conditions of the war enabled the Dutch to maintain over them. The Dutch inhabitants may be described as altogether Protestant, while the Belgian populations were Catholic, and the differences of faith and feeling which in later years led to the separation of the two peoples were already beginning to make their influence evident. The conduct of the war, so far as the United Provinces were concerned, was placed in the hands of Dutch commissioners, and the Dutch commissioners were not in general very conciliatory in their demeanor towards the Catholic populations. On the other hand, the Catholic populations were disposed to resent the sort of dominion asserted by the Dutch, and to see in some of the movements of camps and armies a desire on the part of the Dutch to make the interest, the comfort, and the convenience of their own co-religionists a chief consideration in their military arrangements. Some of the Catholics had their minds filled with the dread that as soon as the war came to an end with advantage to the allies the Dutch would make themselves absolute masters of the whole country which contained the two populations, and it is said by some historians that many leading men among the Dutch were rather outspoken in their avowal of such a purpose.

The condition of growing disaffection among the Catholic populations of the Low Countries towards the alliance was beginning to be well known to the French, and the comparative inaction of the allies during recent months had roused a hope in the statesmen of King Louis that the war spirit was dying out among their leading and most formidable opponents. The effect of all this was that the French determined to make a great effort at some immediate success, and they were further inspired to enterprise by the fact that Bruges and Ghent gave the French troops a welcome into their walls. There was something like trouble and disaffection in Antwerp itself, but Marlborough had received timely intimation of this growing danger, and was ready by the interposition of his influence to prevent it from becoming a reality.

The inspirited French resolved to take advantage of what seemed to be in every way a golden opportunity by a strong attempt to obtain possession of Oudenarde. This place was a fortress on the Scheldt, very strong in itself and holding an important position between Brabant and the French frontier-line. If the French army could get possession of this fortress it would, at all events, keep the way open for them to retire into their own country in the event of strategic reasons rendering that course desirable. The army of the allies, which was commanded by Marlborough himself, was not so strong in numbers as the French army; and the French, therefore, did not seem to have any fear that Marlborough might hasten up to interrupt their movements by beginning the attack. The French army, however, suffered from the disadvantage which was commonly imposed upon French armies at that time: it had a real and a nominal commander. The nominal commander was the Duke of Burgundy, a prince of the royal family, but the real commander was the daring and brilliant Duke of Vendôme. The understanding in such an arrangement as this was that the royal prince should be the figure-head of the campaign, but that he should take the advice and act upon the suggestions of the general who had more experience in military affairs, and who, in this case, had a special genius for the work. In this instance the two commanders did not get on very well together. The nominal commander was not disposed to regard his position as merely nominal, and had not wisdom enough to see the immense superiority of Vendôme. The Duke of Burgundy had, moreover, a strong personal dislike to his companion-in-arms, a dislike which may well be accounted for by Vendôme's character and habits, but which came in with unlucky influence where the great object ought to have been to work out the best possible plan of campaign.

In the meanwhile Marlborough obtained one especial advantage over his opponents, in the fact that he was joined by a colleague with whom he could always work in the happiest union of counsels and with the most satisfactory results. This colleague was Prince Eugene, who had no further work just then to do in Italy, and who was therefore sent to join Marlborough. Eugene was in command of a large imperialist force, but the plans of the Emperor were hindered in their execution by the all too familiar delays, and both Marlborough and Eugene soon began to find that, if Eugene were not to come until he could bring the whole force at his command along with him, he might

WHAT THE WAR WAS COMING TO

come too late to be of any immediate assistance. There was some rapid exchange of communications between the two commanders, and the result was that Eugene left the main body of his cavalry and infantry behind him, and, accompanied only by his personal staff, came at the top of his speed to Marlborough's camping-ground. Marlborough was delighted to welcome the new arrival, and he told Eugene, with truth as well as with graciousness, that the mere presence of so brilliant a soldier would be a fresh encouragement to the whole army.

There was no feeling of jealousy or rivalry between Marlborough and Eugene. Each man recognized to the full the military genius of the other; each man thoroughly appreciated the help which he must receive from the counsels of the other. Marlborough lost no time in explaining all his plans to Eugene, and Eugene had no hesitation in approving them and co-operating with them. The two generals agreed that their march should be between the French frontier and the French army, so as to cut the French off from that line of retreat which it might be supposed that Vendôme would especially desire to keep open in the event of any possible discomfiture to his movements. This was, indeed, somewhat of a daring policy on the part of Marlborough, and if the purpose he had immediately in view should by any chance be frustrated might have led to a most serious disaster. But the policy of Marlborough at a critical emergency was almost always a policy of sudden daring, for no other man could calculate so quickly and so accurately as he the relative proportions of the risk to be run and the advantage to be gained. Where Marlborough saw that a stroke could successfully be made it might always be taken for granted that the risk could safely be run for the sake of the advantage to be thus, and thus only, obtained.

When the French commanders became aware of the approach of the allies they determined at once to give up the siege of Oudenarde for the time. But they were far from expecting an immediate and direct attack from Marlborough, for they knew that the allied forces had been kept on the march for a long time and over a fatiguing country. It did not come into their calculations that even Marlborough would feel inclined to enter upon a great engagement after a march of nearly twenty miles. The French, therefore, settled themselves in a strong position, with much rising ground between them and their enemies, and we may presume that the nominal and the real commander began to dispute as to the best plan of operations. Marlborough did in this, as in many other instances, the very thing which his opponents had made up their minds that he was likely not to do. He rushed into action at once. Even before he had got his whole forces into position he ordered his cavalry to charge, and the French commanders saw that the game was a desperate one; that they had no choice left in the matter; that they must either fight it out to the end or give up the battle. Marlborough put his English troops at the left and gave the command of that part of his army to Eugene, in whom he well knew that the English soldiers had the most perfect confidence. He himself directed the centre of the force, which had no English troops in it, but was made up altogether of the other forces serving the Grand Alliance. Marlborough no doubt felt good reason to believe that the soldiers who were not English would fight all the better because they had such a man, and not one of their own commanders, to lead them in the field and show them the

WHAT THE WAR WAS COMING TO

way to victory. It should be mentioned that in the first charge, that which may be called the preliminary charge, George, the Electoral Prince of Hanover, who was afterwards to rule over England as King George the Second, showed himself, as he did on a later battlefield, a brave and resolute soldier.

In the first encounter of the two armies the French attacked, with some apparent success, the left wing of Marlborough's army, which for a while seemed to be driven back, and the French pressed on all the more persistently in the hope that they were about to win a victory. Marlborough, according to his usual fashion, turned this seeming disadvantage to great account, and directed a rapid movement to cut the French off from any possible retreat by occupying the heights behind them. The movement was perfectly successful, and the battle went on until nightfall. It may almost be described as a regular hand-to-hand fight, for the two armies were so close together that the cannon was hardly employed on either side. Eugene did his work splendidly, and the old Dutch commander, Marshal Overkirk, whom Marlborough had sent to cut off the French retreat, carried out his orders with remarkable skill and resolve, and fully accomplished his purpose. Owing to the fact that the day was one of hand-to-hand fighting for the most part, and that the artillery was seldom used, the slaughter on either side was not very great, but a large number of the French were taken prisoners.

In those days the coming on of night usually brought to a close the most hotly contested battle, and when darkness came on the allies were not quite certain whether they had won an absolute victory, and, indeed, were making resolute preparations for a renewal of the struggle with the return of light. This day was

July 11, 1708. The battle was not renewed by the French on the following day—Marlborough and Eugene had won their victory. Vendôme, the real commander of the French, was burning to renew the battle next day, but the nominal commander, the Duke of Burgundy, was not inclined for such a measure, and most of his generals shared his disinclination. There was nothing for it, then, but to order a retreat, and we learn on good authority that Vendôme was furious in his wrath against this policy, and expressed himself in words which could hardly have been grateful to the feelings of the prince who was in nominal command. The battle, it should be said, was fought splendidly by the French soldiers, and it is to their honor that when night came on the result might still have been regarded as a drawn game. Most assuredly if Vendôme had had his way Marlborough and Eugene would have had another day of hard fighting before they could have claimed a victory. But the more cautious counsels of the nominal French commander prevailed, and the field of Oudenarde was a lost battle for King Louis of France. The prince who represented the lost cause of the Stuart family fought at Oudenarde on the side of the French. The representative of the dethroned and exiled dynasty was in the one army—the representative of the house now appointed for succession to the rule of England was in the other.

Once again Marlborough desired to carry on a bold and forward policy. His idea was that the allies, disregarding every temptation to turn aside for the capture of this or that strong place, should march right on to Paris and dictate terms of peace there. Eugene, however, was of opinion that the fortress of Lille on the French frontier should be captured and secured before the allies set out to make their way

WHAT THE WAR WAS COMING TO

into the heart of hostile France. Marlborough was always willing to give full consideration to any counsels coming from so capable a commander as Eugene, and there was a good deal to be said for the practical wisdom of Eugene's policy. In any case it would have been difficult for Marlborough to persuade the Dutch commissioners into an agreement with his views. The idea of leaving not only the remains of a French army, but also the commanding fortress of Lille behind them, when setting out upon their march into a country the whole population of which would be hostile with one mind and heart to the English invasion, seemed to the Dutch commissioners an enterprise of the most hopeless nature. Marlborough, therefore, readily consented under all the conditions to adopt Eugene's scheme, and it was determined to lay siege at once to the fortress of Lille. The command of the actual siege operations was assigned to Eugene. Marlborough himself undertook the direction of the covering army which was to deal with any attempt for the relief of the besieged place. It was of the utmost importance that Marlborough should take charge of this part of the work, for the French army, even after Oudenarde, was still in considerable strength, and it had been joined more lately by the Duke of Berwick with a large force under his command. It should be said that Eugene's troops, which their commander had left behind him in his eagerness to take part with Marlborough, had by this time come into the field, but the proportions of the two contending armies remained much the same as before, seeing that the troops of Berwick on the one side had to be set off against those of Eugene on the other.

The siege of Lille began at once, and it may truly be said that the eyes of all Europe were soon turned upon it. In other fields of the great and wide-spread war there had not been much important fighting going on of late, and Lille became for the time the centre of universal interest. The defence of Lille was splendidly maintained by the French, and there were many incidents on both sides of the struggle which afterwards gave rise to keen personal and political controversy. Some brilliant displays of daring and skill were made by French officers and soldiers to keep up supplies for the beleaguered fortress, and even to keep the garrison in possession of the news of all that was going on outside it. For sixty days Lille held out, but at last it became clear even, it is said, to King Louis himself and those around him, that a further loss of gallant lives would be only a futile sacrifice. The garrison had run so short of supplies that nothing was left to feed on but scraps of horse-flesh, and no gunpowder remained with which to fire a shot of defiance at the enemy. Eugene behaved with characteristic gallantry and generosity. He allowed Marshal Bouffleurs, the officer in command of the garrison, to name his own conditions of surrender, and the conquerors and the conquered parted on terms of reciprocal admiration.

France was now reduced to a condition which might almost be described as desperate. The treasury was all but emptied; the public debt was increased by an enormous amount; the drain upon the population to fill the ranks of the army had left most of the country places absolutely without cultivation, and there were threatenings, not vague or remote, of a famine in the land. The government found it almost beyond their power to keep up the pay of the soldiers in the field, and to add to all other troubles, the winter was one of extraordinary severity. King Louis began to think that there was nothing left for him but to propose terms

WHAT THE WAR WAS COMING TO

of peace to the conquering allies. The condition of inactivity into which the allied armies appeared to have fallen was now succeeded, so far as the French could judge, by a sudden reaction of temper and an energetic forward movement. Louis actually went so far as to open negotiations with the allies. He sent an ambassador to The Hague, by whom conditions of peace were to be offered which at an earlier stage of the campaigning would probably have seemed well worthy of consideration. The substance of his offers was that his grandson, Philip, should give up all claims to the crown of Spain itself, and should withdraw from the Peninsula altogether, but with the stipulation that Naples and Sicily, which were then parts of the Spanish dominion, should be formed into a separate kingdom, of which Philip was to be created the sovereign.

Now, it must be owned that this offer, if we consent to view it for the moment from the French side of the political field, might have seemed an almost absolute concession to the overpowering strength of the allies. Spain itself was to be declared free of all claim on the part of the Bourbon prince, and when the war began the especial declaration of policy made by the allies was that it would be impossible for them to give their consent to any arrangement which would practically make the kingdom of Spain an integral part of the dominion of France. The allies had never professed any particular interest about the manner in which the populations of Naples and Sicily were to be governed, and an independent kingdom of Naples and Sicily combined could hardly be likely to offer any serious trouble to England or Holland or the states of the Emperor. As to the feelings of the Neapolitans and the Sicilians themselves, no very formidable difficulty could be expected to arise, for the arrangements of international diplomacy in those days, and even in days much later, did not usually profess to take account of the sentiments entertained by mere populations. But the allies were not just then in a humor to be liberal in their acceptance of conditions from an enemy whom they believed to be reduced almost to the end of his resources. No one was better informed than Marlborough as to the degree of strain which the maintenance of the war had put upon the armies and the exchequer of France. Marlborough, however, like nearly all great soldiers, was not eager to prolong a war merely for the excitement and the glory of war, and he, if left to himself, would probably have gone further than many of his colleagues on battle-field or in council to bring about a peaceful and speedy settlement of the whole struggle. But under the conditions which prevailed just then the proposals of King Louis had no chance of acceptance. Each of the allied powers had some separate advantage to obtain for itself, and each was willing to support the claims of all the others as long as this did not involve giving up any part of its own demand.

Marlborough and **Lord Townshend** were appointed as plenipotentiaries on the part of Queen Anne and her government. The English plenipotentiaries were instructed to make very large demands. First and foremost, it was insisted that the whole of the existing Spanish dominion must be set quite free from any claim on the part of France. Then it was further stipulated that France must completely change her policy with regard to the exiled Stuarts, that she must recognize the sovereignty of Queen Anne and the rights of the Protestant succession, and that the Stuart family must be banished from French soil. Finally, a condition was made that the French works at Dunkirk, which were regarded as a menace to England, must be at once demolished. Holland had some stipulations of her own to make, which were not likely to be welcome to the French government, and it is said were thought somewhat too exacting by Marlborough himself. The Dutch demanded that they should be allowed to possess and maintain as fortresses a line of frontier towns, which they declared to be necessary to the existence of the United Provinces as a state, in order to secure them against the risks of any future invasion on the part of France. The Emperor, too, had terms to make on his own account which sounded harshly in the ears of the French negotiators. In fact, the combined conditions of the allies were such as could only be offered with any hope of acceptance to a state already beaten to its knees, and France even yet did not feel herself reduced to that abject condition.

One incident of the negotiations deserves special mention, if only for the curious light it throws on the processes of persuasion which European statesmen were ready, even at so recent a period, to employ for the purpose of gaining their ends. The French Minister for Foreign Affairs, M. de Torcy, was sent to conduct negotiations on the part of France. M. de Torcy had some private interviews with Marlborough, and has himself told with charming frankness that he offered, with the authority of his government, a huge bribe to Marlborough if the latter would only help him to obtain a favorable consideration for the terms offered by France. Now, it is quite certain that during the course of his career Marlborough was more than once accused by his enemies at home and abroad of having accepted bribes, and even of having been guilty of actual peculation. But in this instance we may unhesitatingly acquit Marlborough of any corrupt act, for M. de Torcy has himself told the world that Marlborough would not listen to the proposal. The enemies of Marlborough would probably have insinuated that the great soldier knew well how little chance there was for acceptance of the French proposals, and therefore declined to run the risk of entering into any such futile compact.

However that may be, it is certain that no pressure brought to bear upon the allies had the effect of inducing them to make their conditions more easy for King Louis to accept. Indeed, the result of the discussions at The Hague was that the allies began to make their demands harder and harder the longer the argument was kept up. By the time M. de Torcy was able to return to the court at Versailles he had to bear with him an ultimatum that the whole of the Spanish dominion should be handed over as a kingdom to the Archduke Charles, and that if this was not done within two months King Louis must himself join with the allies in compelling his own grandson, by sheer force, to renounce all his claims to the Spanish throne, and take himself, bag and baggage, out of Spain. This latest condition was especially added because it was seen that Philip had undoubtedly made himself welcome to the Castilian population at least, and that no efforts of mere diplomacy, even if supported and pressed on by King Louis himself, would be likely to prevail on the King's grandson to renounce his claim on the Spanish throne.

Bishop Burnet tells the story in his own way, and some parts of his narrative are well worth quoting: "The foundation of the whole treaty," he says, "was the restoring of the whole Spanish monarchy to king Charles, within two months: Torcy said, the time was too short, and that perhaps it was not in the king of

France's power to bring that about: for the Spaniards seemed resolved to stick to king Philip. It was, upon this, insisted on, that the king of France should be obliged to concur with the Allies, to force it by all proper methods; but this was not farther explained, for the Allies were well assured, that if it was sincerely intended by France, there would be no great difficulty in bringing it about. This therefore being laid down as the basis of the treaty, the other preliminaries related to the restoring all the places in the Netherlands, except Cambray and St. Omer; the demolishing or restoring of Dunkirk; the restoring of Strasbourg, Brisack and Huningen to the Empire; Newfoundland to England; and Savoy to that duke, besides his continuing possessed of all he then had in his hands; the acknowledging the king of Prussia's royal dignity; and the electorate in the House of Brunswick; the sending the pretender out of France, and the owning the succession to the Crown of England, as it was settled by law."

Up to this time the representative of the French King had put on the appearance of willingness to enter into negotiations on the basis laid down by the allies, and hopeful persons among the allies were ready to believe that the serious difficulties were over, and that the ratification of the terms of peace might soon be expected. No such hopes, we may be sure, existed in the mind of Marlborough; no such idea could have been in the mind of De Torcy, although he put on the manner of a negotiator ready to listen to any propositions tending towards peace. When he was returning to Versailles to make known the final decision of the allies he could have been in little doubt about the decision of the French King. It would, in fact, have been absolutely impossible for King Louis to accept such terms without a complete acknowledgment of utter defeat. The King, it must be owned, exhibited on this occasion a spirit not unkingly. Louis made up his mind at once to reject any proposals founded on such a basis. Some influence was brought to bear upon him in his own family in order that a peace, even at this price, might be obtained. It was said that the Duke of Burgundy urged the King to accept the proffered conditions on the ground that the continuance of the war would mean the absolute ruin of France, and Bishop Burnet seems to give credit to the statement commonly believed that Madame de Maintenon brought her influence to bear upon the King with the same object in view. But that article in the proposed treaty which would have bound France to join with the allies in expelling Philip from Spain was too much for the King and most of his advisers.

"The people in France," says Burnet, "were much wrought on by this pretended indignity offered to their monarch, to oblige him to force his grandson to abandon Spain; and even, here in England, there wanted not many, who said it was a cruel hardship put on the French king, to force him into such an unnatural war." Burnet himself does not profess to be one of the Englishmen who held such opinions, and he puts it in a cool and matter-of-fact sort of way that if King Louis "was guilty of the injustice of putting him in possession of that kingdom, it was but a reasonable piece of justice to undo what he himself had done: and it was so visible, that king Philip was maintained on that throne, by the counsels and assistance of France, that no doubt was made, but that, if the king of France had really designed it, he could easily have obliged him to relinquish all pretensions to that crown."

Burnet goes on to provide illustrations from the

former history of dealings between England and France to show that it had been a common habit among French sovereigns to open up negotiations with English rulers without having any serious desire that the negotiations should come to a peaceful settlement, and only with the object of gaining time so that hostilities might be renewed at a moment of less advantage to England. We find in the history of wars much more recent than the War of the Spanish Succession that the process of negotiations on both sides of the quarrel tends to fill the disputing parties with the conviction that the statesmanship of the other side is always inspired by a perfidious motive, and conducted by a treacherous policy. This is one of the evils of war, and not the least of its evils, that the opponents are always ready to credit each other with false pretences and treacherous schemes, even in the conduct of negotiations which profess, on both sides, to be initiated only with a desire to procure an honorable peace. At the time when so many English people at home and abroad were assuring one another that the King of France was merely pretending a willingness to enter into some arrangement, while in his secret heart there was no purpose but to secure delay and to gain time for renewed and more advantageous action, the general opinion in and around the court of France was that the allies were playing just such a game and with precisely similar motives. Looking back on the whole transaction, the present generation of Englishmen may fairly admit that King Louis could not, under all the conditions, accept such terms as those which the allies sought to impose upon him.

Louis seems to have risen to the occasion with a spirit and resolve which would have been well worthy of a better man. He declared to those around him that, if he must fight, he would much rather fight against the enemies of his country than against a member of his own household. His determination prevailed with the statesmen who were his immediate advisers. He was not content with the acceptance of his resolve by the members of his own ministry, but he went so far as to address his appeal to the country at large. He had an address, a sort of public proclamation, prepared, which he sent round to the governors of all the French provinces, with the order that its contents should be made known to the populations within their jurisdiction. In this address he made very much the same complaint as to the purposes and the action of the allies which the allies were making at the time about him. He assured his people that the allies did not really wish for peace, that their object was to prolong the war and to force their way into the very heart of France. He declared that the more he showed willingness to carry on a sincere negotiation with the view of restoring peace, the more determinedly did the allies keep on raising their terms, so that every concession he offered brought out from the other side only increased demands and sharper exactions. Nothing was left for him, he said, but to call upon his people to stand by their country and by him, and to prove that France had still strength and spirit enough to encounter all the allied powers of Europe rather than allow her soil to be occupied by foreign conquerors. The appeal from the King brought an echo from almost every part of France, and once again new recruits from all provinces were filled with alacrity to offer their services in the field for what they believed to be the defence of their country against foreign invasion. The negotiations were over, and the war was to begin again.

WHAT THE WAR WAS COMING TO

Some mention must be made of the help which Marlborough received, during these negotiations and at all periods of the war, from the counsels and the efforts of the distinguished Dutch statesman, Anthony Heinsius. Heinsius, in the earlier part of his career, had been inclined to favor the policy of an alliance with France against William the Third. He studied the question, however, at the court of Versailles, and there became convinced that Holland could expect no real support or genuine friendship from the French court and French statesmen. He became a close and a trusted friend of William the Third, and in later days was a close and a trusted friend of the new English government and of Marlborough. Heinsius was, at the time with which we are now dealing, the Grand Pensionary of the United Provinces. His position was very much like that of an English prime-minister, but at this time Holland was passing through one of the intervals when she had no actual Stadholder or sovereign head of the state, and his influence was, therefore, all the greater in directing the policy of his country. Marlborough could trust him, and his influence was ever on Marlborough's side.

CHAPTER XX

JONATHAN SWIFT'S VIEWS

ALL this time there was a keen, although not by any means unprejudiced, observer taking close account of the events which were passing in political life and of the changes which were made in the ministry of Queen Anne, and this observer followed the useful and wholesome practice of making notes of the events themselves and of the impressions which they produced on his mind. This observer was Jonathan Swift, a man of intellectual gifts not surpassed in his time, of some intellectual gifts not surpassed at any time, a man of passion and of prejudice, of love and of hate; conscious of his own power, and, we may do him the justice to believe, anxious always to make the best use of it, but peculiarly subject to the distorting and distracting influences of an over-sensitive nature and a spirit which seldom brooked the counsels of moderation. Swift, it should be said, finds fault with himself for not having carried out his system of note-taking with anything like the regularity or fulness which he had always believed to be necessary and had recommended to other men. "I was always too negligent," he says, "in taking hints or journals of every thing material as it passed, whereof I omitted many that I cannot now recollect, although I was convinced, by a thousand instances, of the weakness of my memory." Swift, however, promptly finds a characteristic and sarcastic excuse for his frequent failure to keep up the practice which he believed to be right, and had blamed others for not keeping up: "But, to say the truth, the nearer knowledge any man has in the affairs at Court, the less he thinks them of consequence or worth regarding."

The reader who reads Swift's "Memoirs relating to that change which happened in the Queen's Ministry in the year 1710," written in October, 1714, will probably come to the conclusion that, whether Swift was right or wrong in the judgments which he formed as to the political events and personages of his time, he does not seem to have omitted from his notes or his recollections very much that was of material import to the study of that historical period. "Having continued," Swift tells us, "for near the space of four years, in a good degree of confidence with the ministry then in being, although not with so much power as was believed, or at least given out, by my friends as well as by my enemies, especially the latter, in both Houses of Parliament; And this having happened during a very busy period of negotiations abroad, and management or intrigue at home, I thought it might probably, some years hence, when the present scene shall have given place to many new ones that will arise, be an entertainment to those who will have any personal regard for me or my memory, to set down some particularities which fell under my knowledge and observation, while I was supposed, whether truly or no, to have part in the secret of affairs."

These observations have a very keen and vivid interest for the student of history. They come from a man who played an important, if not always a very conspicuous, part in the political events of his time— a man whose intellect was acknowledged, and whose advice was confidently sought by some of the most famous and influential men and women who belonged to the court of Queen Anne. Swift had a peculiarly happy faculty of description, and he was master of the art which can suggest a whole figure or a whole character by a few easy and apparently quiet touches of portraiture. One must not rely on Swift's description as in every case a fair and true picture of the personage whose characteristics he touches off for our instruction. The reader must form his estimate of this or that statesman who belonged to Swift's time by the help of observers and authorities less prejudiced and less partial than Swift. But we may take it for granted that when Swift ascribes certain peculiarities to this or that public man, such peculiarities must have formed a part of his character or demeanor, however much they may have been modified or overborne by other qualities of nature and of temper.

Whether Swift is dealing with friends or enemies, it will be found that he can generally put before the reader a living picture of the man as he showed himself to the outer world, although not perhaps of the man as he actually was in heart and in purpose. One seems to move among the people whom Swift describes, even when we cannot accept his judgment as to their motives and characters. But there is a charm about Swift's political pamphleteering, if we may apply that word to such essays as that with which we are now dealing, quite outside any question as to the accuracy or inaccuracy of his pen portraits of other men. That charm consists in the light they throw on Swift's own temperament, feelings, and character. The more we read them, the more we are impressed with the fact that their chief interest for us is found in the opportunities they give us of studying Swift himself.

JONATHAN SWIFT'S VIEWS

"It may probably enough happen," Swift writes in this same essay, "that those who shall at any time hereafter peruse these papers, may think it not suitable to the nature of them, that, upon occasion, I sometimes make mention of myself; who, during these transactions, and ever since, was a person without titles or public employment. But, since the chief leaders of the faction, then out of power, were pleased in both Houses of Parliament to take every opportunity of showing their malice, by mentioning me (and often by name) as one who was in the secret of all affairs, and without whose advice or privity, nothing was done, or employment disposed of, it will not, perhaps, be improper to take notice of some passages, wherein the public and myself were jointly concerned; not to mention that the chief cause of giving myself this trouble, is to satisfy my particular friends; and, at worst, if, after the fate of manuscripts, these papers shall, by accident or indiscretion, fall into the public view, they will be no more liable to censure than other memoirs, published for many years past, in English, French, and Italian." Then Swift thinks it right to inform us, accepting the possibility that his papers may somehow or other get into the hands of readers, that "the period of time I design to treat on, will commence with September 1710, from which time, till within two months of the Queen's death, I was never absent from court, except about six weeks in Ireland."

Very few readers are likely to find any fault with Swift because he introduces his own personality into some of these papers and takes the opportunity of defending himself against what he regards as the malice of his enemies in both Houses of Parliament, by telling us what he thinks of them and letting us know what poor figures they made of themselves in his impartial eyes. Whether we agree with his judgments or not, we feel ourselves growing better acquainted with at least the outer aspects of the political struggle from the reading of these papers than we should be likely to become from the study of the most grave, erudite, and judicial volumes of history. Swift is always himself, and never seems to write with any consideration as to the most expedient manner of putting a case, or the most plausible method of persuading readers to accept his guidance. We can see in these papers telling and ample illustration of the genius which created the travels of Lemuel Gulliver. We do not stop to inquire whether Gulliver really did full justice to the character of the various personages, great and small, whom he encountered in his travels; our interest is in the descriptions themselves, and we do not care to ask whether the narrator was always justified in his likings and dislikings. We have in a certain sense something of the same feeling about Swift's political pamphlets, and the clearest evidence that he was mistaken or even unfair in his estimate of this or that particular man or woman does not take away in the slightest degree from the fascination exercised over us by the description itself, and by the light which all the descriptions throw on the moods and nature of the writer.

Swift is careful to tell us that he had "often with great earnestness pressed the Earl of Oxford, then Lord Treasurer, and my Lady Masham, who were the sole persons which brought about that great change" in the Queen's household as well as in the kingdom, to give him a particular account of all that had happened during that historical episode. He also assures us that this anxiety on his part did not "proceed from curiosity, or the ambition of knowing and publishing important secrets; but, from a sincere honest design of justifying the Queen, in the measures she then took, and after pursued against a load of scandal which would certainly be thrown on her memory, with some appearance of truth." Some appearance of truth, it must be owned, does still adhere to the charges made against the Queen of acting too often on purely personal impulses, and the appearance of truth does not seem to be entirely removed even after Swift has given his explanation. The reader is often inclined to believe that Swift, in his own mind, must have thought that there was a good deal of truth in the accusations, and that certain sly touches given every now and then in his descriptions seem as if they were put in by a man who means us to understand that he has really said all he can on the side of the defence, and that if there is nothing more to be said it is no fault of his. The impression which will certainly be conveyed to the mind of almost every reader is that those sly touches are more peculiarly characteristic of Swift than some of the grave statements and ingenious arguments with which he accomplishes his work as a friendly but truthful historian.

"What," Swift asks, "would be more easy to a malicious pen that to charge the Queen with inconstancy, weakness, and ingratitude, in removing and disgracing the Duke of Marlborough, who had so many years commanded her armies with victory and success; in displacing so many great officers of her Court and kingdom, by whose counsels she had in all appearance so prosperously governed; in extending the marks of her severity and displeasure towards the wife and daughters, as well as relations and allies, of that person she had so long employed and so highly trusted; and all this by the private intrigues of a woman of her bedchamber, in concert with an artful man, who might be supposed to have acted that bold part only from a motive of revenge upon the loss of his employments, or of ambition to come again into power?"

There might, undoubtedly, seem to the ordinary observer, whether looking on with his own eyes at that time or studying from books at the present day, something more than mere malice to warrant the adoption of such opinions, and we cannot but admit that Swift was perfectly right when he endeavored to induce the Queen and those in her counsels to furnish a full exposition of all the facts in their knowledge which could tend to dissipate such a delusion. "These," says Swift, "were some of the arguments I often made use of with great freedom, both to the Earl of Oxford and my Lady Masham, to incite them to furnish me with materials for a fair account of that great transaction, to which they always seemed as well disposed as myself. My Lady Masham did likewise assure me, that she had frequently informed the Queen of my request, which her Majesty thought very reasonable, and did appear upon all occasions as desirous of preserving reputation with posterity, as might justly become a great Prince to be."

Swift was not able, with whatever effort and perseverance, to carry his point with the Queen and Oxford, and to inspire them with that due care for their reputation which he believed, and they said they believed, to be imperative under all the conditions. Swift does not attempt much excuse for this negligence on the part of his illustrious friends. He expresses his sentiments very clearly. "But, that incurable disease, either of negligence or procrastination, which influenced every action both of the Queen and the Earl of Oxford, did in some sort infect everyone who had credit or business in Court. For, after soliciting near four years, to obtain a point of so great importance to the Queen and her servants, from whence I could propose nothing but trouble, malice, and envy to myself, it was perpetually put off." In fact, Swift explains, he went so far as to offer to undertake the task of writing the history of Anne's reign, and he was ready to accept the office of historiographer, " although of inconsiderable value, and of which I might be sure to be deprived upon the Queen's death." Even this offer, however, did not induce the Queen, Lord Oxford, and Lady Masham to take any serious interest in the matter, and this indifference on their parts is, he tells us, " the cause that I can give but an imperfect account of the first springs of that great change at court, after the trial of Dr. Sacheverell, my memory not serving me to retain all the facts related to me; but what I remember I shall here set down."

Swift begins his story by telling us that " there was not, perhaps, in all England, a person who understood more artificially to disguise her passions " than Queen Anne. The reader will already have seen that the essay in which this passage occurs was not written till after the Queen's death, and without ascribing to Swift any taint of servility or undue loyalty, we may safely assume that his comments on the Queen's peculiarities are all the more free and frank because they were not to come under the eyes of Anne herself. The impression which Swift formed with regard to the Duchess of Marlborough's ascendency over Anne was that it only continued in full force while Anne was a princess, and that by the time she had come to the throne she was already growing to be quite weary of the Duchess's domination. Even during the later part of her life as a princess, Anne, according to Swift's opinion, was already growing impatient of the imperious ways and rude manners which she could not but observe in her self-opinionated friend. " This Princess," he remarks, " was so exact an observer of forms, that she seemed to have made it her study, and would often descend so low, as to observe in her domestics of either sex, who came in her presence, whether a ruffle, a periwig, or the lining of a coat, were unsuitable at certain times."

The ascendency remained for a time one which, as Swift tells us in his effective and characteristic way, the Princess Anne " had neither patience to bear, nor spirit to subdue." The Queen was also beginning to feel a strong dislike towards the Earl of Godolphin. One reason for this, according to Swift's interpretation, was that the Duchess of Marlborough, who had long been Godolphin's friend, got into the way of prevailing upon him to solicit the Queen " upon things very unacceptable to her," and the Queen liked the solicitations all the less because she felt sure that Godolphin was put on to them by the overbearing Duchess. Swift further informs us that Godolphin, " although he endeavoured to be as respectful as his nature would permit him, was, upon all occasions, much too arbitrary and obtruding."

To the Duke of Marlborough we are told that the Queen " was wholly indifferent . . . as her nature in general prompted her to be," and it may well be something of a new sensation to a modern reader to think of Marlborough as a personage to whom any one could be wholly indifferent. The indifference soon changed into another sentiment, for we learn that Marlborough's "restless, impatient behaviour turned her against him." The Queen, we learn, " had not a stock of amity to serve above one object at a time; and further than a bare good or ill opinion, which she soon contracted and changed, and very often upon light grounds, she could hardly be said either to love or to hate anybody." "She grew so jealous upon the change of her servants, that often, out of fear of being imposed upon, by an over-caution she would impose upon herself." This is a telling touch of description, whether it fairly applied to the Queen or not, for one must have seen little of real life who has not met again and again with persons who, out of mere over-caution against being imposed upon by others, have got into the way of imposing upon themselves. Swift was not much of a respecter of persons, even when these happened to be of royal rank, and his loyalty to the Queen never led him into any desire to regard her little weaknesses with greater deference than he would have shown to those of any ordinary woman. "She took a delight in refusing those who were thought to have greatest power with her, even in the most reasonable things, and such as were necessary for her service; nor would let them be done till she fell into the humour of it herself." For such reasons as these Swift believes that the Queen grew into a rooted dislike of the Duke and Duchess of Marlborough and of Lord Godolphin, and "this I take to have been the principal ground of the Queen's resolutions to make a change of some officers both in her family and kingdom; and that these resolutions did not proceed from any real apprehension she had of danger to the church or monarchy."

Thus does Swift quietly proceed to divest poor Queen Anne of any credit for grave and public purpose in her manner of dealing with those immediately around her. She might have been totally indifferent to Marlborough and might have allowed him, with perfect unconcern on her part, to go on conquering her enemies and extending her power, if only he had not taken to pestering her over-much with his suggestions and solicitations, even when these might reasonably have seemed to him to be for her own advantage. Swift will not allow us to be under any delusion on that subject. His mind is clear that, although the Queen had been strictly educated in the faith of the state Church, " and very much approved its doctrine and discipline, yet she was not so ready to foresee any attempts against it by the party then presiding. But, the fears that most influenced her, were such as concerned her own power and prerogative, which those nearest about her were making daily encroachments upon, by their undutiful behaviour and unreasonable demands." There was not much of the courtier's spirit in Swift, and it seems very likely, indeed, that he had got at a clear understanding of the woman herself, just as he might have done if she had been the mistress of an ordinary household who came now and then under his keen observation.

Swift goes on to narrate an incident which happened about a twelvemonth before the death of Prince George, the Queen's husband. "This Prince had long conceived an incurable aversion from that party"—the party represented by the Duchess of Marlborough— " and was resolved to use his utmost credit with the Queen, his wife, to get rid of them. There fell out an incident which seemed to favour this attempt; for the Queen, resolving to bestow a regiment upon Mr. Hill, brother to Mrs. Masham, signified her pleasure to the Duke of Marlborough; who, in a manner not very dutiful, refused his consent and retired in anger to the country. After some heats, the regiment was given to a third person: But, the Queen resented this matter so highly, which she thought had been promoted by the Earl of Godolphin, that she resolved immediately to remove the latter. I was told, and it was then generally reported, that Mr. St. John carried a letter from her Majesty to the Duke of Marlborough, signifying her resolutions to take the staff from the Earl of Godolphin, and that she expected his Grace's compliance; to which the Duke returned a very humble answer."

So far as this part of the story goes, it is not difficult to find some excuse for the apparently inconsistent course taken by the Duke of Marlborough. Marlborough was commander-in-chief of the forces, and the Duke, as Swift tells us, was soon to embark for Flanders. Marlborough may well have thought that the officering of his army was a matter entirely for his own judgment and decision, and that not even the personal influence of the Queen ought to be allowed to dictate to him; while, on the other hand, the disposal of the Queen's political offices was a matter properly to be settled by the Queen's own authority, and one which he was bound to meet with a respectful compliance.

Swift is very severe on the proposal made by Marlborough himself that the command of the forces intrusted to him should be converted into an appointment to last during his lifetime. He turns from other subjects to comment on the fact that "the Duke of Marlborough, whether by a motive of ambition, or a love of money, or by the rash counsels of his wife the Duchess, made that bold attempt of desiring the Queen to give him a commission to be general for life. Her Majesty's answer was, that she would take time to consider it; and, in the mean while, the Duke advised with the Lord Cowper, then Chancellor, about the form in which the commission should be drawn. The Chancellor, very much to his honour, endeavoured to dissuade the Duke from engaging in so dangerous an affair; and protested that he would never put the great seal to such a commission. But the Queen was highly alarmed at this extraordinary proceeding in the Duke, and talked to a person whom she had then taken into confidence as if she apprehended an attempt upon the crown. The Duke of Argyle, and one or two more Lords, were (as I have been told) in a very private manner brought to the Queen. This Duke was under great obligations to the Duke of Marlborough, who had placed him in a high station in the army, preferred many of his friends, and procured him the Garter. But, his unquiet and ambitious spirit, never easy while there was anyone above him, made him, upon some trifling resentments, conceive an inveterate hatred against his general. When he was consulted what course should be taken upon the Duke of Marlborough's request to be general for life; and whether any danger might be apprehended from the refusal; I was told, he suddenly answered, That her Majesty need not be in pain; for, he would undertake, whenever she commanded, to seize the Duke at the head of his troops, and bring him away either dead or alive."

Swift does not seem inclined to give much credit to the Duke of Argyle for a declaration which the ordinary observer might well regard as dictated by loyalty and public spirit. He prepares us for the Duke's heroic utterance by taking care to let us know that Argyle had already conceived an inveterate hatred against his general. It is one of Swift's prevailing peculiarities that he loves to spoil anything like a melodramatic attitude or situation. He is a sceptic as to the sincerity of heroics, and he delights to show us what very ordinary and selfish creatures are most of those great personages with whom history brings us into contact. Swift may have been right enough about the motive which mainly inspired the Duke of Argyle's declaration, and it is quite possible that the same critical way of examining into realities might have knocked much of the grandeur out of many of the noble speeches recorded by Thucydides or Livy. We must take Swift as we find him, and not make it a cause of complaint against the author of *Gulliver's Travels* that he does not deal with his living figures as the author of *Télémaque* might have done. It is perhaps something of a comfort to remember that Swift, too, had his favorite heroes, and that he saw in Harley, for instance, exalted and even sublime qualities of mind and heart for which history from that time to this has certainly not given that statesman full credit. Yet, even when dealing with some passages in Harley's career, the peculiar genius of Swift leads him now and then to exhibit his chosen hero under conditions which might almost be called ridiculous. When commenting on "The Famous Trial of Dr. Sacheverell," Swift observes that the impeachment "arose from a foolish passionate pique of the Earl of Godolphin, whom this Divine was supposed, in a sermon, to have reflected on under the name of Volpone, as my Lord Sommers, a few months after, confessed to me; and, at the same time, that he had earnestly, and in vain, endeavoured to dissuade the Earl from that attempt."

Now Mr. Harley comes upon the stage. Harley arrived in town during the time of the impeachment, and by the intervention of Mrs. Masham he was brought into private conference with Queen Anne. "It was not," we learn from Swift, "without a good deal of difficulty, that Mr. Harley was able to procure this private access to the Queen, the Duchess of Marlborough, by her emissaries, watching all the avenues to the back-stairs, and upon all occasions discovering their jealousy of him; whereof he told me a passage, no otherways worth relating, than as it gives an idea of an insolent, jealous minister, who would wholly engross the power and favour of his Sovereign. Mr. Harley, upon his removal from the secretary's office, by the intrigues of the Duke of Marlborough and the Earl of Godolphin, as I have above related, going out of town, was met by the latter of these two Lords near Kensington Gate. The Earl, in a high fit of jealousy, goes immediately to the Queen, reproaches her for privately seeing Mr. Harley, and was hardly so civil to be convinced with her Majesty's frequent protestations to the contrary."

Ordinary human beings might well imagine that the Queen could have taken some measures to impress, even upon the Duke of Marlborough and Lord Godolphin, that she had a right to see anybody she pleased at any time and in any way convenient to her. But Swift proceeds to inform us that the suspicions entertained by these two eminent persons made it hard for the Queen and Harley to have any private interview. It might be a case of Romeo and Juliet, or of the Nouvelle Héloïse and her lover, for all that the reader could gather from Swift's description of the difficulties and dangers interposed in the way of these meetings. "The Queen, hemmed in, and as it were imprisoned, by the Duchess of Marlborough and her creatures, was at a loss how to proceed." Sometimes, indeed, the situation had its ludicrous aspects. "One evening, a letter was brought to Mr. Harley, all dirty, and by the hand of a very ordinary messenger; he read the superscription, and saw it was the Queen's writing; he sent for the messenger, who said, he knew not whence the letter came, but that it was delivered him by an under gardener, I forgot whether of Hampton Court or Kensington. The letter mentioned the difficulties her Majesty was under, blaming him for not speaking with more freedom, and more particularly; and desiring his assistance. With this encouragement he went more frequently, although still as private as possible, to the back-stairs; and from that time began to have entire credit with the Queen." It certainly was no part of Swift's purpose to throw ridicule on the principle and the conditions of royalty, but there is not much in *Gulliver's Travels,* and in the descriptions of court intrigue which they occasionly contain, more thoroughly ridiculous than this story of the dirty letter delivered by the under gardener and of the great statesman sneaking his way to the back-stairs.

Nothing could come in more appropriately in our study of the politics of Queen Anne's reign than to learn something of Swift's first efforts to come to a thorough understanding of the difference between the principles of the Whigs and those of the Tories. He tells us when and how the consideration of this difference first began to occupy his attention, "having formerly employed myself in other, and, I think, much better speculations." He sets out some of his difficulties with the clearness which belongs to his intellect and his style, and at the same time with an ingenuous simplicity which hardly seems to be a part of his nature.

"I talked often upon the subject with Lord Sommers; told him, that having been long conversant with the Greek and Roman authors, and therefore a lover of liberty, I found myself much inclined to be what they called a Whig in politics; and that, besides, I thought it impossible upon any other principle to defend or submit to the Revolution. But as to religion I confess myself to be an High churchman, and that I did not conceive how anyone, who wore the habit of a clergyman, could be otherwise: That I had observed very well with what insolence and haughtiness some Lords of the High-church party treated not only their own chaplains, but all other clergymen whatsoever, and thought this was sufficiently recompensed by their professions of zeal to the church. That I had likewise observed how the Whig Lords took a direct contrary measure, treated the persons of particular clergymen with great courtesy, but showed much ill-will and contempt for the order in general: That I knew it was necessary for their party, to make their bottom as wide as they could, by taking all denominations of Protestants to be members of their body: That I would not enter into the mutual reproaches made by the violent men on either side; but, that the connivance, or encouragement, given by the Whigs to those writers of pamphlets, who reflected upon the whole body of the clergy, without any exception, would unite the church as one man to oppose them."

Swift appears to have made an analysis of certain conditions then existing in the two great parties with something like scientific precision. The Tories held to a certain dogma, and assumed that their acceptance of it relieved them from the necessity of taking too much trouble to put it into practice in their daily intercourse with their fellow-men, and especially with those who were not exactly their fellows in rank. The Whigs, on the other hand, had taken on themselves the assertion of unfamiliar doctrines, and were anxious to recommend themselves and their doctrines, as far as they could, by making themselves personally agreeable to individual members of that order which they were accused of a desire to disparage. We soon learn in the course of this essay how Swift was induced to occupy himself as a writer for a political newspaper.

"Upon the rise of this ministry, the principal persons in power thought it necessary, that some weekly paper should be published, with just reflections upon former proceedings, and defending the present measures of her Majesty. This was begun about the time of the Lord Godolphin's removal, under the name of the *Examiner*. About a dozen of these papers, written with much spirit and sharpness, some by Mr. Secretary St. John, since Lord Bolingbroke; others by Dr. Atterbury, since Bishop of Rochester; and others again by Mr. Prior, Dr. Friend, &c., were published with great applause. But these gentlemen, grown weary of the work, or otherwise employed, the determination was, that I should continue it, which I did accordingly about eight months. But my stile being soon discovered, and having contracted a great number of enemies, I let it fall into other hands, who held it up in some manner until her Majesty's death."

The *Examiner* may be described as the first of the entirely political newspapers which began to exercise an effect upon parties and the public in the reign of Queen Anne. Its earliest number made its appearance on August 3, 1710, and it bore as its full description *The Examiner, or Remarks upon Papers and Occurrences,* but, of course, it was always known in ordinary conversation as the *Examiner*. This precursor of the political journalism which has been an ever-growing power down to our own time gave itself out almost avowedly as an inspired organ of ministerial opinion, and professed to tell the public what her Majesty's advisers intended to do, and how her Majesty's advisers believed that loyal subjects ought to think, speak, and act. We shall hear more of this paper and of other new and remarkable enterprises in the field of journalism before this history advances much further.

Swift has something to say about the once famous October Club. This name, he tells, was "a fantastic appellation, found out to distinguish a number of country gentlemen, and their adherents, who professed in the greatest degree what was called the High-church principle. They grew in number to almost a third part of the House, held their meetings at certain times and places, and there concerted what measures they were to take in parliament. They professed their jealousy of the court and ministry: declared, upon all occasions, their desire of a more general change, as well as of a strict enquiry into former mismanagement: and seemed to expect, that those in power should openly avow the old principles in church and state. I was then of opinion, and still continue so, that if this body of men could have remained some time united, they would put the crown under a necessity of acting in a more steady and strenuous manner. But Mr. Harley, who best knew the disposition of the Queen, was forced to break their measures; which he did by that very obvious contrivance of dividing them among themselves, and rendering them jealous of each other. The ministers gave everywhere out, that the October-club were their friends, and acted by their directions; to confirm which Mr. Secretary St. John and Mr. B——, afterwards Chancellor of the Exchequer, publicly dined with them at one of their meetings. Thus were eluded all the consequences of that assembly; although a remnant of them, who conceived themselves betrayed by the rest, did afterwards meet under the denomination of the March-club, but without any effect."

JONATHAN SWIFT'S VIEWS

These extracts from Swift's commentaries on the events of the time may be brought to a close by the remarks which he makes on the beginning of the misunderstanding between Harley and Bolingbroke, to which allusion has been made in a former chapter.

"I have some very good reasons to know that the first misunderstanding between Mr. Harley and Mr. St. John, which afterwards had such unhappy consequences upon the public affairs, took its rise during the time that the former lay ill of his wounds, and his recovery doubtful." This, of course, refers to the injuries sustained by Harley from De Guiscard's penknife. "Mr. St. John affected to say in several companies, that Guiscard intended the blow against him; which, if it were true, the consequence must be, that Mr. St. John had all the merit, while Mr. Harley remained with nothing but the danger and the pain. But, I am apt to think, Mr. St. John was either mistaken, or misinformed. However, the matter was thus represented in the weekly paper called the *Examiner,* which Mr. St. John perused before it was printed, but made no alteration in that passage. This management was looked upon, at least as a piece of youthful indiscretion in Mr. St. John; and, perhaps, was represented in a worse view to Mr. Harley: Neither am I altogether sure. that Mr. St. John did not entertain some prospect of succeeding as first minister, in case of Mr. Harley's death; which, during his illness, was frequently apprehended. And I remember very well, that upon visiting Mr. Harley, as soon as he was in a condition to be seen, I found several of his nearest relations talk very freely of some proceedings of Mr. St. John; enough to make me apprehend, that their friendship would not be of any long continuance."

Swift's commentaries form an interesting and a

peculiar part of the history of that time. To say the least of it, they have the effect of rubbing the gilt off the showy and ornamental parts of court life and political combinations. Swift shows us how very like ordinary men and women were the great leading figures in that historical drama. We see the petty likings and dislikings, the small vanities, the mean rivalries and jealousies, the self-seeking motives which the satirist familiarly illustrates in the persons of commonplace men and women, animating and governing the august lives of sovereigns and princes and the stately careers of peers and political leaders. Nobody was a hero to Swift, and yet the famous repartee to that proverb will not apply, for Swift, assuredly, had not the soul of the valet whom it describes as incapable of approaching the heroic.

END OF VOL. I.